The Return of
the Ainu

Studies in Anthropology and History

Studies in Anthropology and History is a series that will develop new theoretical perspectives, and combine comparative and ethnographic studies with historical research.
Edited by Nicholas Thomas, The Australian National University, Canberra.

This book is part of a series. The publisher will accept continuation orders which may be cancelled at any time and which provide for automatic billing and shipping of each title in the series upon publication. Please write for details.

Katarina V. Sjöberg

The Return of
the Ainu

Cultural mobilization and the
practice of ethnicity in Japan

hoap harwood academic publishers
Australia * Canada * China * France * Germany * India * Japan * Luxembourg * Malaysia *
The Netherlands * Russia * Singapore * Switzerland * Thailand * United Kingdom

First published 1993
Second Printing 1997

Amsteldijk 166
Ist Floor
1079 LH Amsterdam
The Netherlands

LIBRARY OF CONGRESS CATALOGING-IN-PUBLICATION DATA

Sjoberg, Katarina, 1949 -
The return of the Ainu : cultural mobilization and the practice of ethnicity in Japan / Katarina SjÖberg.
p. cm.-- (Studies in anthropology and history : 9)
Includes index. 1. Ainu. 2. Japan-- Ethnic relations. I. Series.
ISBN : 3-7186-5401-6
DS832.S66 1993   93-16634
305.89'46--dc20   CIP

DESIGNED BY   Maureen Anne MacKenzie
Em Squared Main Street Michelago NSW 2620 Australia

ALL INK DRAWINGS BY
Mrs Miwako Kaisawa

ALL MAPS DRAWN BY
Claes Nordstrand

ALL PHOTOGRAPHS BY
the author

TYPESET BY
Duro Datek, Lund (Sweden)

Contents

List of Illustrations

Preface

This is a revised version of my doctoral thesis, entitled *Mr Ainu: Cultural Mobilization and the Practice of Ethnicity in a Hierarchical Culture*, presented at the University of Lund in February 1991. In connection with a recent invitation to contribute an article supporting a programme on "Indigenous People and Asia" which I received from St. Anthony's College, Oxford, it came to my knowledge that Japan has now recognized the Ainu as a religious and cultural minority. This recognition could imply a great step forward for the Ainu people. Given Japan's position, however, it is unlikely that much will come of this concession. The prospect of contemporary Ainu being accepted as Japanese on the same level as the Wajin is a bleak one and will, no doubt, remain so until such a time as Japan decides to bring its minority groups into the mainstream.

This book is the outcome of a project called "Intercultural Relations in Japan with Special Reference to the Integration of the Ainu", sponsored by the Swedish Research Council in the Humanities and Social Sciences (HSFR) and the Nordic Association of Japanese and Korean Studies (NIAS).

My interest in the Ainu people originates from a more general interest in Japan and Japanese culture. My main concern, however, is the phenomenon called Fourth World Populations. After having read a book entitled *Aiona* by the French linguist Pierre Naert, I decided to take a closer look at the Ainu people and their integration into the Japanese nation state. The result of my investigation is presented in this book. What distinguishes the Ainu from other indigenous groups is the fact that the Japanese government and its Wajin functionaries relentlessly deny what is taken as the basis for contemporary state policies *vis-à-vis* aboriginal peoples. Not only does this denial severely obstruct Ainu attempts to revive and preserve their cultural heritage, but it also makes them different to other minorities. While other minorities put more stress on political and economic factors in their struggle for better living conditions, and are less concerned with the way in which the majority people evaluate their beliefs and customs, the Ainu are primarily concerned with the judgement of the Wajin and rely on this rather than relying on their own judgement. Persistent in her view that the Ainu have forgotten their former customs and practices, Japan considers a practicable maintenance of Ainu customs outside the tourist arena to be unrealistic and severely circumscribes the efforts of the Ainu to celebrate, revive and preserve the customs of the past.

xi

This book is dedicated to my husband, Claes Nordstrand, who is largely responsible for the maps and who has been a stimulating support during my work. I am also deeply grateful for his constant readiness to help, inspire and encourage me. He also knows this book by heart after endless proof-readings.

I am particularly grateful to Dr Kajsa Ekholm Friedman, head of the Department of Social Anthropology at the University of Lund, and her husband, Dr Jonathan Friedman, for their invaluable help in the process of writing this book. Their intellectual support in the formulation of my ideas was an essential ingredient in every stage of my research. I wish also to express thanks to Professor Sven Tägil from the Historical Department at the University of Lund for his expert advice and valuable comments on the historical section in particular. I was very fortunate in having Professor Roger Keesing from the Department of Anthropology, McGill University, Quebec, Canada, as my opponent at the time of my dissertation and his intellectual support has been indispensable in this revised version.

The Ainu people of Hokkaido have contributed to my work in numerous ways and I would like to express my special thanks to them both collectively and individually. I am particularly grateful to Mr Kayano and his staff, Mr and Mrs Yoneda and Mr and Mrs Narita who assisted me in and around Nibutani, my fieldwork base. I am in special debt to Mrs Miwako Kaisawa for her fine illustrations to this book. My thanks are due to the staff of the Anthropological Departments of Sapporo, Otaru and Asahikawa Universities and to the staff of the Historical Museum of Hokkaido and the Ainu museums at Abashiri, Asahikawa and Hakodate, as well as the various Ainu Exhibition Halls in Hokkaido. Special gratitude goes to my assistant Mrs Hisako Kawakami Preston and her family and relatives who received me with warmth and hospitality.

I should like also to thank all my colleagues at the Department of Social Anthropology in Lund who have provided a stimulating intellectual environment through the years. I am grateful to Alfredo Pernin for the setting and for his expert advice on technical matters and to Anders and Inger Ekström for the photographic reproductions.

My mother-in-law Vera Nordstrand has provided me with both intellectual and practical assistance and I am greatly indebted to her for this. I am also deeply grateful to my son Nicolai Tschofen, my mother Sonja Grip and my father Krister Sjöberg for their unfailing family support.

Finally, I send my thanks to the late Dr Pierre Naert whose work, *Aiona: Det Vita Folket i Fjärran Östern*, aroused my interest in the lives of the Ainu people.

CHAPTER ONE

Theme and objectives

Before the tremendous shock of present-day civilization, with
all its harassing worries, vexatious rules, unbending laws,
burdensome taxes, and crowds of immigrants came upon us,
our fathers had an easy time of it… but now all is change and
the struggle for existence is wiping us out
(Batchelor 1971: 35).

The starting point of this work was to find out whether harassing
worries, vexatious rules, inflexible laws, burdensome taxes and floods of immigrants, in
short, the struggle for existence, is actually wiping out Japan's indigenous population, the
Ainu, and their culture. When discussing their present situation it is usually claimed that
Ainu culture has largely disappeared and it is argued that they exist as a poorly acculturated
and economically and politically marginal minority.

The Ainu are Japan's, *Nihon's*, indigenous population, also known as *Kyuudojin*
(aborigines) or *Dojin* (natives) in the colloquial language, and they are "traditionally"
assigned by the anthropological literature to the general category of hunters and gatherers,
primarily inhabiting the northern island of *Hokkaido*.

Since 1868, with the annexation of their native land, Hokkaido, formerly *Ezo*, the
Ainu are officially incorporated into the Nihon nation, *Nihon*, on equal terms. Although
they differ culturally, linguistically and biologically from the majority population, the
Wajin, they are not officially recognized as a distinct ethnic group by the latter. As a result,
matters concerning the Ainu fall under various social service institutions. Despite preoccupation with questions related to social work and welfare, the living standard of the
majority of the Ainu is far below the average of the nation. This is a circumstance that, as
Cornell (1964: 287) points out, places them among the frontier poor in Nihon, a group
in which, apart from the Ainu, we also find the *Burakumin*, the *Ryukyujin*, the *Koreans*
and several other minority peoples from Russia.

Fruitless attempts to raise the living standard of the Ainu resulted, in 1974, in the
establishment of a separate welfare policy on their behalf, called "The Hokkaido Utari
Welfare Policy". This policy does not come under the category of ethnic policy but rather
general welfare policy (Utari Kyokai 1988: 6).

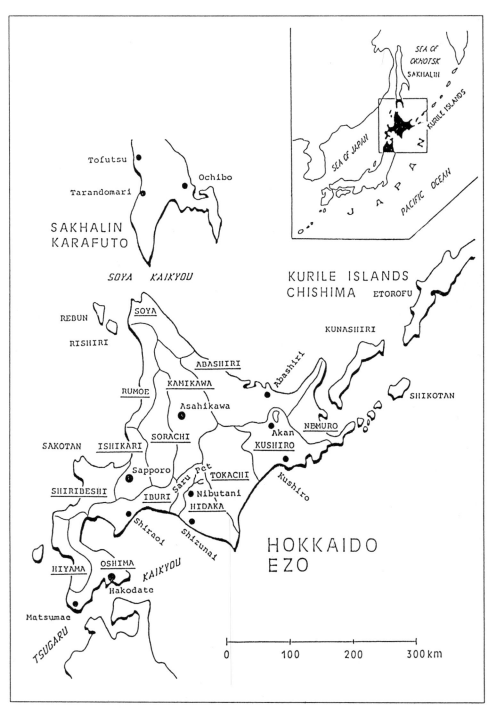

FIGURE 1   *Map of present-day Hokkaido*

The attitude of the authorities to the Ainu as part of the larger society is based on the assumption that the Ainu have to reject ethnic status and adapt to the non-ethnic premisses of state ideology as defined by the highest authority. According to this definition all peoples, natives to Nihon, are to be addressed by the term *Nihonjin*. This concept is a non-ethnic concept and it is linked to the ideology of the Meiji Restoration, *Meiji Ishin*, established in 1868, when Hokkaido was annexed by Nihon.

Today there is a change in the relationship between the Ainu and the Wajin. This change consists primarily of a shift in Ainu attitudes to the official policy of assimilation, which seeks to acculturate the Ainu and to de-emphasize ethnic features. This policy aims at transforming the Ainu into farmers. Today, the better part of Hokkaido land and natural resources are used for bean, corn and rice cultivation, cattle and racehorse breeding, or other economies introduced from Nihon proper, that is *Honshu*. In recent years the Ainu struggle to alter this condition is intensified.

The contemporary relationship between the Ainu and the Wajin originates in the two groups' conflicting interests with respect to the policy of assimilation. This is a rather recent phenomenon but with roots in constantly unsatisfactory conditions for the Ainu dating back several centuries when the Wajin settled in Hokkaido on a large scale and restrictions on both freedom of residence and hunting and fishing grounds first began. Previously the Ainu had little or no objection to the policy of assimilation. On the contrary, they devoted much of their time to becoming "properly" assimilated and much effort was spent on forgetting their Ainu heritage altogether. In a way they tried, as Refsing (1980: 87) puts it, to "become even more Japanese than the Japanese". Today, however, there is resistance both to the policy of assimilation and to the way in which their land and natural resources are used.

Among the Ainu, there is a cultural mobilization taking place today, characterized by its emphasis on ethnic features. Yet, this does not imply a general wish to seek departure from the Nihon nation but a wish to remain part of the nation on terms different from those that prevail today, and there is a notable stress on a land use that corresponds with the values and beliefs that belong to their own cultural tradition. Generally speaking, this means that the better part of Hokkaido land and natural resources are no longer to be used exclusively for introduced crops and economies.

They express their plans for the future in *Counter Plan to the Proposal for Legislation Concerning the Ainu People* (Utari Kyokai 1984, 1987a). These are documents which they have drawn up in cooperation with *Utari Kyokai*, the Ainu association in Sapporo, the "capital" of Hokkaido. The main ambition is to replace some of the imported economies with economies linked to the values of the Ainu. In the proposals there are plans to make national parks of the forests and mountains in areas which formerly were both famous and revered. In this way the flora and fauna of the once most powerful Ainu areas would be preserved. Another of their proposals is to use part of the land to grow Ainu crops and vegetables. In this way Ainu dishes and cooking traditions would not be lost altogether. There are also plans to establish centres for the study of Ainu history, material culture, language and religious beliefs. These studies are to be supervised by the Ainu themselves. To establish such centres is a matter of high priority among the Ainu, because, according to them, previous studies by Wajin and foreign scholars are biased.

The attitudes described above indicate changes in Ainu identity formation. These include a strengthening of their own values and beliefs, a renewed interest in their Ainu inheritance and a questioning of "historical facts" about their culture when described as "backward and static" and they themselves as "Paleolithic remnants".

Today there are Ainu who are unwilling to believe existing "scientific" interpretations of their historical and ethnographic past, and take an active part in critical analyses of foreign as well as Wajin writings about them. In some cases, their own interpretations may even compete with those made by researchers. One example is that which has been presented by Mr Shigeru Kayano, an Ainu from the Hidaka region in the southeastern part of Hokkaido. His criticism is directed against the absence of an Ainu view in matters concerning their own cultural tradition. Such neglect leads, according to him, and others, to conceptual misreadings of their customs and beliefs. This in turn, he claims, has resulted in a presentation of their history and ethnography where Ainu culture has been used mainly as an "uncivilized" contrast to Wajin "civilized" culture. His alternative picture does not go unchallenged and it has been accused of being too narrow, in the sense that the studies undertaken by Kayano are locally restricted, that is, to the region in which he himself lives. He has, among other things, been accused of emphasizing his own culture (Kayano culture) and not the Ainu culture, his own history and not the history of the Ainu. It has also been argued that the form his work takes does not live up to scientific standards but rather belongs to the genre of the novel. Nevertheless, today his reputation as an expert in Ainu material culture, history and language extends beyond the local context and he is frequently consulted by Wajin and foreign researchers about Ainu matters. In addition, his work has become a source of inspiration to the Ainu throughout Hokkaido.

However, among the Ainu today such activities as those described above are small-scale enterprises and they are also for the most part locally restricted. Nevertheless, the mere fact that opposing versions of history and ethnography do exist, unthinkable some decades ago, shows that the efforts of the Ainu of today, expressed not only in a renewed interest in their Ainu inheritance but also in an active revitalization of Ainu customs and beliefs of the past, have much in common with the general awakening among minority and indigenous peoples that is taking place throughout the world today. This is characterized by a loss of faith in the progress of modernization and a corresponding explosion of new cultural movements, from cults and religious revival to primitivism, a new traditionalism, a striving for the re-establishment of a new culturally defined identity (Friedman 1983).

Due to the fact that Nihon is considered by its authorities as inhabited by one single homogeneous population, this creates great hardship for the Ainu in their attempts both to cope with their present situation and to alter it for the future.

The highest authorities in Nihon have made themselves governors and spokesmen of the Nihon nation. Within the state governing group there is a strong belief in the value of a homogeneous nation. Such a national self-representation with no room for the identification of minority peoples as having distinct cultures is not generally accepted by minority peoples living in Nihon. Today, the policy of assimilation is strongly criticized by these peoples because of the above, but also because of the prevailing asymmetrical relationship between the majority people and its minorities, where the latter are excluded from the national political and economic arena.

Since the Wajin maintain this policy and as there are signs of resistance to it among the Ainu today, the field of my enquiry will primarily be directed towards such questions as Ainu production of a separate cultural identity – its specificity and how it differs from other groups – and Ainu strategies of adaptation to the larger national context.

The aim of this work is to understand a specific kind of cultural change, that is, a cultural mobilization, whose content is ethnic in its essence. It comprises a wish of getting to know one's own history and ethnography, a revival of old-time ideologies which includes attempts to introduce crops and economies that correspond with these, and to make their oral language a compulsory subject for pupils of Ainu descent. But it also comprises attempts to present one's history and ethnography in a way that corresponds with one's own view. The former is expressed by organizing lectures about Ainu history, material culture and language, participation in lessons about how to manufacture Ainu items, such as gathering bags, clothings, offering sticks and the like, participation in ceremonial gatherings of different types and learning of Ainu dances. The latter is expressed by way of questioning previous writings of Ainu history and ethnography and in the organization of critical studies of the methods and approaches used in these writings.

In order to grasp the specific kind of cultural change that is taking place among the Ainu today and the circumstances that have given rise to this, Ainu culture cannot be treated as totally self-contained but must be seen as integral to the nation of which it has been part since 1868. The intercultural relations that exist between the two are themselves embedded in Nihon's changing position within the larger world system, one that has clear effects on its culture. It is therefore necessary to maintain a broad perspective when analysing these local changes.

In my work I have focused on strategies and thus I have attempted to lay bare the multiple nature of agency that characterizes the interaction between Ainu, the larger society and the state. As there are several actors in this arena there are also several strategies in dialogue and encounter with one another and one way of understanding cultural change would be to understand it as an outcome of the multiplex interaction between the Ainu, the larger society and the state.

My work deals with processes of integration and fragmentation that characterize the relationship between the Ainu and the larger society. Today the Ainu are to be found throughout Nihon, although Hokkaido still remains the main Ainu territory. However, in my work I do not deal with the entire Ainu population as such, but with a specific kind of cultural change and the process that has led to the present situation of ethnic awareness among the Ainu, that is, from a situation of virtual lack of interest in ethnic factors to the present emphasis on the same. This is a phenomenon which has been described by other groups (cf. Clifford 1988).

The material for this study consists of archival material, written and taped sources, and field material. However, this is not an ordinary ethnographic monograph since the reality which I seek to capture is in no sense traditional. I have concentrated on two principal areas in my field research. The first area has dealt with the cultural mobilization that is taking place among the Ainu today, which is a complex phenomenon. It comprises people who register as Ainu and identify themselves as Ainu as well as those who do not: some people are actively engaged in activities and practices that belong to the Ainu, whereas others are occasionally or seasonally engaged; some people's engagements is on an individual basis others are on a group level; some people hide their interest, when among Wajin, but show it when among their own people; some people are engaged because they see an opportunity to achieve ethnic status, others are engaged because they have an interest in getting to know their own ethnography, seeking their roots so to speak. This complexity of factors involved in personal engagement implied that it was necessary for me to explore the different milieus where I could find representatives of different views. The second area of research has dealt with the Ainu view of the way they have been identified in historical and ethnographic writings. Previous Western and Wajin representations of Ainu history and ethnography constitute a field within which the Ainu have constructed and debated their identity. As such, analysis of their relationship to "others" identification of them is crucial to an understanding of the process of cultural mobilization. To illustrate aspects of the inconsistencies among the various views of the Ainu as they are "written" I used my field research to incorporate Ainu views, comments and criticism with respect to others identification of them.

BACKGROUND AND DELIMITATION OF THE FIELD OF STUDY

The Ainu people and their territory, known in their own language as *Ainu Moshir* and in the colloquial language as Hokkaido, the northernmost Nihon island, were, in 1868, officially incorporated into the Nihon nation to be. This was the result of a long-term penetration of their territory and society by people from the mainland,[1] Honshu, that began when a powerful Wajin *Han*, the *Matsumae*, first settled here in 1514.

For convenience, when discussing the contact period and the periods that follow, I propose the following division:

1514–1868	A period of intrusion.
1869–1899	A period of colonization.
1899–1968	A period of assimilation.
1968–	A period of reorganization and revitalization of the values and beliefs that belong to the Ainu.

The incorporation of Hokkaido, which took place without negotiation with the Ainu, was in effect a colonization. During the actual colonization period, *Kaitakushi*, which lasted from 1869 to 1899, the Meiji government assumed direct administrative and juridical control over the Ainu and an official policy of assimilation was begun, which included legislation against the maintenance of Ainu customs, religious beliefs and language. The land and natural resources of the territory of the Ainu were to be used in conformity with the purposes of the newly established Nihon nation where agricultural activities were encouraged, which did not allow for the continuation of the Ainu hunting and fishing activities.

The intention of the restoration, Meiji Ishin, which means, "enlightened government", was to unite the leaders in feudal Nihon and to make a nation of the Nihon islands. Oligarchy, the dominant form of government that maintained political and military control in old Nihon, was abandoned in favour of a democratic government.

Prior to the Meiji Ishin the population of the mainland was divided into four social strata, referred to as the *Shi-nou-kou-shou*, and Nihon proper was divided into fiefs, controlled and owned by lords whose obligation it was to support an elite (courts and nobles). This was achieved by collecting taxes from retainers bound to the various fiefs. The retainers constituted a peasant group, *Nou*, who served as the foundation of the economy and who looked to the lords for protection in exchange for taxes rendered. Artisans, *Kou*, and merchants, *Shou*, who were almost identical in their status constituted another group, bound to the fief for protection and with obligations to fulfil towards their lords. Since this group was not as economically essential as the peasant group for the maintenance of the system, its members were lower in rank. Essential indeed were the warriors, the *Samurai*, or *Bushi*, whose duties were to protect the fief against intrusion and

---

1 "Although all of Japan is insular, time, history and distance somehow ingrained in the Japanese mind the idea that Hokkaido was an 'island' as against the 'mainland' of Japan" (Takakura 1960: 6)

whose position was second in rank to the lords, *Daimyou*. Within the system as a whole each individual was identified with and responsible to some particular individual higher than himself.

The ideology of this system connects to the concept of *Giri* which literally means "burden" – a sense of moral obligation to one's superior (Matsumoto 1960; Nakane 1970; Smith 1983). Under the reign of the *Tokugawa* family regime (Edo period 1603-1867) the moral code of the Giri was rigidly followed. After a full century (1500-1600) of endemic wars and endless feuds between powerful lords, the Tokugawa military administration, *Shogunate*, imposed a system of social order and moral doctrines so that it would not break down through mutual aggression and hostility (Matsumoto 1960: 13).

Apart from lacking social mobility, the system gave no room for people outside the mainstream such as the Burakumin, the Ryukyujin and the Ainu, that is, the peoples that constitute Nihon's minority peoples and who today, as well as earlier, are classified by reference to their place of birth and not, as is the case with the Wajin, to their function within the hierarchical system.

However, the incorporation or colonization of Ezo was essential for the realization of the restoration, not least because the notorious feuds between powerful lords in Honshu had severe effects on the arable land and its cultivators, the peasants, a considerable number of whom had fled to Ezo. Besides, Russian competition for the territory of the Ainu during the previous years had become a serious threat to the mainland interests in Ezo (Baba 1980: 63; Kreiner & Oelschleger 1987: 30). In short, Ezo territory was needed both as an outpost to the north and for the management and development of the economy of the nation-to-be.

Historically, the study first covers the Wajin violation of Ainu land and the succeeding extension of their own land resources, from the beginning of the sixteenth century to the close of the nineteenth century. During this period, *the period of intrusion*, the relationship between the Ainu and the Wajin changed from a friendly commercial relationship, where the chief objective was profit from trade, to a lord-vassal relationship, *Shujin-Ienoko*, where the chief objectives were the possession of land and Ainu allies. The latter period was characterized by Wajin attempts to control the Ainu and their land and natural resources as well as Wajin attempts to settle permanently in Ainu territory.

The first part of the period is characterized by the Matsumae attempts to fortify mainland settlements throughout the southern parts of Ezo. In the following part of the period the mainland tried to gain control over the Matsumae influence in the southern parts of Ezo and to expand the controlling influence to the eastern parts of Ezo, that is, *Higashi Ezochi*. This was followed by Matsumae attempts to regain control, and the period ended with mainland attempts to gain control both over Matsumae influence and the remaining western parts of Ezo, that is, *Nichi Ezochi*.

The mainland policy, as it was maintained throughout the period, alternated between a policy of segregation and a policy of assimilation, and the relationship between the people from the mainland and the Ainu changed accordingly from one of equality to a lord-vassal relationship.

In the next period that my work covers, from 1868/69-1899, *the period of colonization,* Ezo was renamed Hokkaido, which means the "Northern Sea Circuit", and annexed to Nihon. During this period Wajin surveyors were sent to Ezo to map the island. The succeeding *period of assimilation* lasted until 1968 and during it a policy of assimilation was applied and the vast hunting areas of the Ainu were distributed as "land plots". The Ainu themselves were in accordance with *Kyuudojin Hogoho, Law for the Protection of Native Hokkaido Aborigines* (LPNHA), established in 1899, encouraged to agrarianize their hunting and fishing areas. For this purpose the Ainu were "given" 15, 000 *Tsubo,* which were taken back if they were not cultivated.

The investigation ends with the period beginning in 1968 and the following years of the establishment of Ainu associations and the reorganizing and revitalization of Ainu customs and beliefs.

Geographically, my work focuses on Hokkaido, formerly Ezo and usually referred to as "Ainu native land", in Wajin as well as in foreign literature. However, there still is insufficient evidence as to the reliability of this assumption (Naert 1960; Takakura 1960; Kodama 1970). It could well be that all of Nihon is, in fact, Ainu native land, as well as some Russian areas such as Sakhalin and the Kurile islands.

My study will be restricted to the Hokkaido region since, due to historical circumstances, the majority of the remaining Ainu population now live here. More specifically the emphasis will be on *Nibutani* village in the *Hidaka* region in southeastern Hokkaido, once the most powerful Ainu territory.

My reason for choosing Nibutani relates to the fact that this village, nowadays, is regarded both a centre for the studies of the Ainu material culture and a place from which cultural innovations and "dynamic thinking" emanate. This is a point on which both Ainu and Wajin agree. Nibutani is the sole Ainu tourist centre in the Hidaka region, and many of the Ainu living here are continuously engaged in activities tied to the Ainu culture.

Since the concern is both changes in Ainu identity formation and the variation in the degree of personal engagement in Ainu activities – areas where these activities have a low profile – it is also important to study suburbs to larger cities, such as *Hakodate, Sapporo* and *Asahikawa* in the *Oshima, Ishikari* and *Kamikawa* regions, respectively. The Ainu people in these areas take, when interviewed in their suburban environment, no interest at all in their own culture. Yet, in the case of ceremonial Ainu gatherings they appear dressed up in Ainu-style garments. These people live on the outskirts of the larger society. Many of them have no permanent occupations but are dependent on seasonal work and welfare.

Further, the *Iburi* and *Kushiro* regions, where Ainu activities are concentrated to the *Shiraoi* and *Akan* areas, but where the Ainu population are spread over the regions as a whole, except during the tourist season (early May till late October), were other areas of importance to the investigation as a whole.

Ainu activities in these areas are seasonal only and the people engaged in them represent local and regional variants of Ainu culture. In these areas we find a mixture of Ainu local and regional culture items for sale at the various tourist centres, and the ceremonial performances the Ainu put on here also represent a mixture of Ainu local and regional ceremonies.

Finally, in addition and of value to the investigation as a whole, it was important for me to maintain contact with the centre. Its most monumental appearance is to be found in Sapporo, where, apart from the governmental building, "The Red Brick" in the colloquial language, we also find the Hokkaido colonial museum, *Katakinenka*, the Sapporo State University, *Hokudai*, and the Ainu association, *Utari Kyokai*.

Ethnically, my work includes, on the one hand, Kyuudojin (aborigines) or Dojin (natives) that is, the Ainu and, on the other hand, the Kazoku (the family) that is, the Wajin.

"Kyuudojin" or "Dojin" are concepts forced upon the Ainu by the Wajin authorities. These concepts not only include Ezo natives in historic times, but also Ainu people from Sakhalin and the Kurile islands. These people came to share the same territory, Hokkaido, through treaties settled, revoked and resettled between Nihon and Russia during the years 1875-1945.

Wajin as an ethnic concept derives from or relates to *Yamato* descendants. Yamato in turn relates to the people (in ancient Nihon) who in prehistoric time adapted the *Yayoi* culture, characterized by a simple weed-made pottery, agriculture, including rice cultivation using the techniques of irrigation. This culture has its origin in China and was first adopted by the people in ancient Nihon who lived in a country called *Yamato* (Reischauer & Craig 1973: 4).

The country of Yamato is mentioned in Chinese as well as in ancient Nihon records as the seat of the dominant authorities in ancient Nihon (*Nihonshoki* [*Ancient Nihon Chronicles*] compiled A.D. 720 and *The Account of The Three Kingdoms* (*Chinese Records*) compiled before A.D. 297). This people are in Nihon history writings referred to as the "rightful" inheritors of the Nihon nation (Munro 1911: 11). The Ainu were referred to by this people alternately as the *Ezo, Emishi, Ebizu* (Takakura 1960; Munro 1962; Kodama 1970). To depict this people the Chinese sign *Toi* was used, which means "non-continental people". This sign was originally used by the Chinese to depict non-continental peoples in general, that is, all the peoples who lived in the Nihon islands (Takakura 1960: 10). The Wajin were at this time described by the Ainu as *Shi(n)sham* (Batchelor 1938: 446) which means "fellow tradesmen". Today, the Ainu use concepts such as *Wajin, Shamo,* (impolite form of Shi[n]sham meaning "people whom one cannot trust"), *Nihonjin* and *Kazoku* to describe or identify the national majority people.[2]

The concept of *Ainu* was used by Nihon authorities to distinguish mainland settlers in Hokkaido from the natives. Ainu means "human being" and was used in old times by the Ainu to distinguish "people" (Ainu) from "gods" (*Kamuy*)[3] and "beasts" (*Chikoikip*). In old times the Ainu used the concept *un-guru,* which expresses a sense of belonging (cf. Nibutani un-guru, Shiraoi un-guru, that is, people belonging to such and such a settlement), to distinguish people from different settlements, *Kotan.*

---

2   In *Batchelor's Dictionary* (1938: 446) the word "Shamo" is translated "A Japanese" and the synonym is "Shinsham(o)". However, according to the Ainu at present, they used the concept Shinshamo to denote "fellow tradesmen" in general, that is, people from the mainland, meaning China, Russia and Nihon with whom one bartered. Of late the term Shinshamo underwent a change of meaning and the word used today to depict Wajin has lost its honourable prefix "Shi," hence Shamo which is a negative word today. According to the Ainu it should be translated "People whom one cannot trust" (interview with Ainu male, aged 52, Iburi, 1988).

3   Some scholars write "Kamui" instead of "Kamuy" and "un-kur" instead of "un-guru". According to linguists Kamuy and un-kur are the correct words (see Refsing 1986: 68 ff.). When I use Ainu words I consistently write them as they sound when the Ainu pronounce them and as "un-kur" is pronounced "un-guru" I prefer to write it un-guru.

CHAPTER TWO

The ethnographic encounter

My material is obtained from archives, written or taped sources and field material, the latter being particularly essential for answering the kind of questions that I have posed. The main methods employed are fieldwork, including participant observation, census, case studies, interviews, some structured, but mainly unstructured, and the collection of life histories. With respect to archival material and other written or taped sources, these are essential for the understanding of the official picture of the Ainu. They are also necessary for comparison with the picture of the Ainu obtained through my field material.

The fieldwork, which was conducted in Hokkaido, the main Ainu territory, was divided into three phases consisting of two shorter periods of three months each in 1985 and 1986, and a longer period of six months in 1988. At the beginning, a considerable amount of my time was spent in archives connected with various Ainu museums and exhibition halls and in the company of people attached to *Hokudai*, the Sapporo State University, *Katakinenka*, the Hokkaido Colonial Museum, and *Utari Kyokai*, the Ainu association in Sapporo. Much time was of course also devoted to travelling in Hokkaido in order to obtain an overview of where the Ainu lived, their occupational, situational and social context, differences in milieu, their participation in associations of different types, how they spent their free time, what priorities they made and the like - in short, knowledge of what parts of Hokkaido suited my investigation best.

LOCATION OF FIELD RESEARCH AND CRITERIA FOR SELECTION

The concern with respect to the selection of communities was variation in the degree of personal involvement in the cultural mobilization in the Hokkaido area. However, it is difficult to make a representative selection, partly due to the uncertain population figures (the discrepancy between official and unofficial figures is close to 275,000), and partly due to the variety of factors that might be relevant as criteria for selection such as intermarriages with Wajin, occupational situation (tourism, rural and industrial sectors), economic situation (unemployment, social welfare dependency), participation in Ainu associations, and the like.

This took a considerable amount of my time. It was almost impossible to decide what places would suit my purpose best from the mere appearance of the various tourist centres or the rural communities and the people who were inhabiting in them. For such reasons I had to make minor surveys at several places before I settled for the ones which seemed best to live up to the criteria that I considered most relevant at that stage of my field research.

It was clear to me that my study had to extend beyond the community level. A minority people, like the Ainu, who exist on the outskirts of a larger society can hardly be studied as if isolated from the centre. How they use their resources and their employment situation are, to a considerable extent, decided above their heads and in the interest of the nation as a whole rather than in their own interests. The researcher's concern must be both their attitude to this and their attitude to their present position in the larger society and whether these differ with respect to occupational and situational context. Therefore I did not settle for a permanent stay in just one area, but stayed for prolonged periods in three separate areas, namely *Nibutani, Shiraoi* and *Akan.*

Of these three areas, Nibutani functioned as my field base. In addition I also stayed for shorter periods in other Ainu areas, such as the suburbs of larger cities, notably *Sapporo, Hakodate* and *Asahikawa.* These areas were not selected at random but on the basis of the information I had gathered from key informants.

The use of key informants as a source of information about specific cultures is one of the mainstays of anthropology. It is a methodology indispensable not only for recovering information about ways of living that have ceased to exist, or are sharply modified, but also for obtaining information about present-day living conditions (Pelto & Pelto 1978: 71-75).

As regards my choice of operative concepts with respect to what terminology would be adequate, I am somewhat ambivalent. I could of course adopt such terms as "atypical" and "typical". I chose, however, not to. The use of such terms does not serve my purpose. "Atypical" would generally be regarded as the most adequate term for those Ainu who are employed full-time in activities and practices rooted in their own cultural tradition, and "typical" would be regarded as the most adequate term for those who are seasonally or occasionally employed. The use of such terms better serves a view where the centre is regarded as the logical starting point and since I do not hold such a view I also refrain from using concepts that belong to this view. For want of something more adequate I have simply settled for "strong" versus "weak". For this purpose Nibutani and its Ainu inhabitants were chosen to represent one extreme and the suburbs another. Shiraoi and Akan were selected to represent the "in between".

Nibutani is a rather small village. It is located in *Hidaka*, the most densely populated Ainu region. Hidaka is divided into nine autonomous towns, *Cho*, of which *Biratori Cho* is one. Biratori Cho in turn consists of several villages, *Mura*, of which

Nibutani Mura is one. Nibutani belongs as far as administration is concerned to Biratori Cho, and here we find the town office with twenty-four elected town officers. They belong to the different villages which are subordinated to Biratori Cho. The number of representatives in each village is dependent on its population. Nibutani has only one representative, Mr Shigeru Kayano. The various Chos in the Hidaka region are politically self-governed.

Hidaka, with a total population of 99,930,[1] is a unit in name only. The various Chos of the unit are self-governing, as are also the remaining thirteen regions which together with Hidaka make up the Hokkaido prefecture.[2] The division of Hokkaido into such regions, *Schichou*, originates with the Meiji restoration. Before that Hokkaido consisted of three prefectures, called *San Ken Douchou*, namely *Nemuro, Sapporo* and *Hakodate*, but no regions. Before that Hokkaido was divided into two areas, namely *Higashi Ezochi*, East Ezo, that is, the area controlled by mainlanders, and *Nichi Ezochi*, West Ezo, that is, uncontrolled areas (Takakura 1960: 3; Kodama 1970: 36), and before that Hokkaido was divided into various Ainu communities, settlements or *Kotans*, of which a thorough knowledge is lacking (see also *Hokkaido Encyclopedia* 1981).

Nibutani is the tourist village of the Hidaka region, and the majority of its Ainu population is settled here. In addition, the Ainu living here place strong emphasis on their cultural uniqueness, and several of them are engaged full-time in matters concerning their own cultural heritage. These people identify themselves as Ainu. They arrange courses in Ainu language, material culture, history and religious beliefs.

Besides, there are today advanced plans to make this village "a genuine Ainu knowledge centre". This is an idea supported by national, regional and local funds, that is, from the Nihon state government, the Hokkaido prefectural government and the Biratori Cho administrative unit. During my stay in Nibutani I was allowed to attend a meeting where issues concerning the distribution of Biratori Cho cultural funds were discussed and I learned that there are plans to open a historical museum (the *Saru Kawa Ainu Hakubutsukan*, [*the Saru River Ainu Historical Museum*]) in Nibutani. The museum is to be surrounded by *Chise*,[3] Ainu-style dwelling houses, in which Ainu products will be hand-crafted in the old-fashioned way. Further, there are also plans to make a National Park of the surrounding forests and mountains, to preserve the fauna and flora of the once

---

1   Statistics about population in the chapter are taken from Utari Kyokai 1988: 4; Hokkaido Government 1988: 13.
2   The fourteen regions are: Nemuro, Kushiro, Tokachi, Hidaka, Iburi, Oshima, Hiyama, Shiribeshi, Ishikari, Sorachi, Rumoi, Souya, Kamikawa and Abashiri.
3   According to linguists the proper word is "Cise" yet the Ainu pronounce it Chise so I prefer to write it Chise.

most powerful Ainu territory in Hokkaido. In addition there are plans to replace farming products, such as bean, corn and rice, imported from Honshu, with Ainu crops and vegetables. Finally, there are plans to establish a centre for the study of Ainu history, material culture and oral language with lectures conducted by the Ainu themselves.

Shiraoi and Akan, in the *Iburi* and *Kushiro* regions, respectively, are also what one might call strong Ainu areas. The Ainu here also identify themselves as Ainu and the Ainu profile is strongly emphasized, at least during the tourist season, which lasts from early May till late October. This is a time when Ainu from all over Hokkaido join and take an active part in various Ainu performances and activities, such as ceremonial gatherings, Ainu dances and the like.

The Kushiro and Iburi regions, like Hidaka, are described in tourist guides as famous Ainu centres, with a dense Ainu population. This is only partly true; 42.6% of the total Ainu population in Hokkaido are to be found in the Hidaka region, 27.0% in the Iburi region and only 8.6% in the Kushiro region. Further, in the Kushiro and Iburi regions the Ainu population is spread out, whereas in the Hidaka region the Ainu population is concentrated to the Biratori Cho area.

In the Iburi region, with a total population of 454,387, and with the Shiraoi village and its Shiraoi Historical Ainu Museum as the centre for Ainu activities, we find Ainu from various regions coming together in the tourist season. During the tourist season Ainu activities, such as making and selling Ainu souvenirs, such as wooden bears, key-rings, cloth with Ainu motifs, as well as replicas of culture items exhibited in the museum, are at their peak. Performances of Ainu dances and ceremonies are other activities partaken in and publicly presented. The rest of the year, Ainu activities here show a low profile. Shiraoi as a centre for Ainu activities derives from the richness of this village in archaeological finds. As a result, the authorities in Nihon decided to build a museum here. Later this museum came to constitute the core around which the culture of the Ainu is displayed.

In the Kushiro region, with a total population of 306,707, and the Akan village as a centre for Ainu activities, the situation is much the same, except that there is no Ainu Historical Museum here, nor do we find anything with a similar function to an exhibition hall.

Akan has only recently (in the 1970s) become a centre for Ainu activities. In Akan, as in Shiraoi, the Ainu population more than triples during the tourist season. Akan village is named after Lake Akan and this lake has as powerful a traditional ring to the Ainu as the Saru River in the Hidaka region. However, because Nibutani village, through which the Saru River flows, is the most "researched" Ainu village and because of Shigeru Kayano's work with the local customs of the Ainu in this region, this specific river and village have come to overshadow other places of equal importance to the Ainu. As a result, Lake Akan and Akan village were ascribed less importance by researchers. Since the Ainu living in Akan have, to a considerable extent, been "left alone", that is, research into their local

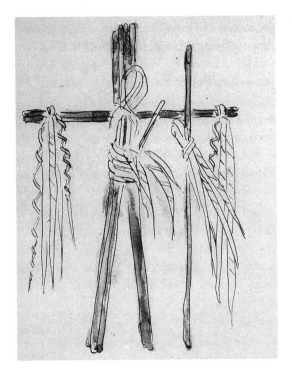

FIGURE 2   Inau *(offering stick)*

customs has never been frequent here, they were less reminded of their former customs and beliefs and the majority of them therefore tried to adapt themselves to the conditions introduced by the authorities in Nihon (interview in Akan, 1988).

In recent times, however, the Ainu in Akan, inspired especially by Kayano and his work, began their own reinvestigation of Ainu customs and beliefs tied to Akan village and Lake Akan. In a way the Ainu in Akan started, so to speak, to take matters into their own hands and among other things they invented a Lake Akan festival, the *Marimo* festival. The Marimo is, according to the beliefs of the Ainu, a powerful lake god, *Kamuy*, whom the Ainu here feared because it was believed that it fed on humans. To please the Kamuy, the Ainu offered special *Inau*,[4] offering sticks, to the Kamuy. This offering was performed on an individual basis. Today, however, it is transformed into a collective ceremony, and Ainu come from all over Hokkaido to join in.

---

4   According to linguists the proper word is "Inaw", but the Ainu pronounce it "Inau" so I write Inau. Naert (1960: 177) is of the opinion that the word Inau is connected with the Giljak word "Nau" and the Orok word "Illau".

Although the activities in "strong Ainu areas" include purely commercial aspects and, except for Nibutani, show a low profile outside the tourist seasons, the Ainu engaged in them claim that their commitment is social more than anything else. Hence, the tourist villages can be viewed as centres, or market places, where not only material needs are fulfilled but also and mainly, social and cultural ones. The centres may therefore, in their present guise, be looked upon as based on shared feelings of mutual understanding and friendship, which emanate from a conscious sense of "belonging" and are consolidated by joint participation in a common culture.

The tourist villages also function as a sort of public sphere for the Ainu. They have become places where the Ainu, by "putting themselves on show", express their group or collective identity. These villages have become places where the conscious reconstruction of an Ainu identity is noticeable. In a way it emphasizes the distinctive content of Ainu ethnicity for the tourists and the larger public who are invited not only to buy Ainu products, but to see how they are made, and even to experiment in making them themselves. They can also learn about Ainu mythology, ritual and history, taste Ainu food and live in Ainu homes, especially when the boarding-houses are full.

Finally, the suburbs of the cities of Asahikawa, Hakodate and Sapporo, which in my study represent "weak" Ainu areas, were chosen for study because of people's apparent lack of interest in their Ainu heritage. In the suburban environment the people are more concerned with hiding their Ainu inheritance than emphasizing it.

Sapporo was chosen to represent the centre in a bureaucratic administrative sense, that is, where rules and regulations, rather than common sense, determine what actions should be taken and how, in relation both to the preservation of legal rights and to power. As regards the bureaucratic administrative meaning of the concept of centre, it is used to facilitate such formalities as registration of place of birth, land ownership, marriages, employment and the like.

PARTICIPANT OBSERVATION

Participant observation is necessary in understanding the basic interaction discussed above. In constructing models for the understanding of different cultures in general and the actions, behaviour and attitudes of the people in particular, "practical experience" of the culture is an absolute necessity. By being there, living there, it is possible to accumulate knowledge about the people and its culture from "the natives' point of view". Attaining an inside view not only brings new knowledge for the description analysis of different cultures, but also allows the establishment of a dialogue between ourselves and other cultures, especially useful for evaluating them in other than value-laden time-bound terms.

The advantage of prolonged stays is obvious, not least for this reason, but also because they make it possible both to compare the information gathered from various interviews, and to observe what people actually say (to each other) when not interviewed. In addition it allows for a comparison of ways in which their actions actually correspond to the opinions expressed in the interviews. Take for instance such a question as: "What word, or words, do you use when addressing non-Ainu people here in Nihon?" Answer: "Nihonjin". This turned out to be correct, but only on occasions when non-Ainu people were present. Otherwise they used "Shamo". In addition they claim to address people from abroad (Westerners) with the term *Gaikokujin*, whereas in practice they used *Gaijin* which is, if not impolite, not as neutral as "Gaikokujin".

Other illustrative examples were the many recommendations of important Ainu happenings, gatherings and meetings, occasions which they themselves never miss. In the end, however those occasions least spoken of turned out to be the most frequented. One example of this is the invented Marimo festival in Akan, a festival that turned out to be "the happening of the year", although in the interviews the Ainu spoke of it with contempt because it was invented and not "genuine". The *Shakushain* festival, on the other hand, which is held in the honour of Ainu ancestors, did not attract that many people, although it is regarded as one of the most important Ainu festivals by the Ainu. Later, I found that this turned out to be linked to the type of place – *Shizunai* for the Shakushain and Akan for the Marimo festival – rather than to the type of festival, and the following explanation was given to me by one of my Ainu informants in Nibutani:

> We enjoy being together with our own people, I mean Ainu who have the same interests as we have. People from Akan, Shiraoi and Nibutani take a great interest in Ainu gatherings of all kinds. When we come and visit each other's places we have so many things to discuss, so it is not only because of the festival we gather. The festival gives us an opportunity to meet. In Shizunai where the Shakushain festival is held people gather because they think that it is expected of them since Shakushain is an Ainu hero. Of course we are proud of him but we feel that the festival does not give us the same opportunity to discuss other things that are our concern. I think this has to with the fact that there are not many Ainu in the Shizunai area and we rarely see them on other occasions. In a way we do not think of this place, Shizunai, as belonging to the Ainu. According to our traditional customs, when Ainu travel to other Ainu areas they are the honorable guests. We do not feel that way in Shizunai (interview with Ainu male, aged 59, Nibutani, 1988).

The following example may be used to illustrate another point. When I first came to Nibutani and said that I was going to stay there more or less permanently for six months, people laughed. The information below was given to me by an Ainu woman who, as my stay went on, not only became one of my best informants, but also a very dear friend.

That we would like to see. We have had so many of your kind [anthropologists] here and not one of them stayed for more than two weeks. To be on the safe side, you can ask me, and other people I will recommend, your questions and then you do not have to stay for such a long time. There will be no problem, we are used to your kind of questions. If you insist on staying here, you will get into trouble. I do not mean to say that we do not like you, we do not know you, but what I am trying to say is that it is unwise to say that you are going to stay for such a long time, when you are not. Take for instance the boarding-house, you mean business to them, if you do not keep your word you disturb things for them. No, it is very unwise of you to say that you are going to stay here for such a long time (my first interview in Nibutani, 1988).

Of relevance here is that I had to face major problems in connection with my change of residence. I learned that this had to do with the fact that "business" was disturbed. This was an explanation which was not accepted by my various hosts. They simply said that my new host was "unreliable". This situation turned out to be the rule rather than the exception.

Central to my fieldwork was the collection of life histories, attitudes, ideational systems and beliefs. Life histories were used as a source of data for the investigation of Ainu old-time history, especially useful as a complement to the reconstruction (reinterpretation) of Ainu history going on today.

Further, the value of collecting qualitative data as a method for illustrating ongoing processes should not be underestimated. Compare for instance contemporary Ainu attitudes to the policy of assimilation, which are predominantly negative, with previous attitudes which were mainly positive. On this point their own explanations showed a great variety as regards causes and effects and differed in many respects from the official Nihon one.

With respect to "attitudes", especially their attitudes to their own situation, it turned out that they varied according to the situational context, which means that people adopted what they judged "appropriate attitudes", in the sense that their pattern of behaviour varied according to the company they were in. When tourists were around they adopted one specific model, when researchers were around this model was replaced by another and among "friends" there was yet another model, and so forth.

What these attitudes had in common was that each model corresponded to what the Ainu thought served both themselves and the "party" best. In a way they adopted the view of the company they were in, since, generally speaking, they contradicted each other on several points.

In the company of Wajin tourists, the Ainu made great efforts to explain how things had improved for them since the annexation of their land. In the company of researchers their main concern was to convince them that they were well read in literature written about themselves and that their own view contrasted in many ways with the views presented in these writings. Points of inconsistency between their own views and the picture emerging from the texts written about them were a constant topic of debate in my relationship with them. In the company of "friends", a status which I gained at the very end of my stay in Nibutani, they made efforts to explain why they had adopted these models. Their explanation can be summarized in the words of one of my informants, an Ainu who, in connection with the Second World War, had spent several years of his youth in Russian imprisonment. "It is our way of coping with reality without losing both pride and dignity, a matter of survival I suppose" (interview with Ainu male, Nibutani, 1988).

The collection of quantitative data was not ignored altogether. The form was that of basic census (Pelto & Pelto 1978: 78-79) and it was restricted to a simple enumeration of household composition. I used it in Nibutani in particular, because of its reputation as a centre for the study of their culture. In order to discover how many Ainu inhabitants in Nibutani village actually took part in activities rooted in their culture I found it useful to make a register. In combination with my notes on marriage alliances, divorces, employment and migration, the register was of great value, not only for understanding conditions here, but also the interdependence of Ainu individuals, and conditions both in Ainu provincial areas and in the suburbs.

During my stay in Nibutani I did not make use of structured interviews, such as questionnaires or interview schedules, since they imply a thorough contextual and conceptual knowledge of an inside view, which was difficult to attain for an "outsider" like myself. I decided to settle for in-depth interviews with open-ended questions that allowed me to discuss things unfamiliar to me. Further, the issues discussed arose for the most part out of the social context which I happened to join. In short, I made use of the topic discussed during these social events and in this regard my own participation in the dialogue influenced both the topic discussed and the outcome of it. When I was involved in the conversation they had a tendency to insert Ainu words when they spoke. I also noticed that they were "on their guard", as if they did not know whether I could be "trusted". When they discussed a topic which they for some reason judged "delicate" or if their opinions differed on a specific topic, they either changed the topic or the group broke up. On other occasions the conversation took the form of an interview, but they interviewed me. The topics of such interviews varied, but for the most part it concerned my family life, things about living in Sweden, and so on. They were also interested in gaining as much information as they could about my own attitude to the customs and beliefs of the Shamo, how much I knew about their manners, their present-day way of life, how much contact I had with Shamo scholars and what these scholars said about them off the record, so to speak.

During my stays in 1985 and 1986 I used what can be classified as a type of interview schedule. At that time I had not gained sufficient knowledge in Nihongo, the Japanese language, so I wrote down my questions in English and an assistant helped me to translate them into Nihongo. Because of my poor Nihongo I could not add any comments during these interviews, which were conducted with the help of a tape-recorder. I then took the tapes to my assistant in Sapporo and she translated the answers. Using a tape-recorder is not very popular among the Ainu and many people refused to be interviewed if I used it. They never gave me a clear answer on this particular point so I was unable to find out why they did not like to be recorded; however, such attitudes are not unusual among people in their situation.

Unstructured interviews were carried out both with key informants like government authorities, Kyokai, Hokudai and Kaitakinenka representatives, and with *Ekashi*[5] (elders) in Ainu provincial areas.

As regards the representation of suburban informants, I faced major difficulties. These people seek to hide their identity and often I had to rely on secondary information obtained through friends and relatives, and such social conversations as described above. It was practically impossible to reach these people without assistance from their kin in the village.

The problem that I faced was the following: these people hide their identity in their suburban environment and their kin in the villages have accepted this. For such reasons they did not willingly take me to visit their kin in the suburbs and I could not simply walk into their lives without notice. After all, the only way I could have obtained information about their whereabouts was from their relatives and that might have resulted in distrust between them. I managed, however, to get some direct information on occasions when they visited relatives or when they took part in the various activities arranged at Ainu tourist centres or in the villages.

FIELDWORK APPROACH

In the field of anthropology there are different ways of interpreting or reading the ethnographic material. In my approach I put emphasis on the emic. In the initial phase of my fieldwork, the tables were turned. I was the one who was questioned about my culture, my family life and so forth, everything I was trained to ask my informants about. While I willingly answered their questions, they either put up a blank face or answered me in the most stereotype ways when I asked them anything about themselves.

It was evidently the case that the Ainu objected to a view of themselves as "anthropological objects". It was obvious that they wanted a "cultural dialogue" to take place and preferred a view where not only my cultural evaluations and their own cultural evaluations were treated in a more "equal" way but where their own cultural evaluations

---

5 According to linguists the proper word is "Ekas", but the Ainu pronounce it "Ekashi" so I write Ekashi.

were predominant. This I thought had to do with them being long-term objects of anthropological interest, a position which they obviously did not like and had their own ideas of how to escape. Besides, I also knew of an incident that took place a year before my own stay. It concerned a Wajin anthropologist who was forced to give up her investigation because of "uncooperative and hostile Ainu" (a quotation from one of my informants). I decided then that I had to play it their way.

I presented them with extended versions of my daily life, gossip, Swedish history, modern as well as ancient, national scandals (there were many at the time of my fieldwork, such as bugging and racism), the welfare and pension system, unions, vacations, the educational system and so on. In this way the Ainu came, at least as far as unstructured interviews are concerned, to play the anthropologist's part, whereas I was their subject. The more extended my answers were, the more comments they gave on the subject. In this way I was able to find out which subjects were of interest and why. In a way they selected essentialities of their own culture, through the role they had given me as storyteller. Their own role, that of pathfinders, helped to guide me through their conceptual jungle.

Another phenomenon well known to anthropologists today is the risk of becoming trapped in a "child position". This position is often restricted to rules of etiquette and ranges over a short period, and my case was no exception. I decided, however, to stay in it for as long as I myself thought necessary, which meant that I broke conventional rules on purpose. Thus I was given information about the hierarchy in the rule-breaking system, what was serious and what was less serious. Through my "bad behaviour" I was able to compare what I was told was serious with what was actually viewed with grave disapproval.

It is of some relevance that the Ainu, trained in what is expected of them as anthropological subjects and accustomed to keeping details to themselves, made it difficult for me to proceed in a "traditional" manner as fieldworker. Besides, the fact that the Ainu are inimical to anthropologists – not just Wajin – in general and to those using Wajin assistants particularly created difficulties in the initial phase of my investigation. Such difficulties affected my work in more than one way. First, it was not possible to have my Wajin assistant accompany me in Nibutani. She had to remain in Sapporo and her main acivity was reduced to helping me with my bookings when I travelled in Hokkaido, doing paper work for me and keeping me informed of Ainu activities advertised in the local papers. Later, however, she was invited to the village and they even discussed arranging a welcome party for her.

Second, since the Nihongo I had learnt through my contact with my assistant and her relatives in Sapporo and my contact with Wajin scholars varied from the Nihongo spoken in Nibutani, there were a many problems at the beginning. The type of problem that arose is somewhat difficult to explain, since one has to have at least some knowledge of how the Nihon language is structured.

Nihongo is what one might call a hierarchical language, with strict rules for proper ways of expressing oneself, depending on one's function in society. As a rule you speak about yourself, and matters concerning yourself, in a humble way (I, a person of small importance, versus you, a person of great dignity), especially when dealing with university personnel, government authorities or administrators, but also with ordinary people. Your inferior position can be expressed either by using synonyms, varying in degree of politeness, or with the help of suffixes/prefixes. In Nibutani, people were not accustomed to this way of speaking. Accordingly, my way of speaking appeared very odd to them. Later I learned that they found that my way of expressing myself made them feel as if they were a bunch of administrators, something which discomforted them, because they could not figure out why I used such language. Often they could not understand me at all. In trying to work out what I meant they suggested a number of synonyms of which I had not the slightest understanding. Later, I found out that their synonyms were those used when addressing children, or females,[6] whereas those synonyms I was accustomed to were those used when expressing one's inferior position, since this was what I had been taught through my previous contacts. As my stay went on they took great interest in my linguistic progress and it often occurred that they asked me about what my "posh" Shamo friends had to say about my Nihongo acquired in Nibutani.

Although the advantages of an inside view can never be over-emphasized there is a specific disadvantage, which relates to the fact that one can never be sure of to what degree the inside view one has acquired, through sharing the lives of the people one is studying, actually corresponds to an inside view acquired by inheritance. Nevertheless, inside views may serve as a guide to understanding Ainu resistance to the policy of assimilation, simply because the actions taken by the Ainu in the integration situation could never have been predicted by outsiders such as the Wajin. This is not totally neglected by researchers with an interest in the present situation of the Ainu. The lack of an inside view in the Ainu case has unfortunately been used as an excuse in explaining "why Ainu community life collapsed". Peng and Geiser write:

> A possible reason why Ainu community life collapsed, when other groups faced with duress have remained viable, may be explained by the relation between symbolic meaning and group solidarity. There is a close connection between the effectiveness of symbols in maintaining group identity and the functioning of institutions that are sources of symbols. Upon the disappearance of institutional functions, the symbols become "free-floating" and thus in turn foster the individ-

---

6   Before my stay in Nibutani I was not much trained in the "female" language. Most of my contacts were males and those who were females addressed me in much the same way as the males did.

ual's detachment from group-life. Such was the case for the Ainu. The Japanese were apparently unaware of the degree to which the Ainu's cultural apparatus was entangled with what appeared to be a simple hunting and fishing economy. Very early in the relations between the Japanese and the Ainu, severe restrictions were placed upon the Ainu's use of the lands and the seas and those were replaced by Japanese colonial exploitation. The meaningful symbols connected with these ancient Ainu practices were now purposeless (1977: 20).

The authors' explanation that "the Japanese were apparently unaware of the degree to which the Ainu cultural apparatus was entangled with what appeared to be a simple hunting and fishing economy" is as poor an excuse as it is convenient. Further, it gives us a distorted picture of "the course things took", what actually happened and why. In addition, it prevents us from discovering incentives in Ainu society and culture since the inherent dynamics are either not recognized at all or else they are interpreted as blockages. In my own approach I will concentrate on how the Ainu at present reinvent, restore or reorganize "their once meaningful symbols", since the fact that the symbols, as Peng and Geiser state, are "purposeless" does not necessarily imply that they actually became purposeless for the Ainu. Rather, their "purposeless condition" may be restricted to the context in which Peng and Geiser put them.

The ethnographic encounter comprises more than an encounter with modern Ainu, what they do for a living, how they see themselves today, their goals and wishes, attitudes and the like. It also comprises the encounter with their methods of approaching written and verbal accounts of their history and ethnography and how they incorporate this in the reality in which they live today.

The Ainu of the past and present, as we see them and as they perceive themselves, are, of course, not simply a product of the way others have interpreted them, their society, symbols, actions, activities, behaviour and history, but of their own way of responding to this. The image we as well as the Ainu have of themselves, both past and present, is also the result of their specific history, the interpretation of which, to a considerable extent, is dependent on who the author is and how he interprets the reality of history. There is thus no "natural" continuum in the process of building an image of oneself in the general sense, but rather a wide spectrum of possible constructs, due not only to the above but also due to the fact that people learn from experience and reconsider their views. This affects of course our own as well as the Ainu view, of the historic Ainu over time.

The Ainu do not look upon themselves in the same way today as they did some hundred years ago. There was a time when the Ainu were eager to forget their own customs and beliefs in order to become Nihonjin. One reason for this was that they thought that the gods of the conquerors were more powerful than those they themselves worshipped. Today there are few people who would connect Ainu strategies for achieving ethnic status to a view that the Ainu have come to realize that their own gods were, perhaps, not that bad after all. Today their attempts to become accepted as Ainu, getting to know their own cultural tradition by reconsidering values and beliefs that belong to the past, are related to other factors and need to be looked upon in a different light; our approach and that of the Ainu are modified accordingly.

Today the Ainu make use of the information gathered about them not only to reconstruct, reorganize and reinvent their own values and beliefs but to gain an understanding of why they acted in the way they did and why they became marginal in their own domains. Their approach is one where the modern Ainu try to understand how the mind of the historic Ainu operated by questioning the conceptual tools of others who have interpreted it.

Since the information gathered by researchers makes up the basis on which the reconstruction of their history and culture is built, a proper approach would be to deal with these as (re)constructions and this is exactly what the Ainu do. The question is how to deal with this? One possible way is to let the Ainu comment on the texts produced about them and use this information to make the ethnographic picture we have of their social and cultural past more complete.

CHAPTER THREE

Analytical framework

This chapter is divided into three parts. In the first part I will deal with previous research about the Ainu. The works to which my attention is drawn include purely descriptive works by missionaries and explorers, community studies concerned with cultural and social change and works about Ainu oral tradition, material culture, religious beliefs and kinship.

In the second part I will present an alternative framework. The use of well-received constructs as receptacles for field data may seem both secure and attractive. The idea of simply adapting what has been called classical realism that has been amply criticized (Clifford 1986; Marcus & Fisher 1986; Van Maanen 1988) as their works enact a specific strategy of "authority" is not the best approach. The latter approach tends to reduce the heterogeneity of ethnographic realism to univocal homogeneity. My own approach marks a departure from this view and is in line with a model developed at the Department of Anthropology at the University of Lund. In my approach the concern is to grasp the heterogeneity and my focus is on the encounter between strategies of the state and local strategies. A perspective that focuses on strategies best suits the analysis of a multi-vocal reality. This approach allows for an incorporation of the individuals and their actions in the dialogue that exists between the Ainu and the larger society.

In the third part I will consider workable definitions of the concepts that are central to my work. These are nation, state, culture, ethnicity, discrimination, assimilation, acculturation and integration.

OVERVIEW OF PREVIOUS WORK

Before discussing my own approach let us consider the approaches of previous research.

First, some general remarks about the works made by missionaries (Batchelor 1901, 1902, 1924, 1932, 1971; Hilger 1967; Kodama 1970: 13 ff.), explorers (Bird 1881; Landor 1893; Kajima 1895; Fisher 1949), and colonizers from Nihon proper, to be found in archives annexed to Hokudai (Sapporo State University) and in archives connected with the various Ainu museums (see also Takakura 1960: 82-88). These writings take on something of an institutional voice and their authority rests on the background expectations of an audience of believers. These expectations rely, in turn, on the rather exemplary status of the authors as objective judges of the society, customs and behaviour of the people they encountered, quite regardless of the fact that the objective character is contaminated by personal bias, political and religious goals, or moral judgments. Common to their works is that they served to set the agenda for the style, scope and subject matter of anthropological debates and were for the most part preoccupied with the origins of modern institutions, rituals, customs and habits of thought through the contrasts of evolutionary stages in the development of human society. Their picture was a negative one. The people were described as "barbarians", their customs as "primitive" and their social life as "crumbly". The observer saw himself both as a superior being and as a saviour.

A FUNCTIONALIST VIEW

Let us now consider the studies made of the cultural and social tradition of the Ainu. The form of most of these studies is that of ethnographic realism, of which the most striking characteristic is the almost complete absence of the author from most segments of the finished text – after having finished the job of collecting data he vanishes behind a steady descriptive narrative justified largely by the respectable image and ideology of ethnographic practice.

Unlike the writings of missionaries, colonizers and explorers, these writings pass on more or less objective data. The authors are identified as scholars with graduate training, academic affiliations and impersonal disciplinary interests that legitimate access and inquiry within the target culture. The people and the material are organized according to topics and problems relevant to the authors conceptual and disciplinary interests.

When considering the studies of the kinship organization of the Ainu, attempts have been made to bring order into the system that governed the social structure of the Ainu in the past and a number of interesting studies have been made (Seligman 1962; Sugiura & Befu 1962; Ohnuki-Tierney 1974, 1976). It should be pointed out that although the structure of the Ainu social system has been subject to much debate in anthropological circles and regardless of attempts to bring order into the system that governed the social structure of former Ainu societies, it remains as obscure as ever.

In the medical-oriented field, Ohnuki-Tierney has contributed to important discoveries for the understanding of Sakhalin Ainu symbolic interpretations. Her research on their medical beliefs (1981), illustrates how illness relates to their view of the universe, how the medical system is intimately interwoven with their moral cosmology and social network and how illness and health in the universe of the Sakhalin Ainu can be interpreted as symbolic aspects of the social order in their culture.

In her work she explores such issues as the status of women in hunting-gathering societies and the relation between the symbolic structure of a people and their more practical social life. She questions what kind of classification system or systems we can find in a given culture. The objective of her investigation is the perceptual structure underlying behaviour, verbal and non-verbal, but not behaviour itself (1981: 15). She sees structure as an abstraction and points to the fact that structure does not correspond to any one specific incident of behaviour. Her concern is how thought influences behaviour and vice versa and she points at the fact that a misfit between thought and behaviour tells us something about both.

The studies undertaken to investigate the social and cultural change, whether historical or ecological-evolutionary, that has taken place among the Ainu, show a notable stress on endogenous factors in accounting for the cultural and social situations of the Ainu at present. They have attempted to demonstrate that apart from agriculture, which must have been imported, the Ainu have not been capable of development (Munro 1911; Saito 1912; Takakura 1960; Kodama 1970), or that their ecological adaption is itself an example of a less-developed form of existence (Watanabe 1972, 1975).

In *The Ainu Ecosystem* (Watanabe 1972) important discoveries have contributed to an understanding of the former Ainu lifestyle in the context of their environment. Watanabe's research illustrates means and mechanisms within the context of the system of activities that incorporates them and he analyses the way in which they contribute to the maintenance of their individuals, the group and the species.

In "Subsistence and Ecology of Northern Food Gatherers with Special Reference to the Ainu" (Watanabe 1975), he analyses the relations between group structure and subsistence activities and their spatial correlates and he discusses the arrangement of settlements with reference to resources. His ambition is to clarify the concepts of nomadism and sedentarism. He also discusses the allocation of subsistence activities by sex and age, with an attempt to reconsider the issues of division of labour and how it evolved.

The problem with his view is that he treats the Ainu way of life as a closed system. This is inadequate to understanding the Ainu cultural and social existence whether in the past or in the present. His preoccupation with the ecological adaptation of the Ainu reduces mechanisms within the Ainu society to a way of illuminating how the ecological adaption of the Ainu fits their activities as hunters. Accordingly, the Ainu way of life has been analysed to fit this category, regardless of the fact that a proper definition of hunters and gatherers with respect to the Ainu is missing.

When considering works on the Ainu language, *Ainu Itak*, (Pilsudski 1912; Gjerdman 1926, 1959; Batchelor 1925, 1938; Chiri 1956, 1962; Naert 1958; Kindaichi 1960; Lindquist 1960; Tamura 1983; Voi 1983, 1987; Refsing 1987), it is important to note that Ainu in general do not think highly of the studies made of their language.

The problems connected with the language of the Ainu are considerable. The Ainu Itak is oral and it differs in many ways from *Nihongo*, the Japanese language. The main problem is that it is difficult to use Nihon characters, in this case *Katakana*, when transcribing Ainu Itak into Nihongo and as a result many Ainu words have been corrupted. Recent research has come to realize this and favours Roman letters instead of Katakana.

AN ALTERNATIVE FRAMEWORK

The point of departure I use in my approach is in the modern situation and the scope is extended to the wider political and economic structure to which the Ainu belong. My concern is to understand the situation of the Ainu as it is today, including the process that has led to today's situation of interest in ethnic factors. Essential to my research are issues such as the asymmetrical relationship between the majority people, the Wajin, and the indigenous people, the Ainu. This is a context in which matters concerning Ainu affairs fall under various social service institutions, primarily because of the comparatively high proportion of Ainu who rely on social welfare.[1]

The method chosen by me to illustrate ongoing changes in the interaction situation puts emphasis on the efforts of Ainu individuals to exploit various niches, opened to them through their contact with the larger society. As there are several actors in the arena there are also several strategies in dialogue and encounter with one another. One way of understanding the cultural change that takes place would be to understand it as the outcome of the multiplex interaction between the Ainu, the larger society and the state. In other words, a perspective that ascribes more importance to strategies of various kinds insofar as they are collective actions for altering old conditions and creating new ones.

---

1   In 1973 Mr Saito, Minister of State, stated that:

"The Ainu fall far behind economically, occupationally, educationally and also in terms of welfare ... we feel obligated to help raise their living standard ...and improve welfare services for them" (Draft from the 71st Diet, the Third Subcommittee of the Lower House Budget Committee Session March 5, 1973, Utari Kyokai 1987b).

This statement was based on *An Investigation of the Actual Conditions among the Ainu in Hokkaido*, financed out of the budget of the Ministry of Health and Welfare, and conducted in 1972. The report reveals that:

"30.9% of the households are in the lowest bracket of income, including those on welfare. This means that 3 out of 10 Ainu people have to live in complete destitution" (Utari Kyokai 1987b).

In a more recent report, *The Report on Actual Condition of the Ainu People in Hokkaido*, made by Hokkaido Local Government and conducted in November 1986 we find that:

"Population on public assistance in Hokkaido is proportioned thus: Ainu 60.9%, Non-Ainu 21.9%" (Utari Kyokai 1987b).

Above all, this perspective assigns more importance to conscious will and practices of both individual and collective existence.

It is thus no longer a question of observing or being involved in a normal process as an agent of the changing conditions of which one is part, nor is it a self-propelling process that needs only to be freed from the fetters of tradition, or whatever structures may be holding it back, and it cannot be taken as normative. In understanding the cultural mobilization that takes place focus is thus put on "actually existing change", including an awareness that there is no universal movement from "traditional" to modern but a multitude of regional transformation processes. In the Ainu case, the advantage of this approach is obvious, because at present there is no "Ainu society" in the general sense, which makes it impossible to look at its structure. What we have instead is a network of Ainu individuals who, with the aid of a variety of strategies, try to adapt themselves to the changing conditions.

By employing a perspective that focuses on strategies rather than structures it is possible to incorporate individuals and their actions in the dialogue that exists between the Ainu, the larger Nihon society and its authorities. If not, we might find ourselves in the situation of previous research and likewise arrive at the conclusion that the policy of assimilation, such as it is maintained by the authorities, is a success, led astray by official statistics regarding their present occupational situation and the total number of the Ainu population. These so called "facts" are backed up by Wajin authorities who use these as signs indicating that the assimilation actually is a success.

THE PROCESS OF CHANGE

To start with, I judged it very likely, as Hall (1987), points out, that "traditional" societies were experiencing their own dynamics before they were disrupted by intruders, and that the intrusion itself represented a change in the processes of change. In the Ainu case, recent research by Crawford and Yoshizaki (1987) provides evidence that the Ainu hunting and fishing economy was, if not a recent phenomenon, at least not as ancient as previous research suggested. This would indicate that the Ainu were at one time a hierarchical society with a mixed economy and that their present status, including the image of hunters, is a product of a long and painful interaction.

Many of the societies that anthropology used to characterize as "traditional" (original) were in fact late phenomena, created through contact with an expanding Europe (Fagan 1986; Wolf 1986). Many of them were also, as has been pointed out by Ekholm Friedman (1991), products of global historical processes, which for their part meant gradual disintegration and peripheralization and in some cases even complete elimination. They were "primitivized" by the position they occupied within the global system (Friedman 1983; Ekholm Friedman 1991).

The process of change consists of modifications, often analysed as processes of contraction caused by specific reactionary cultural traits within the structure of "traditional" societies. As regards the Ainu, compare for instance their previous position as part of feudal Nihon, where they were supposed to contribute to the economy of a feudal system rather than to one which existed in their own territory, with their contemporary position in one of today's leading capitalist nations, where their land and natural resources are essential but where their skills and knowledge, whether inherited or acquired through contact with the larger society, are of minor importance. In this situation it is important to note that the actions taken by the Ainu are neither irreversible nor one-directional. Examples are today's alternative land use which has introduced Ainu crops and the change of the profile of Ainu tourist centres.

As I understand it, this development is a result of a dialectical process between the Ainu and the larger society, whereby the strategies employed by the Ainu actively change the very structure that gave rise to them. The intervention of the Nihon nation, via different development programmes and activities, may not only trigger various responses by collective and individual actors, but may also create new networks, as is the case with the Ainu tourist centres.

THE NECESSITY TO INCORPORATE THE PERSPECTIVE OF THE AINU

If we wish to understand the situation of the Ainu, as it actually is to the Ainu, we have to make use of the conceptual and explanatory tools of the Ainu themselves. Otherwise our interpretations easily become ethnocentric and encourage researchers to emphasize what we, as researchers, perceive as signs of "incapability" (ecological specialization) attached to cultural and social forms rather than to inadequacies in the methods employed by us (community studies in a functionalist tradition). If we make use of the perspective of the Ainu we will also be able to present a picture of the interaction with the Ainu as actors and active subjects, thereby opposing the usual picture of them as sleeping partners or passive objects.

The present-day Ainu engagement in activities and practices tied to their culture and a consequent change in their attitude to the policy of assimilation, can best be understood if we take a closer look at the role they themselves, their land and natural resources play(ed) in interaction with the Wajin. As for their present situation, we have to consider that their land and natural resources are essential to the nation as a whole, whereas their skills and knowledge are of minor importance and that the holistic and hierarchical identity of the Wajin makes it difficult for them to enter the larger society.

Finding themselves as part of the process of change, the Ainu react and they interpret the events around them. The actions they take relate as much to the interaction situation as to values rooted in their own culture. Within this framework, Ainu contact with the larger society teaches them not only how to go about restoring these values but also what niches they can successfully exploit. But it has to be remembered that their actions also relate to the restrictions placed upon them by the larger society of which they are part and where they feel that their land and natural resources are properly integrated whereas they themselves are left with circumscribed possibilities to enjoy their fruits.

Interaction with the larger society provides alternative or new ways of displaying and strengthening their ethnicity. An example of this is that tourist production and display have become a central process in the conscious reconstruction of Ainu identity. In several areas they have established village structures for the express purpose of producing. hand-crafted goods. The have also built Ainu-style houses, *Chise*, where important village activities, such as the teaching of history and language and Ainu dances, weaving and wood-carving occur on a weekly basis.

It has been argued that the way the Ainu display their cultural tradition is folklore, that is, alienated from their identity, because of its emphasis on cultural artifacts. For the Ainu the act of putting emphasis on cultural artifacts is in itself an act of creating an image of oneself as an ethnic entity. Among the Ainu there is no interest in political autonomy but a wish to function politically and economically within the larger system and socially and culturally parallel to it.

While this might appear simple to the Western observer, it is a very serious problem for a state whose acceptable principle of reasoning is endangered by the existence of multi-ethnicity. All inhabitants native to Nihon are Nihonjin and as such the Ainu are perceived as just one variant of a dominant and sole ethnic group, the Wajin. It has been claimed that the position of the Ainu can only be changed in Nihon official ideology via a fuller integration into the larger economy and society and they must enter contemporary Nihon society on terms defined by the highest authority in Nihon, which implies a rejection of ethnic status.

A theoretical consequence of this is that the Ainu of today, officially, exist in what might be called a cultural vacuum. A practical consequence of this is that it has given rise to a variety of ways for the Ainu to manoeuvre their ethnicity, ranging from, on the one hand, the emphasizing of themselves as a unique cultural group, to the emphasizing of cultural similarities between themselves and the Wajin, on the other. A main feature of them all is that contact with the Wajin is presupposed and the main goals are to gain equal opportunities and equal rights in a society dominated by a group of people other than themselves.

SELF-PERCEPTION

The picture, as it has been presented by previous research focusing on the condition of the Ainu today, does at best oppose the highly discriminatory treatment of the Ainu by Nihon authorities, the national majority in particular. This in turn, is related to the preoccupation of the researchers with issues related to the Ainu as a "marginal" minority people, where the focus is on their peripheral position within a centre-periphery context.

The Ainu do not refer to themselves as "indigenous", nor do they talk about themselves as "marginal". To the Ainu, the Ainu are "central" as are their land and natural resources, their activities and their ways of handling their situation. This call for the use of a model where the methods employed by the Ainu are understood in relation to the premisses that govern the reality that exists among them. The strategies they employ in the interaction situation emanate from what they perceive as "the centre", rather than from within a centre-periphery context, where they actually are marginal.

ADVANTAGES OF EMPLOYING AN AINU PERSPECTIVE

By employing an Ainu perspective we add an alternative cause of the previous Ainu attempts to become "even more Japanese than the Japanese" and why they failed. Apart from the fact that we in this way are given an opportunity to explore their cultural tradition from an Ainu angle, there is also a possibility for us to add an alternative explanation both of the present change in the relationship between the Ainu and the Wajin and of its contemporary direction. The fact that the Ainu at the time of the annexation of their land were left in extreme poverty, seems to have been as obvious to the emperor (Hokkaido Government 1899) as it was to the Ainu themselves. The cause of the condition was, however, differently interpreted.

To the emperor, the *Tenno*, "the immigrants and the innocence of the Ainu" have caused this effect, whereas to the Ainu, it resulted from "bad" relations with Nature. They felt that Nature had deserted them, and their own explanation was that they had not fulfilled their obligations towards Nature. Due to their own "disgrace" and the favourable position of the Wajin, the Ainu chose to abandon their own beliefs and customs (Kayano 1988b). After all, the gods of the conquerors had turned out to be the most powerful ones. Now, difficulties and obstacles in achieving this status which they in fact never had, have formerly been interpreted exclusively as "inabilities" on the part of the Ainu, whereas complex mechanisms, such as prevailing hierarchical mechanisms in the Wajin system that make transgression impossible, have, for the most part, been ignored.

The strategy used by the Ainu at that time did not fulfil the promises of a future ideal life, nor did the mere copying of Wajin customs. Instead the Ainu found that their land and natural resources were incorporated into the Wajin system while they themselves were not. Essential to this state of affair is, of course, the hierarchical identity of Nihon which prevents people of non-Wajin descent to enter the political and economic arena in Nihon. In our attempts to understand why the Ainu have come to place emphasis on their own cultural uniqueness and also to understand the strategies that they employ, this aspect is of crucial importance.

Although the picture of the Ainu which appears at first glance may fit the stereotype of a people who have deserted their own customs this picture is illusionary. Although the Ainu no longer live in Ainu-style houses, *Chise*, wear Ainu-style clothes, *Attus*, or speak their native language, *Ainu Itak*, we have several indicators pointing to the fact that the strategies employed by the Ainu stand in direct opposition to the non-ethnic premisses of state ideology. This need not imply that the Ainu are seeking to leave the nation of which they are part, nor that they strive to exist between two sectors, a "traditional" and a "modern". It would be wrong to conclude that their strategies of adaptation contrast with the modern life of the present. Such an interpretation derives from the assumption that tradition and change stand in a dualistic relationship. By employing an Ainu perspective it is possibile to show that in practice there exists a synthesis between the two.

While the history of Ainu relations to the larger society is one of increasing economic and political integration (many Ainu have abandoned their countryside residence and seek a living in the industrial sector and those who remain have adjusted themselves to new conditions, that is, they are engaged in the rural sector), they have not only been able to preserve their own cultural uniqueness but they are also strengthening it in various ways. The change from a subsistence to a market-oriented economy has, quite contrary to what was generally assumed, thus not worked to alienate them from their own cultural tradition.

THE AINU METHOD OF GAINING
PUBLIC RECOGNITION OF THEIR SITUATION

To gain public recognition the Ainu are, at present, engaged in giving lectures about Ainu material culture, language and history, and they are also organizing field trips of different types. These include camping arrangements, where the public can take part in Ainu hunting parties, and field trips where the public is invited to areas which used to be powerful Ainu settlements, *Kotan*. During these events, the participants are told about former Ainu place-names, the way in which they have been corrupted and how this in turn resulted in the loss of essential knowledge about characteristics of the places.

Ainu place-names give information not only about the general topography but also about other characteristics, such as the place where benevolent gods live, the river with an abundance of trout, the place where you may hunt but not settle down and so forth (see also Batchelor 1925). With the hope of replacing the standard picture of the "traditional" Ainu way of life with a picture of diversity, the participants are also informed about local and regional variants of Ainu language, customs and religious beliefs.

The way in which the Ainu now seek to gain cultural recognition should not be confused with folklore. The need to make their existence clear, to put a "face" on their culture, something like presenting a "Mr Ainu", can only be understood if we consider that the potentials of their culture have been underestimated for centuries and that to the majority of the people living in Nihon the "Ainu" concept is something unknown. There are people who think that "Ainu" is some kind of food, or even a computer. What may look like folklore on the surface, reveals, when further investigated, a people trying to bring about a renaissance of their culture.

CONCEPTS AND DEFINITIONS: NATIONALISM AND CULTURE

It is necessary to consider the concepts and definitions that I will use in my work and since my principal idea is to focus on the Ainu as actors, or active subjects, the Ainu interpretation of the concepts used will be given preference. Before I continue I would like to make some initial remarks about the concept of nationalism. The problems connected with a proper definition of this concept are widespread and the idea is neither homogeneous nor simple. Compare for instance the following definition given by Anderson:

> Since World War II every successful revolution has defined itself in national terms – the People's Republic of China, the Socialist Republic of Vietnam, and so forth – and in so doing, has grounded itself firmly in a territorial and social space inherited from the pre-revolutionary past. Conversely, the fact that the Soviet Union shares with the United Kingdom of Great Britain and Northern Ireland the rare distinction of refusing nationality in its naming suggests that it is as much the legatees of the pre-national dynastic states of the nineteenth century as the precursor of a twenty-first century internationalist order (1983: 12).

Anderson's argument that nationalism is as much a legacy of the pre-national dynastic states of the nineteenth century as it is a precursor of a twenty-first century internationalist order, shows that there is much in common to nationalism throughout the world in its cultural and social process.

Kapferer argues, in his latest book *Legends of People, Myths of State* (1988), that:

> Nationalism born in the emergence of European individualism is an exported spiritual commodity which varies around the same ideological themes. From the Marxist point of view it is generally argued that nationalism is a product of European colonialism, capitalist expansion, the creation of international and local bourgeoisie, an instrument in class domination and so on (Kapferer 1988: 3).

In his book he expands the work of Louis Dumont, demonstrating that notions of the state, of the person and the individual take distinctive forms (1981: 8-10).

Kapferer analyses two different concepts of nationalism, the hierarchical nationalist ideology of Buddhist Sri Lanka and the egalitarian nationalism of Australia, and he makes inquiries into the ideological foundations of modern political cultures and the relationship of nationalist ideologies to problems of ethnic identity. As for nationalism in Nihon, it is closer to the hierarchical nationalist ideology prevalent in Buddhist Sri Lanka than to the egalitarian nationalism of Australia, although similarities with the latter are not totally absent, such as the long-standing problems of ethnic intolerance in Nihon society.

In Buddhist Nihon, as in Buddhist Sri Lanka, nationalism, or the national identity, *Kokka-Shugi*, is not separated from the cosmological order. It is constructed out of its myths of history and the deeds of its heroes (in the Nihon case *Nihonshoki* A.D. 720 *Kojiki* A.D. 712 *History of Nihon: Records of Ancient Matters*). Its practice is notably political since it is dictated by the highest authority which contemplates a political symbiosis between the concept of state and the concept of nation.

"*Nihonjin* (Japanese) nationalism", *Kokka-Shugi*, as the name indicates, is closely tied to the *Kokka*. The sign used for Kokka denotes both nation and state. However when referring to nation only, the appropriate word is *Minzoku* or *Kokumin*. The sign used for Minzoku reads nation, race and people, while the sign used for Kokumin reads nation and people. Of these two concepts *Minzoku* is the word the Ainu equate with nation, that is, they speak of the Japanese nation, *Nihon Minzoku*.

The Kokka constitutes the sovereign power in control of the Nihon nation and the sovereignty of the Kokka is founded on the same beliefs that prevailed in Nihon before the Meiji era. The national identity, Kokka-Shugi, in its present guise, is linked to the ideology of the Meiji era when the authorities in Nihon, in an attempt to unite the peoples, decided that all peoples, natives to Nihon, were to be addressed by the term Nihonjin. This was a measure taken to secure the loyalty of the subjects of the nation to be, in order to be able to ward off invasion from USSR and the West. The authorities in Nihon do not recognize any other culture than the one from which they themselves originate, that is, the Yamato culture, and regard all other cultures of the nation as variants of this, that is, other cultures of the nation are ranked.

The national identity, Kokka-Shugi, connects to the assumption that the Yamato people, the ancestors of the Wajin, founded the Empire of Nihon. This assumption has its foundation in Shinto beliefs. The state religion of today's Nihon is Buddhism, but the Wajin of today have not given up their Shinto beliefs altogether, rather, the form their religious beliefs take is more like a symbiosis between the two (Nakane 1970; Smith 1983). The ancestors of the Wajin were Shinto. Shinto was the state religion in Nihon till 1946 when, on account of Nihon's defeat in the Second World War, the emperor, the *Tenno*, was forced to give up his divine status and profess himself an adherent of Buddhism. The highest authority in Nihon before the Meiji era was the leader of the supreme *Uji*, house

FIGURE 3   Itak *(conversation, dialogue)*

or country, and he was considered both a priest and a king, combining both political and religious authority in one person. The son of the sun-goddess *Amaterasu,* Tenno *Jinmu,* is believed to be the first Tenno in Nihon. All the Tennos succeeding him are believed to descend in an unbroken line from Tenno Jinmu and it is from him and the ancestors of his subjects, that is, the ancestors of the Wajin, that the Kokka-Shugi actually originates. Accordingly, the basis on which the national identity is founded implies that one's cultural heritage must be traced to the Yamato people, tne ancestors of the majority people. In theory there is no problem, since the culture of the Ainu is defined as a variant of the Yamato culture and therefore the Ainu are, in fact, Nihonjin.

However there is, if not a theoretical then a practical problem. The Ainu are officially defined as Hokkaido natives, that is, Kyuudojin, and the Kyuudojin are officially recognized to be of Ainu descent not Wajin. Since, the Ainu are of Ainu descent they cannot be identified as Nihonjin, simply because their ancestors are not the Yamato people, but the Ainu.

The guidelines made up in the Kokka classify the Ainu with respect to place of birth, whereas the Wajin, according to the same guidelines, are classified with respect to their function in a hierarchical system, originally called the *Shi-nou-kou-shou* system. This system is frozen into a legally immutable estate structure and it prevents people outside the system, such as the Ainu, from entering it. Hence, in practice the guidelines stated in the Kokka become blurred and create great hardship for the Ainu in their attempts to gain a national identity. The national identity that connects to the Shi-nou-kou-shou concept, which in turn connects to the moral codes of the concept of *Giri*, is also notably political, because the guidelines for its practice are dictated in the Kokka. A practical problem preventing the Ainu from attaining a national identity is that one must first also have the status of ethnic group, which is denied them on the grounds stated in the Kokka.

NATION

First, if we consider the concept of "nation", it is essential to distinguish between, on the one hand, the Nihon (Japanese) nation, *Minzoku*, and, on the other hand, the Ainu nation, *Moshir*. It is difficult to arrive at a workable definition of the term nation, since it has become much too general, yet it is very practical in that it is a theoretical concept of universal validity.

> All that I can find to say is that nation exists when a significant number of people in a community consider themselves to form a nation, or behave as if they formed one (Seton-Watson, quoted in Anderson 1983: 15).

Another factor that creates difficulties is that the Nihon word or sign for nation, *Minzoku*, also relates to race (physical characteristics), that is, people of the same race, and the fact that the Ainu word for nation Moshir relates to "universe", described by the Ainu as a unit or territory, where everything and everybody, dead and alive, continue to interact in eternity.

THE AINU VIEW

According to the Ainu, the Minzoku is synthetic, whereas the Moshir is authentic. The synthetic character of the Minzoku relates, according to the Ainu, to a "man-made" fusion of different or specific cultures and peoples (Ryukyujin, Burakumin, the Ainu), whereas the authentic character of the Moshir relates to the absence of such a fusion.[2]

---

2   In *A Counter Plan to a Proposal for Legislation Concerning the Ainu People* (Utari Kyokai 1984) the Ainu stress the fact that:
    "The Nihon government has incorporated the Ainu Moshir, without negotiating with the Ainu people" (p. 1. in the Report).

According to the Ainu the following definition is applicable to the Minzoku: an aggregation of peoples of more than one culture (distinguished by specific lifestyles, employing specific modes of production) and races (distinguished by peoples with different physical characteristics) who are organized into a single state, in this case Kokka (distinguished by a sovereign power in control).

To the Ainu it is debatable whether sovereignty as a concept relates to the preservation of legal rights or to power. In their opinion the Minzoku has grounded itself firmly in a territorial and social space inherited from the ancestors of a dominant and sole ethnic group denying other groups of people an ethnic status.

An adequate definition of the Nihon nation, in my opinion and for our purpose, is one that includes both a cultural and a political interpretation of the concept of nation. I propose, however, that the Nihon nation, in the sense that has been pointed out by the Ainu, is to be considered synthetic, especially since the Kokka only recognizes cultural and racial "variants" within its national context.

In Ainu opinion, an appropriate definition of Moshir is a community of persons bound together by common descent, language and history, without any external sovereign power in control. Their definition of the Ainu Moshir, is one where their own wish to function politically and economically within the Minzoku and culturally and socially parallel to it is clearly expressed[3]. In view of the absence of a central political institution in the Ainu Moshir, I propose the term cultural group as the most adequate one.

MINZOKU AND MOSHIR AS "IMAGINED POLITICAL COMMUNITIES"

In addition, it is obvious that both concepts of nation (Minzoku and Moshir) in their contemporary guises are invented and as such they are subject to "human construction". Their elements are selected and arranged in order to fulfil or maintain specific aims. They may be distinguished by the style in which they are arranged and imagined. In short, nation may be characterized in the following way: "an imagined political community – and imagined as both inherently limited and sovereign" (Anderson 1983: 15).

The Nihon nation, in its contemporary interpretation, was invented to prevent Russian inroads on specific territories, which were imagined by the feudal lords as belonging neither to the Ainu nor to the Russians.

---

3   The following issues, stressed by the Ainu in *A Counter Plan to a Proposal for Legislation Concerning the Ainu People* (Utari Kyokai 1984):
    "To recognize that the Ainu people with its own distinct culture reside in Nihon, and to respect the ethnic pride of the Ainu people under the constitution of Nihon" (p. 1 in the Report).

The Ainu nation, in its contemporary interpretation, was invented to express a wish to function politically and economically within the Nihon nation, but socially and culturally parallel to it. By applying this interpretation of their Moshir, the Ainu hope to be officially recognized as a distinct national group, the Ainu, instead of a variant of another national group, the Wajin.

THE CONCEPT OF CULTURE

My next issue concerns the concept of culture and how it is interpreted by the Ainu. The concept must be understood as a historical product. The formation of Ainu culture can hardly be viewed as separated from development, past and present, in the Nihon nation as a whole.

Before proceeding, some general remarks about the concept of culture are necessary. This has been the focus of anthropologists since the emergence of anthropology as a science. Hence, the concept of culture, like the concept of nation, has also become much too general.

Culture was at first used to identify "the otherness" of other peoples, and in the most general sense, culture came to refer to tradition, which included anything from material culture and language to social structure and religious beliefs (Boas 1911, 1916, 1924; Kroeber 1920, 1952; Tylor 1958).

One of the approaches to the study of other cultures was to examine national character, and some of the historical writings involved efforts to exemplify the distinctive characteristics of other groups. Basically these are stereotyped, self-serving group portraits which mix together racial, psychological, cultural and social factors. The notion of culture implied in such usages has proven too broad and too blunt to capture essential elements in human behaviour.

Later the categories used when defining the concept of culture were narrowed and culture was perceived as a socio-cultural system distinguished by objective criteria, such as common habits, descent, and religion. Some of these approaches give culture a relatively high degree of autonomy (Geertz 1957, 1973; Morin 1973; Sahlins 1976, 1985).

According to Keesing culture can be restricted to an "ideational system". He writes:

> Culture in this sense comprises systems of shared ideas, systems of concepts and rules and meanings that underlie and are expressed in the ways that humans live. Culture, so defined, refers to what humans learn, not what they do and make (1981: 68-69).

Culture as an ideational system is, however, linked to a culturalistic approach, in which culture is seen to govern behaviour. This is best expressed by Geertz (1973). According to Geertz, "culture can best be understood as a set of control mechanisms, plans, rules, instructions and so forth for the the governing of behavior" (1973: 44).

Culture can thus be used in two different ways, as an "ideational system" and as a "socio-cultural system".

However, by separating culture from its imprisonment in society, that is, a departure from the view where culture is conceived as an aspect of social structure or more or less synonymous with it, the nature and relationship between the two can be explored. One way of achieving this is to interpret culture in terms of culture codes (Morin 1973). Yet an initial difficulty in perceiving culture codes is, as Keesing (1981: 69) puts it:

> that we are not in the habit of analyzing cultural patterns: we seldom are even aware of them. It is as though we – or the people of any other society – grow up perceiving the world through glasses with distorting lenses. The things, events, and relationships we assume to be "out there" are in fact filtered through this perceptual screen. The first reaction, inevitably, on encountering people who wear a different kind of glasses is to dismiss their behavior as strange or wrong.

According to Keesing there is more to be added, and he suggests "that the view of culture as collective phenomena need to be qualified by a view of knowledge as distributed and controlled, that is, we need to ask who creates and defines cultural meanings and to what ends" (1987: 161).

According to Geertz (1973) culture can be read as a text. In his view "melodies, formulas, maps and pictures are not idealities to be stared at but texts to be read, and so are rituals, palaces technologies and social formations" (quoted in "Anthropology as Interpretative Quest" Keesing 1987: 169) If culture is a text to be read, how is it to be read by the natives. The rites, myths and concepts of people are deeply ambiguous. This implies as Keesing phrases it "cultures as texts allow alternative readings and that with our predilection for the exotic we may read cultural metaphors too deeply" (1987: 161).

There is reason to question Geertz's cultural model because, as has been pointed out by Ekholm Friedman (1991), social and cultural change is above all a result of breaking the rules and Geertz's view of Man as a computer, a cultural machine governed by a program, stands in contrast to what we know about human evolution and history, where Man is more innovative and has more freedom than that. In the model created by Sahlins (1985), which resembles Geertz's, in so far as Sahlins also speaks of cultural schemes, "change" is added to the model:

> as the contingent circumstances of action need not conform to the significance some group might assign them, people are known to creatively reconsider their conventional schemes. And to that extent, the culture is historically altered in action (1985: vii).

However, as Ekholm Friedman puts it:

In this model there is only culture and practice, no social structure and no global system penetrating and incorporating his Hawaiian and Maorian arenas. He thinks societies exist side by side, open to be sure to one another, but following their own path into the future. He does not completely deny the existence of global systems, but he ascribes it no major importance (1991: 7).

"Traditional" and modern man – and his cultures – are, in large measure, products of Man's own responses to the images created of him. Essential features in societies and cultures may be circumscribed, corrupted or lost forever over time and attempts to restore them may be futile. Nevertheless, people are continuously trying to recapture "hidden knowledge" and reinvent "true meaning" in order to reconstruct meaningful behavioural patterns. This act in combination with a general ability to reconsider one's views and learn from experiences constitutes the intellectual framework of which cultures are made up. Although the myths and rituals that organize ideas and values in societies are changed over time, they do not become meaningless, rather temporary and arbitrary, which in turn provides possibilities to apply them to cultural and social existences varying in degree of complexity. Since the guises are both temporary and arbitrary they can thus be attributed to a behavioural pattern that suits the "present" circumstances in the best possible way. In this regard they are essential indeed for the production of cultures. The interpretation of them is, of course, likely to vary according to both time and interpreter. The approach to culture must thus include an understanding of how the bearers of a specific culture perceive and apply their own myths and rituals over time and of how people who are bearers of other rituals and myths perceive and apply those of the former as well as their own ones.

CULTURE AND ETHNICITY

At present the concept of culture is also open to subjective interpretations, the way people perceive themselves and are perceived by others as a common (ethnic) group (Barth 1969). Barth's definition of an ethnic group emphasizes its action as a group in interaction with other groups. The uniqueness in this assumption relates to the fact that it is interaction between groups that makes it possible to maintain continuation of the group. Barth also stresses that ethnicity is something socially important for the group and therefore also for its unity:

By concentrating on what is socially effective, the ethnic group is seen as a form of social organization. The critical feature then becomes ... the characteristic of self-aspiration and the ascription by others (1969: 13).

Further:

> Though the members of such an ethnic group may carry a firm conviction of identity, their knowledge of distant communities who claim to share this identity will be limited and intercommunication within the ethnic group … cannot lightly be assumed to disseminate adequate information to maintain a shared body of values and understandings through time. Thus even if we can show that the maintenance of … identity is an overt goal … this will be a goal pursued within the limited perspective of highly discrepant local settings. Consequently the aggregate result will not automatically be persistence of an undivided distinct single ethnic group (1969: 117).

Barth's position is that the maintenance of a shared identity as expressed as the overt goal of the members of an ethnic group does not guarantee a persistence of the group as an undivided distinct single ethnic group. In this view changes in external circumstances can affect but not completely alter identity. Groups of people sharing biological ancestry are readily seen as units, and social units are readily identified as sharing putative ancestry. Blood, seed and transmitted substances figure prominently if not exclusively in determining an individual group's membership.

Orlando Patterson's position is that the members' conscious sense of belonging to an ethnic group is critical and that if this criterion is not met the group does not exist as an ethnic group:

> An ethnic group exists only where members consider themselves to belong to it: a conscious sense of belonging is critical. It implies that where all other criteria are met except this sense of belonging, the ethnic condition is not met – even where other members of the society may regard a group of individuals as an ethnic group. It also implies that where … the assumed bases of group allegiance do not exist the salient condition of ethnicity is met when members subjectively assume the existence of such mythical bases (1977: 104).

Daniel Bell (1975) argues that ethnic identity is something built up as much by one's own view of oneself as by the way others regard one. With this view ethnic identity can best be described as a "strategic" choice. His view is that the background of the choice is dependent on psychology insofar as it need not be founded on facts but on assumptions or myth.

A concluding remark would be that there are indeed alternative schemes of conceptualizing ethnicity. Common to the different approaches is that objectively given cultural and ancestoral differences are at the root of identity ascriptions. Yet when it comes to the application of ethnicity as a scholarly concept they do not all reach the same conclusions, which gives us reason to do some rethinking with respect to conventional assumptions about group identity.

AINU ETHNICITY

The Ainu interpretation of culture is equivalent to ethnic group and, to them, ethnic group is a concept that derives from or relates to a human group having racial (anthropomorphic), religious, linguistic and historical traits in common. People sharing these basic features also share a common identity, which in the context of the Ainu may be defined as an ethnic identity, something which people are born into. In this regard, their ethnic identity is both limited and definite. Their ethnic identity which is based on such features as descent, language, and the like, is also, if not explicitly, distinguished from subcultures, including movements of different kinds, such as youth and religious movements, women's liberation, the greens, and so on, where factors other than the objective characteristics as described above, are stressed (Isajiw 1974; Peterson Royce 1982).

By emphasizing one or more of the elements of which the ethnic group consists, its limited and definite condition will be removed and can thus be transformed into a condition which is neither limited nor definite. Hence, we have what is called ethnic identification, characterized not so much by objective as subjective characteristics, that is, the feelings one shares with others in the group (Barth 1969; Spicer 1971; Bell 1975; Patterson 1977).

As regards the subjective characteristics, these do not have to be based on "facts", but may be founded on assumptions (Peterson Royce 1982) or myth (Patterson 1977). They are dependent on the psychology of a people and built as much by one's own view as by the way one is regarded by others.(See Bell's [1975] discussion of what he describes as "strategic choices" and Spicer's [1971][4] discussion of the different ways of interpreting historical sequences.)

If ethnic identity is something definite and limited, that is, something which one is born into, then ethnic identification, that is, the use one makes of the elements which make up the ethnic identity is both unlimited and indefinite. Hence, the necessity to distinguish between the two concepts. For my purposes, I also propose that the uses that the Ainu make of their ethnic identity, when they use specific elements of it, may best be viewed as some forms of ethnic-based actions. As Peterson Royce suggests:

> Ethnic identity is the sum total of feelings on the part of group members about those values, symbols, and common histories that identify them as a distinct group. Ethnicity is simply ethnic-based actions (1982: 18).

---

4   "I am focusing on history as people believe it to have taken place, not as an objective outsider sees it. It is history with a specific meaning for the particular people who believe it" (Spicer 1971: 796).

In order to realize their aims in a society dominated by a national majority, the Ainu use their ethnicity in various ways in the integration situation. The strategies they use range from, at the one end, the emphasizing of the basic elements in their own definition of culture where they are recognized as Ainu both by themselves and by the Wajin majority, to, at the other end, the emphasizing of the elements specific to their situation where they are recognized as Nihonjin, both by the authorities and themselves, but where they are recognized as Ainu by the Wajin majority.

The extremes are, on the one hand, Ainu people who identify themselves as un-guru, where un-guru, which means "person" or "man", has the meaning of "belonging" to a group, or a place (Nibutani un-guru and Shiraoi un-guru), and, on the other hand, Ainu who identify themselves as Nihonjin.

In this situation there are possibilities for the Ainu, both to use more than one identity and to manoeuvre in different ways. Accordingly, they can clarify themselves vertically (in a political hierarchy), with Nihonjin at the top and Ainu at the bottom, as well as horizontally, including Nihonjin (of Ainu descent), Ainu, and un-guru.

As regards the former way of expression, it includes the possibility of inversion, that is, Ainu at the top, and we actually find such "black is beautiful" tendencies. An example of a step in this direction is that the concept *Utari*, an Ainu word for "comrade, fellow", used since the incorporation of Hokkaido to depict Hokkaido natives, now is replaced by "Ainu", a concept that was previously regarded as stigmatizing.

Historically we can perceive the different ways in which the Ainu have used their identity as responses to the interaction situation where they, to some extent, operate with what Isajiw calls double boundaries (Isajiw 1974: 122), and it is therefore important to emphasize as Cohen (1978: 387) does, that ethnic boundaries are not stable and continuing, but multiple and include overlapping sets of ascriptive loyalties that make for multiple identities.

Looking at earlier Ainu attempts to hide their identity, we see that a concept such as Utari served social purposes, on a national as well as regional and local level, and not ethnic purposes such as the reintroduction today of the concept of "Ainu" and the use of un-guru.

MAJOR STRATEGIES USED BY THE AINU FOR IDENTIFICATION

Speaking in general terms, we may among the Ainu today discern at least two major strategies used for identification. One is used by those Ainu who put strong emphasis on themselves as a distinct cultural entity. The other is used by Ainu who put strong emphasis on similarities of their own culture and that of the Wajin. In common with the latter group is that in a national context they identify themselves as "Nihonjin" whereas in a regional and local context they identify themselves as "Nihonjin of Ainu descent". These people employ what we might call double identities, used in a hierarchical sense. The people who manoeuvre their identity in this way are to be found among those Ainu who seek their living in the rural sector, or in other sectors connected with the various industries in the big cities. The former, on the other hand, identify themselves as Ainu in a national context, whereas, in a regional and local context, they identify themselves as un-guru. These people can be said to use their identity for "clarification" purposes. Hence, the use they make of their identity must be interpreted in a strictly horizontal sense. Ainu people who manoeuvre their identity in this way are occupationally engaged in various Ainu activities and they are to be found both in the countryside and in the big cities.

However we do also have examples of Ainu who reject their Ainu identity in words but reveal it in practice. This can best be exemplified by the way in which Ainu engaged in the rural sector seek recognition as farmers, peasants, and the like, yet, in the case of Ainu festivities or other Ainu activities, many of these people are not only seen as observers, but dressed up in Ainu clothes, they take active part in Ainu activities of various kinds. In addition these people have actually made their Ainu costumes themselves, a fact that reveals that a great deal of both their time and effort is spent in learning the special dressmaking technique of the Ainu.

Further, among the Ainu who have migrated to the metropolis, we have examples of Ainu who repress their Ainu identity and who identify themselves with reference to their (un)employment situation. These people seek recognition as Nihonjin and they claim to have lost contact with their Ainu relatives. Their Ainu relatives, on the other hand, claim to have close contact with them and identify them either as Ainu, which is also used by the Wajin, or un-guru, which is used by Ainu exclusively. Within this context it seems advisable to consider the possibility that their indifference to their Ainu inheritance is a consequence of their inferior social position in the suburban environment where they live, rather than a means to escape their Ainu heritage altogether. These people "turn away", by identifying themselves as Nihonjin, but does not succeed in alienating them from their own people.

A main feature of the pattern that reveals itself today is that it relates to Ainu responses to specific social and occupational contexts. On the one hand we have Ainu who use their identity to achieve a specific purpose, a cultural definition; the two concepts that they use when they identify themselves (*Ainu, un-guru*) are interchangeable. The one concept does not feather one's nest in a better way than the other. On the other hand we have Ainu who use their identity in a chameleon-like way; the two concepts that they use when they identify themselves (*Nihonjin, Nihonjin of Ainu descent*) are not interchangeable. The concepts are used with respect to which purpose they best may serve. One concept is favoured on some occasions and another on others.

When discussing the different ways in which the Ainu use their identity we see a connection between the degree to which they perceive or experience discrimination (85.2% of the Ainu today feel that they are discriminated against[5]), and the extent to which they rely on social welfare. According to the Ainu of the first group their dependence on social welfare determines to a considerable extent the direction of their ethnic-based actions. The position of the Ainu is that the authorities, by denying them ethnic status, promote discriminatory treatment since their position as well as their actions are explained with the help of ideologies and values which do not belong to the Ainu.

It is essential to point out that the Ainu are not trying to become "Wajin", they are trying to become accepted as Nihonjin and Nihonjin of Ainu descent on the same terms as Nihonjin and Nihonjin of Wajin descent are accepted today. As it is now, the two concepts Wajin and Nihonjin have an identical status and because of this they are also interchangeable. This is of course not the case with the two concepts Ainu and Nihonjin. The Ainu are, in fact, only recognized as Nihonjin by people in a situation similar to their own, that is, minority peoples living in Nihon.

This can of course be related to the fact that the Ainu were defeated by the Wajin and after that they became subjects of the nation on terms dictated not by themselves but by the conquerors. Now, since they are incorporated into the Nihon nation they are in fact Nihonjin, because they are actually subjects of the nation. However, since they are also Hokkaido natives, they are entitled to both a native and a national status, which they have although, during the present conditions, neither their native status (Ainu) nor their national status (Nihonjin) render them an ethnic status. This in turn can be connected with the fact that from another angle they are not Nihonjin because they are not of Wajin descent, nor are they Ainu simply because there is just one single ethnic entity recognized as such in Nihon.

Without further attempts to clarify the concept of discrimination I will be content with the fact that the opinion of the Ainu is that it is the absence of an official definition of them as an ethnic entity that makes them feel that they are discriminated against and disadvantaged. According to them this relates to social disadvantages inflicted upon them by such destructive acts as the policy of assimilation, where the efforts made by the Wajin authorities to improve their situation are restricted to social work in general and welfare policy in particular. If the Wajin authorities, the Ainu argue, had been more sensitive to the restoration of ethnic rights, their situation would have been improved a long time ago.

---

5   Compare also:
    "I had been in Hokkaido until the spring of 1962. When I recall the experience I had during my stay, I believe that discriminatory consciousness against those people living in the urban areas was relatively small. But in areas where there were many rural communities, discriminatory consciousness still exists among non-Ainu people. Now I remember I exerted myself to improve the situation" (Mr Ueki, Minister of State in 1976, the 77th Lower House Accounts Committee Session, May 20, 1976 (Utari Kyokai 1987b).

To illustrate this point, the following comparison can be made between their own view and the official one. First the view of the Ainu:

> We feel discriminated against because our skills are not wanted, by the Shamo. They only hire us to do those jobs which they themselves do not want. We are not their equals, since if a person of Ainu descent and another person of Wajin descent apply for a job, they [the employers] will choose the Shamo regardless of qualifications. If we ask for an explanation, they [the Wajin] say we [the Ainu] cannot be trusted. Further, if we want to marry a Shamo, it happens that his or her parents declare the person who will marry an Ainu dead. It may not happen too often, but to me one such incident is enough (interview with Ainu female, aged 19, Furenai, 1986).

The official view:

> On account of the degree to which the Ainu people rely on social welfare, which inevitably relates to the economic, occupational and educational status of the Ainu, there is clear evidence that the Ainu people are disadvantaged. This unfavourable situation of theirs is due to the difficulty they have had in only being able to catch up with development within a century (interview with government representative, Sapporo, 1988).

Without arguing that the above view is representative of the position of the government in general, there exists a kind of racism in Ninon, which permeates administration and officialdom. There is also the question of whether the established official ideology encourages this development. If such is the case there must be something fundamentally wrong with the established official ideology since it promotes discriminatory treatment.

ASSIMILATION, INTEGRATION AND ACCULTURATION

My final issue concerns the concepts of assimilation, integration and acculturation.

The Nihon state, Kokka, organizes power on a basis beyond kinship and, empowered with the ultimate sanction of physical force, it enforces its laws and maintains the existing order of stratification. The Ainu, on the other hand, pursue a policy of getting integrated into the larger society, Nihon, on the basis of group decision-making.

The state pursues an acculturation of the Ainu. Acculturation as a concept is generally defined as one kind of cultural change. It is defined by Keesing as "culture change due to contact between societies: most often used to refer to adaptation of subordinate tribal societies to domination by Western societies" (1981: 507). In the Ainu-Wajin relation acculturation is related to such measures as legislation against the maintenance of Ainu customs, beliefs and language and, further, an incorporation of the Ainu Moshir in the interest of the Nihon nation, something that has resulted in the dispersion of Ainu groups and individuals.

The Ainu, on the other hand, demand the incorporation of Ainu Moshir into the Nihon nation, but in the interest of the Ainu and with an official recognition of them as a distinct ethnic group with its own unique culture, language and history. From their perspective the inhabitants of Nihon consist of Nihonjin of Wajin descent, Nihonjin of Ainu descent and so on. This latter definition gives room for the identification of different cultures (lifestyles) within the Nihon nation, whereas the former leaves a cultural vacuum as regards the lifestyles of the various minority peoples, including the Ainu.

CHAPTER FOUR

The Reconstruction of the "Traditional" Ainu Society

In this chapter I will present the ethnography of the Ainu including both previous ethnographic material and my own. The main aim is to present the ethnography of the Ainu in a way that allows an incorporation of their own view.

The weight I put on this relates to the fact that, if an Ainu view of their own ethnography is neglected, we run the risk of presenting a picture of their ethnography which is unfamiliar to them. According to the Ainu two issues are of importance, (1) why the research is done and (2) whose viewpoints are reflected in the final report. These issues are major problems among anthropologists today (Clifford 1986; Van Maanen 1988) and it is no wonder that the anthropological subjects make these issues their own concern as well.

In recent anthropology the opinion of the natives is given considerably more importance. Some general remarks are required about (1) the temporal modes and (2) the form that I use when presenting the material below. With respect to the temporal modes, I will not consistently use an ethnographic present. The phrase "ethnographic present" is an anthropological technique used to caution readers that the culture, as described when the fieldwork takes place, no longer exists.

The advantage in using an ethnographic present is that the people and the culture appear in a more vivid way. At the same time there is the danger that we forget about the passage of time and those changes that have occurred historically and therefore the advantage of using an ethnographic present does compensate for its disadvantages.

With respect to the form I use when presenting the ethnography of the Ainu, I will present previous ethnographic material in a form that resembles that used in monographs. The information that they give is used here to assist our understanding of the views of the Ainu. After all, the aim of their works is to give us, the outsiders, an intelligible view of Ainu society.

The views of the Ainu, on the other hand, are presented as comments to the view of professionals and the form they take is, for the most part, that of quotations.

As far as my own material is concerned, it is used to elucidate certain aspects of the customs and beliefs of the Ainu and for the most part my own material is presented in the form of comments, both to the views of professionals and to the Ainu views. In this way I hope to be able to create a manifold picture with respect to social and cultural forms that either have been transformed or ceased to exist.

THE "TRADITIONAL" AINU WAY OF LIFE

When presenting information about what has been defined as the "traditional", that is, original, Ainu way of life, it is of some relevance that the basic information on which assumptions about the "traditional" Ainu society is built derives from documents made by feudal lords, administrators and explorers from Honshu and missionaries from abroad. These documents date back about six hundred years. The term "traditional" as it is used by these writers refers both to an Ainu way of life prior to the period when the Matsumae Han settled in Hokkaido and to their way of life during the early days under the control of the Han. As has been pointed out earlier their material has mainly been used to support a view of the Ainu as hunters living in egalitarian societies. This might, in fact, be a product of the interaction with the Wajin. Although it is of great concern, my main aim is not so much to question previous writings about cultural and social forms that have ceased to exist or the way in which the data has been used, but rather to complement the generally accepted view with a picture of the "traditional" Ainu as the modern Ainu interpret them.

In my approach to the "traditional" Ainu, their society, way of life and religious beliefs my concern is, on the one hand, with how the modern Ainu interpret both the "traditional" Ainu and the material written about them, and on the other hand, how they reconstruct the values and beliefs that belong to their culture and how this is applicable to the reality in which they live today. Since there is a certain ambiguity with respect to what "traditional Ainu society" actually looked like and since the concept "traditional" in the minds of contemporary Ainu, does not necessarily correspond to past practices, the concept is, in my study always placed in quotes.

The "traditional" Ainu lived, according to ainulogists, in egalitarian societies with an extensive division of labour both within and between communities. Due to specific historical and environmental circumstances, the Ainu did not constitute a single homogeneous community, but displayed a number of well-defined, regional variations (Watanabe 1975: 69-72). They were mainly hunters[1] with a highly organized system of hunting and fishing rights. Takakura writes:

> There are boundaries, both in the mountains and the sea... Outside one's own boundary one is prohibited from so much as even cutting a blade of grass. The law

---

1   "It is generally agreed to use the term 'hunter' as a convenient shorthand, despite the fact that the majority of peoples considered subsisted primarily on sources other than meat, mainly wild plants and fish" (Lee & DeVore 1975: 4).

is very stringent and anyone violating it is deprived of his catch as a punitive compensation after charge and deliberation (Takakura 1960: 15).

The Ainu staple food consisted of fish, wild plant food and agricultural products, but their highest esteem was for meat, preferably bear meat (Takakura 1960: 19; Watanabe 1972: 21-30, 1975: 71; Ohnuki-Tierney 1981: 117).

Collective hunting and fishing activities, trading, leadership of ritual performances and the manufacturing of ritual objects were male tasks, whereas the gathering of edible and medical plants, food preparation, cloth-making and agriculture with millet, barnyard grass and turnips as the main crops were female tasks.

Although hunting was a male activity women were not excluded. Their contribution consisted of small animals and their hunting grounds were restricted to the immediate surroundings of the dwelling places. Watanabe (1975: 74), mentions that Ainu women also took part in deer-hunting with sticks. The hunting activities of the women were private and carried out within the "domestic" arena, that is, the game they provided was distributed within their own nuclear family exclusively (Watanabe 1975: 75; Ohnuki-Tierney 1981: 86).

The contribution of women to hunting did not extend beyond the profane realm. Their hunting activities were not related to ritual or other religious phenomena (Ohnuki-Tierney 1981: 86). One could say, as the Ainu do, that the women's hunting was, in fact, part to their gathering activities:

> The hunting activities of the women are not classified as hunting but rather as a form of gathering since their hunting activities only include small game on domestic ground. Small animals are neither very important nor very dangerous (interview with Ainu male, aged 56, Hidaka, 1988).

The hunting activities of the men, on the other hand, were collective, that is, hunting parties were arranged and each participant was assigned a specific task. The hunting grounds of the men extended beyond the place where they lived and the game consisted of big and "dangerous" animals, preferably bear but also deer. The hunting activities of the men always went together with elaborate ritual preparations (Watanabe 1972: 72). These were called *Ukosanio* and they included offerings to and communication with supernatural beings, *Kamuy* (Watanabe 1972: 43-56, 75; Ohnuki-Tierney 1981: 84). The hunting activities of the men were connected with the sacred realm. The game, especially the bear, was distributed publicly, that is, they arranged a ceremony and the game was divided among all the participants, the hunters, their kin and also the Kamuy. The distribution ceremony was called *Iyomante*[2] and involved the killing or "sending away" of the souls of the animals brought home by the hunters.

According to most reports, the Iyomante ceremony is the most precious of all ritual performances practised by the Ainu.

According to Batchelor the Iyomante ceremony represented "the outward expression of the greatest racial religious act of worship of the Ainu brotherhood" (Batchelor 1932: 37).

True or not, the Ainu never stopped practising this ritual although it was forbidden by the Wajin authorities in connection with their annexation of Ainu land. The official explanation for this was that the ceremony was very cruel (*Hokkaido Government* 1899), but according to my informants, "the act of placing such restrictions on the Iyomante performance formed an essential part of the continuation of the policy of assimilation" (see also Kayano 1988b).

Although ambitions to understand essential issues in the lives of the Ainu of the past by connecting these with the Iyomante ceremony may seem as adequate a method as any other, there is a danger in such approaches. Their interpretations may, for all we know, turn out to be mere epiphenomena of the approaches used in such research. Considering the fact that the studies of the Iyomante celebration started during the time it was forbidden (restrictions against Iyomante were not lifted until the late 1970s) and the fact that transformations within Ainu society during the years before the annexation were considerable, essential factors tied to the original ritual were no doubt severely circumscribed at such a late time.

Further, there seems to be little sense in hoping for a thorough understanding of the ceremony by studying the way it was undertaken in secret, during the days of its prohibition, since secrecy *per se* includes limitations. In addition, when the Iyomante ceremony was reintroduced officially, in connection with the flourishing tourist industry, it went through an almost total transformation. The purpose of the ceremony was henceforth to attract tourists and consequently it was performed during the tourist season, a time which ill fitted the "traditional" timing, which was in February.

Another male activity was trade. The Ainu traded both among themselves locally and preferably with other Ainu from Sakhalin and the Kurile islands, but also with the

---

2   There is to date no clear evidence about whether "Iyomante" includes the dispatch of the sacred bear only, or whether other sacred animals also can be included:

"The religious killing of the brute creation is called by the general term 'Iyomante', by the Ainu, which means 'a sending away'. This word carries no idea of death by killing in it, but rather a sending of spirit away – a dispatch" (Batchelor 1932: 34).

"Iyomante, a ceremony in which a bear is killed and its ramat sent back to Kamuy Moshiri" (Peng & Geiser1977: 224).

"The ritual killing of the cub, Kamui Iyomante, sending off the bear spirit" (Watanabe 1972: 75).

"The most reverent of all dismissals is that performed at the ceremonial killing of the sacred bear, and it is called Kamui Iyomante" (Munro 1962: 47).

Shishamo, fellow traders from Nihon proper, Russia and China (Kreiner & Oelschleger 1987: 30; Takakura 1960: 24).

Trading was the privilege of male leaders *Ekashi*. The Ainu did not only trade the surplus to their requirements but, according to the chief curator of Batchelor's Museum in Sapporo, "they also traded hand-crafted goods, especially wooden objects, which encouraged the producers to improve their carving skills" and he continues, "contests for the most beautifully carved wooden objects were frequent" (interview with the chief curator of Batchelor's Museum in Sapporo, 1986). This statement was confirmed by my Ainu informants. Trade with Nihon proper consisted of fish and edible seaweed, hawks, bear liver, seal skin, eagle feathers, etc. In return the Ainu were given such things as rice, sugar, sake (rice wine), tobacco, lacquer ornaments and containers, and cotton cloth (Takakura 1960: 24; Refsing 1980: 83). According to Takakura, "those who extended their generosity to the many succeeded in Ainu society, while those unwilling to share their surplus had the lowest status" (1960: 11). The question is why generosity was revered so highly. This is a point on which neither Takakura, nor anyone else for that matter, is clear and as a result the question of what the term "generosity" actually stands for in Ainu society of the past remains.

For clothing Ainu women made textiles from vegetable fibres, elm bark cloth (*Attus*) and helm cloths (*Reteruppe*) but also from animal skin (*Uri*), bird feathers (*Rapuri*) and fish skin (*Akumi*) (Takakura 1960: 14; Hansen 1978: 53, 122). Cloth making and food preparation were female tasks, whereas the making of weapons, such as bows and arrows, fishing utensils and objects for religious offerings, were male tasks (Takakura 1960: 11-13, 19; Munro 1962: 28 ff, 69; Watanabe 1975: 75; Ohnuki-Tierney 1976: 314).

Ainu women of today have not forgotten how to make Ainu-style clothings, and in accordance with the current renewed interest in their own cultural heritage, many Ainu women are attending lessons in the Ainu technique of cloth making and many of them are today manufacturing their Ainu-style clothes in an Ainu-style manner. There are even plans to take up the manufacture of Ainu-style clothes on a commercial basis.

As in the case of clothes making among Ainu women of today, Ainu men show a renewed interest in the manufacture of Ainu male items, and some of them have made this their main source of income.

Spears (*Opu*), clubs (*Isabakiku*), fishing nets (*Ya*), fish traps (*Urai-tes*) and canoes (*Cep*) were used for fishing. The technique used when fishing with traps is described by Takakura:

> Stakes are driven into the stream beds in arrow head form with the point downstream. The spaces between the stakes are fitted with branches while the point is open and covered with a net (Takakura 1960: 13).

For assistance in fishing the Ainu had domestic dogs. These dogs belong to the *Akita* race and resemble the dogs of the Eskimos. The dogs played an important role in the lives of the Ainu and they were also used in hauling and transportation (Watanabe 1972: 27-31).

Furthermore, dog skin was used for clothing and during the winter, if food was scarce, the Ainu used dog meat as food, both for the dogs and for themselves (Ohnuki-Tierney 1976: 306). Today the Ainu use these dogs as guard dogs. (In the villages where I stayed during my fieldwork, every Ainu household had such a dog and in one of them an Ainu woman earned a living by breeding these dogs.)

That the dogs played an important role in the economic life of the Ainu is beyond all doubt, but that they were so important that the Ainu used them to depict themselves, as some ainulogists (see Augusta 1960: 7; Takakura 1960: 8) suggest, is exaggerated and misleading.[3]

The Ainu word for dog is *Seta* or *Reyep*[4] (Batchelor 1938: 444), which is very remote from the Wajin one which is *Inu*. It is thus not likely that the word Ainu derives from "Inu". Besides, "Ainu" means "human being" in the Ainu language and it was used to distinguish "people, humans" (*Ainu*) from "gods" (*Kamuy*) and "beasts" (*Chikoikip*) (interview with Ainu people in the Hidaka, Iburi and Kushiro regions; see also Kayano 1988a). Consequently, those results that the school of thought which Takakura (1960: 8) refers to cannot be taken seriously in the view of the Ainu themselves and recent research, the present writer included. Nevertheless, the assumption that Ainu as a concept derives from Inu (dog) has inflicted much harm to the Ainu today and has encouraged discriminative acts by the Wajin majority.

To fully understand the role of animals and their place within the Ainu universe is extremely difficult since the Ainu do not describe or label them in the same way that is usually done by outsiders. The explanation the Ainu give for an understanding of their religious beliefs has been interpreted as belonging to a primitive stage of evolution. Attempts have been made to fit their perception of the universe to a model of a "cosmological order" constructed by ainulogists.

Before discussing the different aspects of the Ainu perception of their own universe let me present a view given to me by a prominent Ainu leader, who is well read in the

---

3   "Records of the Tsugaru region from the seventeenth century state that Ainu who took Japanese names were distinguished by the addition of 'Inu' [Nihon word for dog] to their names and there is a school of thought which believes that 'Ainu' comes from 'Inu'" (Takakura 1960: 8).

4   According to linguists this word should be "Reyep", but according to Batchelor it should instead be "Rep". However, the Ainu pronounce it "Reyep" so I prefer Reyep.

literature written about his people. When asked if he could explain the essence of Ainu religious beliefs, he expressed himself in the following words:

> When you enter an Ainu house, Chise, you find sacred things, placed where you expect them to be placed. Everything is familiar to you, because of the information you have received through books or other sources. Now you think you know their story. This makes you think that you understand them and the context they are in. This in turn makes you very pleased. You found and understood what was expected. True, you understand more than people with no interest in those things, but you understand very little compared with us. Why is that, you ask. I will tell you. You are involved with theory, but you are not emotionally involved or tied to these things and you have no experience of how they work in practice. Therefore you see them as objects. As objects they have nothing living in them and they are what you call dead matter. To us they are both dead and alive. Let me explain. They live lives of their own. They live because they are in their proper surrounding. Only in this surrounding can they live. When new or other objects take the place of the former, they are placed in harmony with the former. The objects and their order are one and the same thing to us. There is nothing if they do not come together. Therefore, they are both dead and alive at the same time. Alive because they have something to tell us who understand to interpret it properly and dead to those who do not understand what is delivered. The message they hide from you, we can see clearly. Therefore the message they tell you is very different from the message they tell us (interview with Ainu in Chikabumi Kotan, 1986).

It is obvious that the Ainu position is that an emotional engagement is an absolute necessity for a proper understanding of their world. There is also a notable stress on the fact that it is not possible for an outsider to get an inside view of their religious beliefs, no matter how eagerly one tries. Their position is that in order to be able to grasp these things, one has to be born Ainu, or raised among the Ainu since childhood.

THE COSMOLOGY OF THE AINU
IN ITS RELATION TO POLITICS AND RELIGION

The Ainu perception of the universe or, to use their own language, *Moshir*, can best be described as a unit, the territory of the Ainu, where everything and everybody dead and alive continue to interact (cooperate) in eternity. This is a description which research in general approves of. Nevertheless, to do full justice to their perception of the universe is problematic indeed, and there is always the risk that our translation of it is a poor representation of the Ainu view.

Their perception of the universe was spatial rather than temporal-historical, which does not mean that historical time was totally suppressed. Instead historical time was integrated into a larger space, and the deceased persons were "out there". Their world was a real place and for the living Ainu it was concrete, rather than abstract, in the sense that

FIGURE 4   Utarigeh *(family, household)*

communication between the two worlds was mutual, and one could actually visit each other's places. These visits took place in dreams and in these dreams the living were urged by the deceased to visit. The purpose of the visits was to "settle things", that is, give guidance to the living in matters concerning "proper behaviour":

> Because you my son have neglected to take care of leftovers, we, your ancestors have nothing to eat. The Kamuy punish us because you think of today only and take no interest in tomorrow. This is no good way. If you do not think of tomorrow, why should Nature, our Moshir, bother with you and your ancestors? (interview with Ainu male aged 53, Chikabumi, 1986).

The beings, *Kamuy* and *Chikoikip*, that dwelt in the world beyond were thought to have great power and the Ainu envisaged them as fabulous monsters, part human and part animal, animals that talked, flew, married humans and transformed themselves from one species to another.

Culture was not superior to nature as in our ideology and there was no ranking as such, or at least no unambiguous ranking. Women might be considered "impure", because of the fact that they menstruate, but their very impurity was also a sign of their ultimate power, in the sense that the men placed restrictions upon them because of the power they, the men, ascribed to their impurity (cf. Friedman 1983).

The world of the dead or unborn, material objects, and the like, appeared as real to the Ainu as the world of the living, and distinctive features between the living, the dead, the Kamuy and the Chikoikip were not clearly expressed.

Although the Ainu made no clear distinction between things and humans, they did not perceive themselves as things. Ainu were essentially not things. Ainu had wills and intelligence. They expressed their wills emotionally, that is, they loved and hated, and they used their intelligence to interpret signs which they incorporated into a system of law and order.

Their kind of universe contrasted to our universe in that humans were not distinct from things in the same way as in our ideology and consequently the quality of "thing" differed also from our perception. The quality of things was not fully differentiated from their personality. They might not be humans but neither were they entirely things (cf. Douglas 1966).

To define their own position in the Moshir, the Ainu interpreted the Moshir and its components from a human-centred viewpoint. Their perception of the Moshir was related to experiences, inner or outer, known or partaken in, imagined or real.

To interpret the Moshir, to separate the known from the unknown, to distinguish the otherness, the external realm, the supernatural, distant allies and enemies and the like, and to maintain order and harmony, specific regulations and taboos were used. With the help of these the Ainu differentiated Ainu (humans) from Kamuy (deities), but also males and male tasks from females and female tasks (Kayano 1988a b).

At the same time everything and everybody was given both a fixed position and a non-position which the Ainu called *Sak* within the larger context of the Moshir.

According to the beliefs of the Ainu, their own position within the Moshir emanated first and foremost from limitations in the ways of the living. Humans had to adhere to the rules which existed within the Moshir as a whole. These rules concerned proper behaviour with respect to Nature. The basis on which these rules were founded constituted a message that one should take great care returning to Nature what belonged to Nature. According to Ainu beliefs this included sending back the spirit of the game one hunted, the fish one caught, the trees one cut down, and so on. This involved for the most part ritual performances expressed in thanksgiving ceremonies, which varied in elaboration, for the supernatural beings and for ancestors.

In some cases there was no need to arrange ceremonies at all. Instead one could express one's gratitude by uttering some ritual words, or making an *Inau*, offering stick. If the Ainu broke any rules, that is, if the ceremony performed or other preparations were not elaborate enough or even neglected altogether, they took a considerable risk. Although they could never be sure of how and when they would actually be punished they were sure that they would be punished.

The punishment could be in the form of the loss of a child, an unfaithful wife or husband, illness, bad hunting, famine and the like. There was never any doubt that they could escape punishment, although it might happen that they could not recall the reason why they were punished. On such occasions they attached the reason for their punishment to the fact that they were not aware that they had actually offended Nature. The fact that they had offended Nature was however beyond all doubt since otherwise they would not have been punished.

This way of interpreting one's position in the universe is rather common in such societies. Compare for instance the view of the Ainu with what Mary Douglas (1966) states:

> The cosmos is turned in, as it were, on man. Its transforming energy is threaded on the lives of individuals so that nothing happens in the way of storms, sickness, blights or droughts except in virtue of these personal links. So the universe is man-centred in the sense that it must be interpreted by reference to humans (1966: 85).

The Moshir was composed of two main realms. The one occupied by the living, which was called *Ainu Moshir*, and the one occupied by the non-living or unborn, who were equivalent to Ainu ancestors and descendants, and all "things" within its realm. This realm was called *Kamuy Moshir* and at its highest level were the supreme Kamuy or *Pause-Kamuy*, whom the Ainu associated with the reshaping of the Moshir.

The Ainu do not have a creation myth, only a "reshaping myth" (Batchelor 1971: 331, 367; Naert 1960: 162) and in this myth the Moshir consisted of a marshland which the Pause Kamuy decided to "remodel". To the Ainu *Pau* as in *Pause*, was the sound of the Kamuy who decided to reshape Ainu Moshir. Hence, the bear, which the Ainu, among other things, called *Sekuma-Pause-Kamuy*, also belonged to this category (Batchelor 1932: 351; Munro 1962: 22). My fieldwork observation reveals that according to the Ainu the bear Kamuy was included among the Pause Kamuy.[5]

---

5   Ohnuki-Tierney writes:
"The bears are physically more powerful than humans and have the remarkable capacity to survive the winter simply by licking the salt on their paws [as the Ainu believe] the power of the bears as perceived by the Ainu, is above all, their capacity to reign as the supreme deity who determine the welfare of the Ainu, if pleased, they provide abundant food and protect the Ainu… but if offended they can punish the humans by harming them" (1981: 83).

Apart from "the reshaping gods and goddesses", Pause-Kamuy included those Kamuy whom the Ainu associated with their settlements. These were *Kamuy-Huchi* which consisted of two components, *Ape-Huchi* who was their female ancestor goddess and *Huchi*, the goddess who gave birth to the fire and after that protected it. *Chise-koro-Kamuy* which also consisted of two components, *Ape-Ekashi*, the male ancestor god, and *Chise*, the god who protected the village and the house (compare Munro's [1962: 16-27, 35], discussion where he speaks of Ape-Huchi and Ape-Ekashi as "house mother" and "house father"), *Hash-uk-Kamuy*, the god who provided game, and finally *Wakka-us-Kamuy*, the god who provided fish.

All Pause Kamuy were in essence male Kamuy. This may seem odd since Kamuy Huchi, the birth-giving goddess, for obvious reasons must be considered female. In the Ainu opinion, however, Kamuy-Huchi was considered to be both female and male. The Ainu themselves give the following explanation for this view:

> Kamuy-Huchi stands apart from fire and birth, also as a female goddess, Ape-Huchi. Kamuy-Huchi is the supreme Kamuy and the power of Kamuy-Huchi is not only equivalent to the power of other male Pause-Kamuy, but it is also superior. It is true that our belief is that Kamuy-Huchi and Chise-koro-Kamuy are a married couple, we call them Ape-Huchi and Ape-Ekashi, and in this regard, Ape-Huchi is a female goddess and plays the second fiddle as an Ainu wife should do. In our opinion Kamuy-Huchi, which is also Ape-Huchi, is the supreme Kamuy. You see, since Kamuy-Huchi stands for many things, both female and male, Kamuy-Huchi cannot be entirely female, nor can Kamuy-Huchi be entirely male. Although some of Kamuy-Huchi's components are entirely female ones, yet Kamuy-Huchi is neither woman nor man (Interview with Ainu Ekashi, Hidaka, 1988).

The level below consisted of those Kamuy to whom the Ainu ascribed lesser importance, including living things and material objects such as *Kamuy Ni*, trees, *Kamuy Nonno*, flowers and the like (Naert 1960: 157). According to the Ainu, Kamuy of lesser importance were in essence female Kamuy. Their own explanation of this is as follows:

> Since we believe that we need important Kamuy for important tasks we also believe we need less important Kamuy for less important tasks. It is as simple as that. In our society we men take care of important tasks. It is our belief that women, because of their awful smell, which comes from menstruating women, will chase the Kamuy away from us. We cannot afford this. It is too risky to let women handle important tasks. Clearly, you must see that (from the above interview).

I would, however, not go so far as to assert that my own interpretation is coherent to the view of the Ainu whose cosmological order differs from my own. These phenomena were of course related to factors that governed the Ainu perception of how to maintain a cosmological order, yet I can never be sure that my own interpretation of this relationship actually corresponds to an Ainu view.

From my own world view I can always connect the fact that the smell of menstruating women chases the Kamuy away and the fact that male hunting is superior to female hunting with mechanisms used by Ainu males to control their women. I can thus go further and assume that the same mechanism works to maintain their cosmological order as a whole.

MOSHIR IDENTITY

Let us now continue with further information about the classification of the *Kamuy*. The following classification is proposed by Munro. He writes:

1. Remote and traditional Kamui
2. Familiar or accessible and trustworthy Kamui
3. Subsidiary Kamui
4. Theriomorphic Kamui
5. Spirit helpers and personal Kamui
6. Mischievous and malicious Kamui
7. Kamui of pestilence
8. Things of unutterable horror (1962: 12).

The Ainu do not reject Munro's way of classifying their deities, but they are not fully content. I was given the following explanation by one of my informants:

> It is not possible for other people to fully comprehend the weight we put on our Kamuy, or what the concept of Kamuy stands for to us Ainu. There is no Nihon word that covers the "imi" [true essence] of Kamuy. One and the same Kamuy may have many different names. To us, the more names a Kamuy has, the more frequent we make use of its favours, and thus it fulfils several different purposes. We do not value one favour more than the other (interview with Ainu male, aged 55, Asahikawa, 1988).

According to Peng and Geiser, Kamuy Moshir was divided into several layers. These were called:

> "Siniskanto" [the heaven of heavens], "Nociwokanto" [the starry heaven], "Urarokanto" [the foggy heaven] and "Rankenkanto" [the lowest heaven] (1977: 209).

According to Batchelor (1901) there were six layers while Naert (1960) speaks of three layers and so does Hilger (1967). I have no intention of entering the discussion of how many layers existed in the Moshir. The differences seem to have their roots both in highly personal interpretations of the material delivered by informants and in the different ways used by the Ainu of classifying the elements of the Moshir. The latter, according to Kayano, is because:

> the manifoldness in the Ainu belief system, owing to a variety of beliefs in different Ainu areas, has given way to a biased and uniform scientific picture (interview with Kayano, 1988).

This shows that, even though previous research seems to have taken remarkably little interest in the great variation of the beliefs of the Ainu, they themselves were aware of them.

What distinguishes deities from humans was, according to Ohnuki-Tierney, that the former were "super-Ainu". She writes:

> Although these deities are seen as super-Ainu, they are not altogether different from the Ainu. The Goddess of Hearth ... is called Grandmother Hearth, the bear deities are addressed in prayers as grandfather and the bear cub ... as their grandchild ... Further illustrations of the fact that the deities are perceived as much the same as humans are found in folktales... In one tale a human who is married to a bear deity takes along elders from her settlement to the countries of the deities: the elders find their deities to be in human form living with their families in houses just like those of the Ainu (1981: 83).

According to her, the Ainu differentiate themselves from their gods and deities by ascribing these supernatural qualities, and defining them as "super-Ainu". This may give a plausible picture of how the Ainu formerly distinguished themselves from their gods.

Nevertheless, the question remains, whether we, by classifying the deities of the Ainu as "super-Ainu", actually have advanced any further when it comes to an understanding of the reality as it was perceived by the Ainu. As for our understanding of the interpretation of these things among today's Ainu people, we should perhaps, on grounds presented by Kayano (1985), put less emphasis on what means the Ainu used to distinguish themselves from their Kamuy and concentrate instead on the fact that they did make a distinction and use this information to understand the actual purpose of the interaction between the two. In this regard it is advisable to interpret the above, as the Ainu themselves suggest, as "preferred" attitudes towards Nature that are expressed in the form of tales to guide the Ainu. Compare also:

> In spite of the rich natural environment, the Ainu refrained from excessive hunting and fishing to ensure a continued supply for posterity. When the Ainu gathered wild plants for food, they never uprooted them, but left the roots and seeds for the following year ... This attitude was taught through the telling of stories passed from generation to generation. This Ainu oral tradition is called Uwepeker. These tales reminded the villagers of those who had been punished by the gods for abusing

the mountains and the rivers. The Ainu heeded these teachings and lived according to them (Kayano 1985: vi).

In this quotation there is stress on preferred attitudes and this is informative since it gives us an idea of their vision of an ideal model of interaction between themselves and Nature. It seems as if the Ainu attitudes to Nature, rather than distinguishing them from the Kamuy, are essentialities in the dialogue that is conducted between themselves and the Kamuy. Compare also what is said by Chiri Mashio an Ainu himself but who grew up without knowing the Ainu language:

> In the Ainu view all animal deities are actually human in appearance and live as humans do when in their own country. Only when they visit the Ainu country do they disguise themselves in the forms of animals by wearing special fur or leather garments. The purpose of this disguise is to bring a present when visiting as an expression of goodwill (quoted in Ohnuki-Tierney 1981: 84).

According to Peng and Geiser (1977), there were two types of supernatural beings, namely, *Ramat* and *Kamuy*. Peng and Geiser make great efforts to interpret the various relationships which they believe exist between them. They write:

> There are two types of supernatural beings in Ainu religious thinking. One is called ramat [spirit] and the other kamuy [god] … First there is a many-to-one relationship between ramat and the kamuy: it exists between a group of ramat and a group of kamuy in that the former are disguises of the latter… The many-to-one relationship may be inferred to also embrace all animals, e. g. bears, owls, foxes, etc.… Each species has as many ramat as there are animals controlled by a particular kamuy.… Second, also found is a one-to-one relationship that exists between ramat and kamuy in that one ramat corresponds to only one kamuy. The one ramat in this case is that of a human being, which after his departure from the body, may be elevated to become a kamuy.… The third and last relationship is a negative one: There are ramat that stand in no relationship with any kamuy: if preferred, this may be rephrased as one-to-zero relationship (1977: 215).

Peng and Geiser have devoted much time to sorting out Ainu religious beliefs, yet the model they present is in my view artificial. By referring to two different types of supernatural beings, they incorporate the Ainu belief system into their own world view, and use conceptual and explanatory tools that belong to their own mode of thought to interpret them. Such a method may be useful if our aim is to understand the supernatural beings of the Ainu in the context of the researchers, but it does not help to illuminate how the supernatural beings are to be understood in the context of the Ainu, nor can the information be used to gaining an understanding of how and why the Ainu view of their supernatural beings have changed over time.

The general opinion of both the Ainu and scholars is that Kamuy possessed Ramat and that Kamuy were deities or gods, because their souls were powerful and holy. Batchelor's (1901) standpoint on this matter is not clearly expressed and he does not make any distinction between the god, that is, the Kamuy and its attribute, that is, Ramat:

> The Ainu ascribe to every kind of animal, tree and plant a life with power of thought and action, possessing emotion and passion, like their own. They [the Ainu] suppose that every tree has not only its own Kamuy, but that roots, stems, rugged bark, inner-bark or fiber, wood, heart, knots, buds, leaves, twigs, crown and flower with fruit also, each are themselves peopled with innumerable other Kamuy spirits, some of which are good and other evil (1901: 351).

When Ainu spoke of "souls" they used the word "Ramat". The Ainu opinion was further that everything and everybody had Ramat but not everything and everybody was Kamuy. The English word "soul" is of course not equivalent to Ramat but it is as close as one can come. Munro writes:

> Ramat [literally "heart"] is a word that cannot be translated, and stands for a concept not easy to describe. The nearest English equivalents are soul or spirit (ibid: 8).

> Whatever has no ramat has nothing. Ramat is all pervading and indestructible. It varies vastly in amount and concentration (1962: 8).

With the exception of *Aiona*, the goddess who according to Ainu myth (Naert 1960: 160) created and educated humans, all other Kamuy were perceived as deities whose Ramat could enter various organisms in Ainu Moshir.

Munro (1962: 10) shares the opinion that Kamuy, just like humans, could be good (*Pirika*), bad (*Wen*) and something in between (*Koshne*), and so does Kayano, although he expresses it in a somewhat different way:

> To us [the Ainu], all living things, objects, and phenomena were gods, some bringing benefits, some misfortune, and some neither. There was an unwritten law between the gods – that is Nature – and the Ainu, allowing them to coexist in harmony (Kayano 1985: vi).

The reason for their different characters was, according to the Ainu, related to their own human assistance when it came to releasing the Ramat from its deceased body (see also Naert 1960: 180; Munro 1962: 26; Seligman 1962: 132; Peng & Geiser 1977: 211; Ohnuki-Tierney 1981: 116-117).

If the Ramat of the deceased was powerful the ritual performed was elaborate (Ohnuki-Tierney 1981: 102), if not, only minor preparations were made (Ohnuki-Tierney 1981: 86).

In the former case the religious killing was called Iyomante, which means "a sending away". The word does not imply death by killing but rather a dispatch (Batchelor 1932: 37). This was an expression of goodwill and served to please the deity. It is believed that the Kamuy would return to Kamuy Moshir and if treated in the right way, the Kamuy would visit Ainu Moshir again (Ohnuki-Tierney 1981: 83).

If the Ainu failed to assist, the Kamuy could not return to Kamuy Moshir and it was believed that the Ramat would haunt the Ainu by sending misfortunes (Munro 1962: 26; Naert 1960: 180; Peng & Geiser 1977: 211; Ohnuki-Tierney 1981: 83). For the most part, however, the Kamuy were benevolent and took great interest in the lives of the Ainu (Naert 1960: 195).

The Ainu did not believe in the reincarnation of humans. Humans could visit dead relatives, but only in dreams, and the dead could interfere in the lives of the living but they could not be reborn. To be reincarnated was the privilege of animals and deities. Dead Ainu were believed to live their lives in ways which were very similar to those of the living Ainu (Seligman 1962: 132). The place where the dead dwelt was called *Kamuy Kotan.*

According to Naert (1960), dead persons first entered *Pokna Moshir*, which means the world beneath. From here a deceased person was transported either to *Kamuy Kotan* (Paradise) or to *Teinei Pokna Chiri* (Hell) (Naert 1960: 119 ff.). The Ainu themselves do not, however, share this opinion. According to one of my informants:

> We do not make any distinction between hell and paradise [in the way that Naert does]. All dead Ainu people come to the same place. Whether this place turns out to be a hell or a paradise to the deceased person, has to do with kin in the world of the living. If his kin act in the proper way towards Kamuy both the living and the dead are well taken care of. If not both are suffering (Interview with Ainu female, aged 45, Iburi, 1988).

The Ainu communicated with their Kamuy with the help of *Yukar*, odes. Yukar means "to imitate" and the Ainu imitated the voices and movements of their Kamuy (Batchelor 1901: 270; Seligman 1962: 176; Hilger 1967: 272; Peng & Geiser 1977: 224). This special technique was called *Sharante* (Hilger 1967: 182), and it was highly revered and much effort was expended to develop it to perfection.

To communicate with their Kamuy the Ainu relied on Ekashi, honourable male elders, and Inau carvings, handmade objects, sticks to which shavings, *Kike*, are attached and made as offerings to the Kamuy and sacred in themselves (Munro 1962: 7).

Inau were personal belongings and appeared in two categories: *Kamuy-Nomi-Inau*, used in offerings to the deities and gods, and *Shinurapa-Inau*, used in offerings to the ancestors (Munro 1962: 29). Naert (1960: 177) has described them as anthropomorphic gods. One could say, as the Ainu themselves do, that there existed an Inau for each and every incident in the life of the Ainu.

Ainu kept their Inau in groups. These Inau groups were called *Nusa* (Batchelor 1901: 121; Naert 1960: 126) and the Nusa was located in front of the eastern window, *Kamuy-Kus-Puyuara* (Batchelor 1901: 121), which was considered a holy window.

To communicate with the Kamuy was the prerogative of Ekashi and it was believed that these were the only ones who knew the language of the Kamuy, which was called *Kamuy Itak* (Ohnuki-Tierney 1981: 87). According to Ohnuki-Tierney this assumption that women were not able to speak Kamuy Itak "provides the basis for their exclusive access to the role of officials in rituals" (Ohnuki-Tierney 1981: 82).

This way of excluding females from access to the role of ritual officials did not prevent Ainu women from having ritual functions altogether. Ainu women were excluded from ritual activities until they had reached old age. According to Ohnuki-Tierney (1981) the ritual function of old women in healing procedures were ascribed great importance, yet the form it took differs from male ritual activities:

> In female ritual activity communication is two-way and at a close range.... Immediate repayment in form of the healing of the sick person.... Group ritual [male ritual activity] is one-way. Offerings are made and the Ainu convey their respect and ask for general welfare, such as abundance of food from the deities concerned... the deities are asked to repay only at some unspecified time in the future (Ohnuki-Tierney 1981: 101-102).

Speaking in general terms, the combined factors of sex and age brought elderly males closest to the deities and within this framework men, especially the elders, and Kamuy were given an eastern position, which the Ainu associated with the sacred realm, whereas women and youth were given a western position, which the Ainu associated with the profane realm. Important tasks, those of men and Kamuy, were performed within the eastern realm and unimportant tasks, those of women and youth, were performed within the western realm. According to the Ainu these positions originate in mythical time and they are related to the reshaping of the Moshir. The myth, which is quoted by Batchelor, tells us the following story:

> The female had the west ... and the male the eastern parts. But as the goddess was proceeding with her work she happened to meet the sister of Aiona and instead of attending to her duties, stopped to have a chat with her ... the male deity continuing to work away, nearly finished his portion ... the female became frightened ... did her work hurriedly and in a slovenly manner (Batchelor 1901: 39).

It is noteworthy that east and west may be substituted geographical positions such as upstream and downstream. This was first noticed by archaeologists, and anthropologists have tried to make these positions fit the eastern and western positions. It has been argued that upstream corresponds to east and downstream to west, although sometimes, according to Wajin archaeologists, the opposite is the case, as for instance in the Asahikawa area (interview with a Wajin archaeologist, 1988).

Besides west and east or upstream and downstream, the Ainu had a third dimension which was called *Sak*. Literally Sak means "non-location" (Batchelor 1938: 433) and it included "things" which, for one reason or another, could not be identified simply because their location was unknown. Sak could refer to a child who did not know its parents. It could also refer to "things" which took up habits, such as cannibalism, which was not common among the Ainu.

Sak were often dangerous and the Ainu took great care when dealing with them. Since they could not approach them directly, as their location was unknown, they offered them reconciliation by using known Kamuy, preferably *Huchi-Kamuy*, the Fire Goddess, as mediators (Naert 1960; Munro 1962; Ohnuki-Tierney 1976; 1981). In combination with *Kotan*, as in *Sak Kotan*, the concept referred to the hunting grounds of the Ainu, hence "summer village" (Batchelor 1938: 433). These were places from which women and youth were excluded, but where Ainu males spent about half of the year. This arrangement is labelled "semi-nomadian".

The organization of Ainu settlements, Kotan, their dwellings, winter and summer settlements, were closely related to their perception of the universe and so were also the social and political structure in Ainu society.

AINU POLITY: GROUP ARRANGEMENTS, SOCIAL AND POLITICAL

When dealing with the structure of the *social system* of the Ainu we must rely on a rather unsatisfactory body of material. Note for instance the following remark made by Watanabe:

> The structure of Ainu social system is one of the most obscure aspects of the Ainu life. Published data on the subject are scanty and fragmentary (Watanabe 1972: 13).

The general opinion is that the Ainu social system is extremely complicated. This derives from the fact that the Ainu have double unilineal elements in their social system and that both matriliny and patriliny are recognized, but that each sex acknowledges only the line of its own sex. Seligman writes:

> It is difficult to classify the structure of the Ainu social system because it is not a double unilinear descent system … as that implies the recognition of matriliny and patriliny by both sexes for different functions. Nor is it what I have called an asymmetrical system, i. e. single unilineal descent accepted by one sex and bilateral descent accepted by the opposite sex. The Ainu system has double unilineal elements in that both matriliny and patriliny are recognized, but it is unusual in that each sex acknowledges only the line of its own sex. It is asymmetrical in that

exogamy is ruled by matriliny.... Among the Ainu patrilineal territorial grouping, descent and ancestral worship for women is limited to the descent of the great-great-grandmother (1962: 158).

Sugiura and Befu also point out the difficulties that exist when it comes to classifying and explaining the structure of the Ainu social system and their attempts to shed some light on the system resulted in their proposal of the term "parallel descent". They write:

> The most significant feature of Ainu social organization was undoubtedly the unique manner of tracing descent. Men tracing their descent patrilineally and women doing so matrilineally, were organized into separate unisexual groups. What could this type of descent system be called in contradistinction to typical unilinear and double unilinear descent? We propose adoption of the term parallel descent advanced by Davenport (1959: 570) since his discussion suggests a close resemblance to the Ainu rule of descent (1962: 296).

Peng and Geiser are of the opinion that a definition of the Ainu social system by the term "parallel descent" as proposed by Sugiura and Befu is highly speculative and their criticism is formulated thus:

> After considering their investigation one has the impression that their sole purpose is to describe what they call "parallel descent" rather than kinship organization *per se*. They appear to offer credence to a plausible kinship system in order to accomplish that end (1977: 101).

The social structure of the Ainu remains as obscure as ever and this can at least partly be related to previous attempts to remodel the Ainu social system to fit existing models used by anthropologists in societies similar to that of the Ainu. In a way the structure of the Ainu social system has been the subject of descriptive ethnography and in this situation the empirical material, rather than theory, has been their prior interest. Another difficulty is also the fact that the Ainu stopped practising it a long time ago and their own information about the system is limited to, (1) the shape and form of the emblems of the matriliny/patriliny and (2) the material of the emblems.

In Ainu myth, the social system was introduced to them by Aiona, the goddess who created and educated them. Exactly when they stopped practising it, is, however, debatable, and according to some Ainu it goes back as far as "several" hundred years ago, that is, when the Matsumae Han first settled in Hokkaido, whereas according to others, it was abandoned at the time of the annexation of their land, that is, around 1868, which is also the opinion of most researchers.

The reason why they abandoned their social systems is not clearly expressed and the Ainu opinion differs from that of "professionals", who claim that the system died out as a result of the increased contact with people from the mainland. According to the Ainu, the increased contact with the mainland was, in fact, irrelevant. A story recounts under what circumstance they gave it up: they gave it up because a young Ainu girl showed her emblem, *Upshoro-Kut*, a secret girdle, to a Shamo and after that there was no turning back. The reason why this act was ascribed such decisive consequences is not clear, yet as Kayano points out:

> It may be combined with the fact that, because it was introduced by one of our most revered Kamuy, the damage could not be repaired and for fear of a punishment, as for instance a retrogression to Moshir as it looked before the Pause Kamuy remodelled it, if the damage was neglected, the Ainu simply chose to abandon it (interview in 1988).

The concern is what is there to say about the Ainu society and its structure and the question is what we know for certain about it. The Ainu society was beyond all doubt kinship-organized and it was bound together by social ties, moral duties and obligations towards kin. Yet, can we be sure that residence was patrilocal, that is, that women left the Kotan of their parents when they married (Watanabe 1975: 69 ff.; Peng & Geiser 1977: 42-59)? As far as Watanabe is concerned, he does in fact also mention the possibility of inter-Kotan marriages (1975: 70). In the judgment of the Ainu there are no such rules now nor have there ever been:

> People are allowed to settle down wherever they themselves see fit. Maybe the village of the husband is preferred but it is not prescribed (interview with Ainu Ekashi, Hidaka, 1988).

The patrilinies were territorial corporate groups. They were called *Shine-Ekashi-Ikir* and the members of each group claimed descent from a common male ancestor (Seligman 1962: 145 ff.). The overt expression of membership in the Shine-Ekashi-Ikir group was the possession of a common male ancestor emblem, *Ekashi Itokpa* (Watanabe 1972: 13). According to Watanabe there were, besides regular members, also foreign Ainu people, *Anun Utari* in this group:

> They [Anun Utari] fall under two classes ... those from other places who rely on some affinal relationship or kinship with local members had come to stay as a sort of guest. They were usually married and were with their families. To the other class ... there were those who had no relations among the local group members, but pressed by strained circumstances had come to them for aid (Watanabe 1972: 14-15).

The social core of the territorial group consisted of the nuclear family *Chise*, mother, father and their unmarried children. Extended families were the exception rather than the rule and were usually formed by co-resident widowed kinsmen or kinswomen (Peng & Geiser 1977: 86).

The unit, *Kotan*, usually consisted of about five, and seldom more than fifteen, patrilineally related nuclear households, Chise (Takakura 1960: 16 ff, Seligman 1962: 150 ff.; Batchelor 1971: 35; Watanabe 1972: 9-13; Ohnuki-Tierney 1976: 310; Peng & Geiser 1977: 107 ff.). This statement is not unproblematic. Compare for instance the following:

> An investigation of the Kamikawa region showed several scores of hundreds of semi-underground houses [typical Ainu dwellings] formerly used as dwellings. Yet in order to take this as evidence that the Ainu villages were once larger-... it is necessary to prove that all of the caves in the district were of the same period (Takakura 1960: 17).

The view mentioned above that Ainu society might have been much larger than previously accepted is built on the assumption that the Kamikawa region was actually an Ainu-controlled territory. On this point scholars are in disagreement. The finds referred to above date back about eleven hundred years and archaeologists and ainulogists in general are still debating whether the Kamikawa region was actually controlled by the Ainu at this time (Munro 1911; Naert 1960; Takakura 1960; Kodama 1970). Nevertheless, and regardless of whether the Kamikawa region actually belonged to them, the Ainu are convinced that their societies were in fact much larger than researchers care to admit.

> There might have been small Ainu residences, of course, but most Kotan were much bigger [than most scientists admit]. I should say five hundred people to each. You see, in those days, we had chiefs, powerful chiefs, chiefs with a lot of goods. People of such Kotans could welcome outside people, have many children and lead good lives (interview with Ainu Ekashi, Chikabumi Kotan, 1985).

Judging from the quotations above, it seems likely that the size of a Kotan varied to a much larger extent than previously accepted.

The social core of Ainu society consisted of the *Matikir-Esap-Utar* group. This group was composed of males (*Ir-Matainu-Esap-Utar*) and females (*Ir-Matainu*) descended in the uterine line from a known ancestress four generations back. Within the Matikir-Esap-Utar group marriages were prohibited.

The overt expression of membership in the group was that its female members (Ir-Matainu) shared one and the same female ancestor emblem, *Upshoro-Kut*, which was a secret or hidden girdle worn by the women. The females who shared the same Upshoro-Kut belonged to a group called *Shine-Huchi-Ikir* (Watanabe 1972: 17). In the case of the adoption of a child, which was rather common, the child, if a boy, was given the *Itokpa* of the adoptive father and in the case of a girl, the *Kut* of the adoptive mother (see also Naert 1960; Seligman 1962; Sugiura & Befu 1962; Watanabe 1972; Ohnuki-Tierney 1974, 1981).

The Matikir-Esap-Utar group was primarily social and it was also non-territorial. The members were scattered over vast areas but they were bound together by moral obligations such as to help and assist each other in times of hardship (Seligman 1962: 137 ff.). With respect to the Shine-Huchi-Ikir group Watanabe writes:

> It is true that the women who assist a woman in marriage, childbirth, illness and death were her Huchi ikir relatives. These activities of mutual help seem to have been based on a person-to-person relationship (1972: 17).

Seligman writes that "the ability to become a midwife is inherited in the matrilineage" (1962: 150). The female ancestor mark, the Kut, regulated marriage alliances:

> A man could not marry his mother's sister's daughter, but there was no prohibition against marriage with a father's brother's daughter. Further, no man might marry two sisters. Munro was told that sisters having the same kut were regarded as one person. Polygyny was permitted .... Munro does not refer to any example known to him (Seligman 1962: 147-148).

Seligman further writes:

> In former times the Japanese established trading posts in coastal areas, and Ainu would come to these, such men might be accompanied by a small wife (pon machi) (1962: 147).

In Batchelor (1938: 399) *Pon Machi* translates as "concubine". This indicates that Pon Machi may be a rather recent phenomenon, introduced by the Wajin at the time of their intrusion into Hokkaido.

According to Watanabe (1972: 17), there is no evidence of Ainu having more than one legitimate wife. However, it is questionable whether polygamy existed as a general practice among the Ainu. In "Instructions to Officials in Charge of the Management of Ezo, February 10, 1799" we are informed that: "It is said that their [the Ainu] custom is for the rich to have many wives and the poor to have none" (archival records at Hokudai, Sapporo State University).

It is noteworthy, that during my field research I came into contact with one male Ainu who is married to two sisters. I do not know if his marriages are registered. In any case he has four children, two by each of the sisters. The Ainu say: "We do not say that we are not allowed to have more than one wife, only it is not customary" (interview with Ainu male, aged 35, Nibutani, 1988).

Ainu marriage alliances did not require bridewealth, that is, valuables given by a man's kin group to his wife's kin group to legitimate their marriage, that is, to compensate her kin for losing her presence and labour and to give him rights regarding their children. Rather the persons represented in the contract were moral persons acting voluntarily, yet the contracts were strictly obligatory (cf. Mauss 1969: 1).

Let us now consider the rules that governed the political *structure* in Ainu units, Kotan, which were flexible indeed. According to Watanabe (1972) there existed two types of settlement, which he labels mono-settlements, that is, one Kotan one leader, and multi-settlements, that is, several Kotan with the same leader. Watanabe writes:

> The Kotan group did not always constitute a socio-politically integrated territorial unit that is a local group. The presence of the two categories .... labelled by the present writer as settlement group and local group. The local group as a politically autonomous group could either consist of several kotan or only one single kotan. The unity and integrity of the local group were manifested in the presence of a common headman, collective ownership of the named concentrations of the spawning beds of dog salmon, group participation in certain rituals such as the salmon ceremony and cooperation in housebuilding (1972: 10-11).

The type to which the settlement belonged was determined by the existence of an "able-bodied" headman. The Ainu called their headmen *Kotan-koro-kuru* (*guru*) and *Sapane-guru*. These are local variants (Batchelor 1938: 269, 437). The Wajin, on the other hand, called them by various names:

> There were no leaders of the whole island of Ezo but a leader to each village and he was called Otona. But Otona was a name used by the Japanese... Each village had its leader called Bankinnenshippa. There were also sub-chiefs called Shibank-inne. These leaders the Japanese called Otona and Kozukai respectively. Every village had its own chieftain. The more powerful were called Hashio and the less powerful were called Otona (Takakura 1960: 17).

My fieldwork data reveal that the Ainu are unfamiliar with the two concepts *Bankinnenshippa* and *Shibankinne* used in the quotation above. It is, however possible that these words have lost their meaning today. They might have been local concepts.

The Ainu argue that the words and concepts used by the Wajin to describe Ainu leaders do not carry the meaning of leader, at least not in their sense of the concept. To them these concepts are Wajin interpretations intended to fulfil Wajin aims to control them and their territories. In Ainu opinion the most revered quality of the leader is his generosity. Since *Kotan-koro-guru*, *Sapane-guru* and *Ekashi* carry such a meaning, these concepts are the only possible ones.

The following list of a leader's main tasks has been provided by Watanabe:

1. *External affairs*:

   a) observance for rituals for affiliation of a newcomer to his group
   b) ritual sanction of trespasser

    c) ritual permission to nonmembers to exploit resources

    d) negotiation of inter-local group affair

2. *Domestic affairs:*

    a) leadership in observance of dog-salmon ceremony

    b) being kept informed of areas where hunting with springbow [used when hunting big game] was taking place, and, people engaged in it

    c) supervision of the proper observance of ritual taboos by individuals of his group

    d) protection of an individual family short of food

    e) giving advice to individuals of his group in practical and moral difficulties which varied from production-technique to medicine

(Watanabe 1972: 13).

A leader's position was usually passed to his eldest son, but not necessarily. If the son was considered a bad leader, that is, if he was not generous, he might not be elected and if already elected he could be disposed of or even killed (Seligman 1962: 155), and his position handed over to a more suitable person. If no such person existed within the Kotan it could not function as an autonomous political unit but had to be brought together with other units under an able-bodied headman (Seligman 1962: 155; Watanabe 1972: 10-12).

An immediate reaction to such a state of affairs is of course, what kind of circumstance governed a dissolution of political control and what exactly does the term "generosity" mean? After all, it seems rather strange that people simply gave up political control. However, since neither professionals nor the Ainu are explicit on this point the question remains. A possible explanation might be that the absence of political control within each Kotan was considered less destructive for the group and its members than an ungenerous leader was, since an ungenerous leader might bring harm to the order of the Moshir, whereas the absence of political control did not have such consequences. After all, "The Ainu could exist as a group without political control, but how could they exist as part of Nature if their leader was ungenerous, when the Kamuy had decided that generosity was the most revered quality of a leader", which is the explanation Kayano gives (interview, Nibutani, 1988).

Kotan without headmen thus existed locally without political autonomy but with territorial hunting and fishing rights intact (Watanabe 1972: 12). As soon as a local leader was appointed the unit regained its political autonomy. A territory, politically autonomous or not, was called *Iwory*, which means a field of activity for gods, Kamuy, and humans, Ainu (Batchelor 1938: 214).

The Iwory was divided into a permanent winter settlement often located by a river, lake or by the sea and a summer settlement, Sak kotan, with access to game (Takakura 1960: 17; Seligman 1962: 157; Watanabe 1972: 72, 1975: 10-12; Ohnuki-Tierney 1976: 310). The summer settlement was reserved for males, preferably those who were able to hunt, but also those who were not. Included in the non-hunting category were elder honourable males, Ekashi, who were too old to take active part in the hunting parties, but whose ritual functions were considered indispensable (see also Kayano 1988a). No females were permitted (Watanabe 1972: 150-153, 1975: 75, Ohnuki-Tierney 1981: 86).

Takakura provides us with the following picture:

> Although the natives of Ezo possessed their own houses, they never lived at the same place all their lives. Whenever the game was more abundant in other parts of the country they would abandon their houses and carry their belongings to the new land, build another, and settle down. Such were the customs of the Ezo. Moreover, if there were places where hunting and fishing was more promising, according to the season of the year, they did not remain in one place even for a year. They moved with the game and were therefore without a permanent home (1960: 16).

His view of Ainu society corresponds not only to a view of the Ainu as hunters but also to an evolutionary definition of the concept, that is, a reconstruction. After all, at the time of the description the Ainu did not live in a world of hunters, their contacts with other types of societal forms go back about eleven hundred years.

According to the Ainu, the description above is incorrect. They claim that the above view is based on exceptions to the rule rather than on the rule itself and this in turn had to do with the fact that the Wajin had limited knowledge of certain aspects of the "traditional" Ainu society. They did not know that there existed two different types of settlement, one summer and one winter settlement. The way in which the Ainu express their view can be exemplified as follows:

> In Ainu societies there were people who moved about rather frequently, yet this was the exception rather than the rule. The people who were without a permanent home were, for the most part, those who had violated Ainu laws and thus condemned to banishment. Furthermore, since Ezo, at least prior to the Wajin intrusion, was rich in natural resources, which was one reason for the intrusion, shortage of game was rare. Hence there was no need for our people to take up the lifestyles of the nomads. It arose with the intrusion. According to us, the above picture is artificial and corresponds to a picture of us not only as a defeated people but also an inferior one. Since a thorough knowledge of our old-time customs and tradition is lost, the best we can do is to add our own, in the eyes of the Wajin, highly personal interpretations of the conditions of our former life. Now I will give you mine: ...
>
> We stayed for a rather long time, say five, even ten years, more even, at the same place. We only moved when food was scarce, but that did not occur very often. At least not before the Wajin invasion. We seldom starved. If perhaps one family did not have much to eat we always shared. If there was little to share, we shared it. Sometimes a person could not find anything to eat. He then went to visit persons he knew, his kinsmen. They helped him. Most of the time people stayed

where they belonged, where their ancestors lived. It was not good to leave, because then our kinsmen in the other world could perhaps not find them and assist them (interview with Ainu Ekashi, Sapporo, 1985).

Note that the two different views may not contradict each other altogether. It is possible that the Wajin are referring to movements between the territories of the Ainu, that is, summer and winter Kotan, without knowing that they actually had permanent Kotans where they stayed for a considerable length of time.

INHERITANCE

With respect to inheritance, all essential female property, *Huchi-Korpe*, which included bead necklaces (*Reutunbe*), earrings and food preparation utensils, was inherited by daughters from their mother. When it comes to male property, *Maeni-Korpe*, the eldest son inherited the house and the courtyard. The family treasures, such as useful articles (*Iyoibe*), and goods of ritual value (*Ikoro*), ornamental swords (*Shintoko*), lacquer boxes used as receptacles for sacred things (*Itangi*), went to sons, but there were no restrictions about how they were to be divided among the sons. Further, if there was no son to inherit, the treasures went to a son-in-law, a stepson or an adopted son.

The information above is given by Munro (1962: 60-62) and Seligman (1962: 149-150): however the Ainu dispute this saying that it is the youngest son who inherits the house and the courtyard, since it is he who takes care of his parents. According to my informant:

> The best arrangement is for the youngest son to inherit Chise [the house and the courtyard]. Since he is the youngest he is also the strongest, with much power still in his body. He is the one best suited to take care of his old parents. Look around yourself. In this village this custom is still alive and we have no intention to alter it (interview with Ainu male, aged 53, Nibutani, 1988).

Well, I did look around myself. Furthermore, I took the advice literally and refrained from asking "impertinent" questions. During my stay I learned that looking was as much as I actually could do since elder people's whereabouts, i. e. their choice of residence, or rather their youngest son's choice of residence for them, is a delicate matter. Judging from my observations, the majority of the elder people in the village stay either with their youngest son or close to him, that is, they are neighbours. If not, both the parents and the son are the subject of gossip and speculations.

Gossip and speculations reveal that people in general side for both parties in the sense that certain extenuating circumstances are recognized, such as:

They [the youngest son and his family] have a boarding-house. It is too noisy for
old people. They have to make a living and their parents have to have some peace
around them....

It is their [the parents'] own choice. Both parties are more comfortable now.
You see, the parents do not like his wife. We think she is nice, yet they [the parents]
do not"....

The youngest son left Nibutani. He could not find work here. His parents
are too old to move. Now they live in their daughter's house instead....

The son is divorced. His wife left him. They [the parents] will not live in his
house. Maybe they think he will have difficulties in finding another wife (interviews
in Nibutani, 1988).

The alternatives to the parents and the youngest son sharing a household are for
the parents either to live alone, at some distance, or with other relatives, preferably sons
and daughters of all categories – age is not considered important. It is noteworthy that
the results of my census do not correspond to the information obtained through gossip.
It turned out that people are skilled in avoiding direct answers to this particular question
and they use this skill close to perfection.

The reason for the discrepancy may be that the Ainu are well aware of their status
as anthropological subjects. They are familiar with both previous and contemporary
writings about them. If "practical application" does not correspond to "prescribed" rules,
the Ainu may try to give answers that correspond to preferred rules rather than to the way
in which they actually are practised today.

As for Nibutani, this seems to be a plausible explanation. In this village people are
proud of their Ainu inheritance and make great efforts to preserve Ainu customs and
beliefs. For this reason the Iyomante ceremony is now reintroduced in this village and it
seems as if this ritual, at least mythically, stands as a source of stability and security.

IYOMANTE

According to my informant:

The myth [the one quoted above] teaches us how to deal with Nature and whom
we shall provide for. I mean whom we can marry. Yet in this village we have a man
who is married to two sisters - you must know that, everybody knows – which the
myth tells us not to do. He is well off so I think the myth gives us advice which
we can follow if we like. If a person can take care of two wives, I do not think it
matters if they are sisters, do you? The myth also teaches us what actions we shall
take if things are bad. Trade with other people, marry a widow, move to our
relatives, etc....

As you know, it is our belief that we humans cannot exist if Nature deserts us. Therefore we must return to Nature what belongs to Nature. This we do by releasing the ramat of things in Nature....

The reason why we think that the bear is mighty is because it is the biggest animal in our Moshir. For the same reason it gives us plenty of food during the long winter. If we have bear meat we do not suffer from famine. When the bear visits our Moshir it knows that it will be well taken care of. It is not chance that governs when or whom it visits. It is the choice of the bear itself. The reason why it visits is that the bear can see if humans are short of food. It then picks one of us to be its master in the world of the humans. This person must be a generous person and a revered person as well. We know that, and a "chosen man" is very proud of himself. The bear always chooses some kind of leader, Ekashi. If by accident a non-chosen person should be appointed leader the bear will kill him. We then know that the leader is bad. If he tries to catch the bear, the bear will kill him. We then know that the man is to blame, not the bear. The bear knows the future and judges accordingly....

Now, it goes without saying that it also knows that we are going to send it back to Kamuy Moshir when it has finished its duties among us. Otherwise it cannot visit again and we will be deprived of its services. We cannot afford that so we take great care in feeding and entertaining it. If the bear is a small one we nurse it just like we nurse our children. In fact we treat it like a child.[6] It is our adoptive child, we say. When it is time for the bear to leave us we give a great feast in its honour, the Iyomante.[7] During its stay in our place, many people have come to pay it their respect. These people are invited to the Iyomante celebrations which last about three days. The people who are invited are those of our own kin. Sometimes people from distant settlements will come and join. We welcome them. They have heard of our fortune and now they will rejoice with us....

---

6   See also Naert (1960: 183) where he gives the reader a picture of an Ainu woman nursing a bear cub.

7   "I so and so of such a place am about to send away the little cup to its home among the mountains. Come ye friends and masters to the feast. We will then unite in great joy of sending the mighty one off" (Batchelor 1932: 37).

"O thou precious little high one. We salute thee. Hear now, we have nourished thee and brought thee up with great care, all because we love thee so much. Now as thou hast grown big we are sending thee away to thy father and mother. When thou comest to them, speak well of us and make known to them how kind we have been to thee. Come back to us again and we will then have another feast together and once more send thee off" (ibid: 40).

"O Divine cub, we present thee with these sacred things. We offer them to thee. Take them with you to your forebears and say to them: I have been right well taken care of for a long time by an Ainu father and mother. I have been preserved by them from harm and have grown up. Now I come to thee. I bring with me various viands for a feast. Pray let us eat and rejoice! If thou sayest this they will be pleased and happy" (ibid: 42).

In the old days, when there were plenty of bears, it occurred that many households of one single settlement had their own bear-cub. In those days, we had strict rules concerning whom to invite, but I do not think that each and every settlement adhered to the same rules. As for Nibutani, we invite kin on the male side and kin on the female side as well. I think this group is called Matikir esap utar. Munro wrote this. I knew Munro, he lived in our village for many years. Have you visited his museum yet? But, mind you, I have heard of those who invited kin belonging to the female side only, or was it male, I cannot recall. Nevertheless, our customs differ so it might have been both ways. Today we invite everybody, even strangers like yourself, yet, in this village we think that people who think our customs odd should rather not attend. They might write bad things about us. You see, to persons who do not understand our ways this ceremony may seem very cruel. It was forbidden, you know. People who think this ceremony cruel perhaps do not know that the bear is not killed but sent away actually, and we take great care in sending it off properly. We use tree kamui to assist us, and we put the bear's head very very gently between the tree logs which we have prepared very carefully and ornamented with Kike. I tell you something very stupid. When Iyomante was allowed again, some of our villagers thought that we should rather not kill the bear. Can you imagine? Fortunately, Mr Kayano did not listen, so the ceremony was not spoild. Had he not, our Kamuy might have been very angry and we would have made fools of ourself....

Mr Kayano, who is a precocious man, took measures. He videotaped the ceremony. You never know, the ceremony may be prohibited again. My personal opinion is that one can never recall the true feeling by looking at the tape, nevertheless, I think it was a good thing to have it taped. You can watch it and other people as well. On the tape you can see what the bear likes. As you can see, it likes the same things as humans do. It likes things that are shiny, so we offer shiny things to it. But we also dress up in shiny things ourselves. The women have earrings and necklaces. It likes food, all kinds of food, so we offer that to it. It likes sake so naturally it gets sake. It likes to listen to the songs and music of our people and to watch us dance. So we perform. When it is pleased we send it off to its ancestors. All the things which it likes it carries back to its home. Not literally, but in its soul and mind. These things are used as proofs that it has been well taken care of and it is divided among the bear's kin, just the way we divided the bear meat among our kin. Did you know that we give poor relatives and pregnant women double portions? This we did even this time. Once we have sent the bear away we are sorry. We have lost a friend. To remember our friend we place its head on a pole in our Nusa and we put plenty of inau, kike, etc. on and around it. We think this will please the bear. It is its funeral presents. We do the same thing when people die. Such are our beliefs (interview Nibutani 1988).

When my informant spoke of the ceremony he used *Kono Kamuy* which means this god, *Sekuma-Pause-Kamuy* which means the supreme god (Batchelor1932: 37) and *Heper* which means bear-cub (Batchelor 1932: 35).

It is relevant that the bear used to have several other names besides those above. These were:

1. *Utare,* which according to Takakura also, in a figurative sense, means "slave".

He writes:

Although there were men who could not support themselves and became dependent on their chiefs, they were called utare and the word slave was never used (1960: 19).

Watanabe uses the word Utare when he refers to the member of a Kotan. He writes: "Kotan... plus 'un' [of, or to be] 'Kuru' [a man] 'Koro' [to possess] 'Utare' [people]. It means people of such a headman" (1972: 11).

Seligman writes: "Matikir Esap Utar: a group composed of the males and females descended in uterine line from one woman to another for four generations" (1962: 146).

We cannot exclude the possibility that according to the beliefs of the Ainu there was actually a connection between the Ainu word for bear (Utare) and people (Ainu) in relation to a leader or a group of descendants.

2. *Metot-us-Kamuy,* which means the leader of the bears, that is, Utare (Batchelor 1932: 37). In this regard Metot-us-Kamuy is equivalent to Ekashi, that is, Kotan un Kuru Koro Utare.

3. *Kim-un-Kamuy,* which means bears who possess or use magic force. There are two different kinds of Kim-un-Kamuy. Those who are bad, *Nupuro-kes-un-guru,* and those who are good, *Nupuro-koro-Kamuy* (Batchelor 1971: 123-125).

According to the Ainu these bears, that is, Nupuro-kes-un-guru and Nupuro-koro-Kamuy, were those who visited the Ainu Moshir, when Iyomante was held in their honour. Hence, Kim-un-Kamuy were the "gifts" which Metot-us Kamuy distributed among the Ainu in Ainu Moshir. In a way these Kim-un-Kamuy were in essence female, at least if we relate them to the myth "A Woman Changed into a Bear" (Batchelor 1971: 133-140).

Hence, we have the following plausible scheme: (1) Heper = Ainu youth, (2) Utare = Ainu people in general, (3) Kim-un-Kamuy = Ainu women, that is, gifts, (4) Metot-us-Kamuy = Ekashi, leaders, and (5) Sekuma-Pause-Kamuy = the supreme god, that is, Chise-Koro-Kamuy, Kamuy-Huchi.

AINU ATTITUDES TO THEIR AINU HERITAGE

When I asked my informant why he settled for Sekuma-Pause-Kamuy and Heper, and why he did not use Utare, Kim-un-Kamuy or Metot-us-Kamuy, he answered:

Why do you ask such stupid questions? Maybe in the old days people did so, but today it would not be proper. The majority of our people are educated people (from the same interview).

In my opinion this is a very harsh answer, but I understand his reaction. During many hours he had given me information about beliefs that are tied to ancient times, beliefs that have been interpreted as belonging to a primitive stage of evolution. The essence of these beliefs he keeps to himself, possibly for fear of being misinterpreted.

For the same reason outward signs of Ainu inheritance, be it in the suburbs of the larger cities or in the countryside, are rare and people appear, on the surface, to have more in common with the Nihonjin and their way of life. Many Ainu who live in the suburbs claim to have no interest in their culture, and we do not find many signs of an Ainu inheritance, at least not in the suburban areas.

In the countryside, generally speaking, Ainu-style settlements, Kotan, have been replaced by typical Nihon villages, Mura. The majority of the population in most of the villages are Wajin and the Ainu who live here are for the most part engaged in agricultural and cattle-breeding activities.

Outward signs of Ainu inheritance are generally rare. In their everyday life people do not dress in Ainu-style clothes, they do not live in Ainu-style dwelling houses, Chise, nor do they speak their native language, Ainu Itak. Nevertheless, signs of the villages' Ainu origin are not missing altogether. Indicators are bears in cages, tourist shops with Ainu souvenirs such as wooden bears, key-rings, replicas of cultural items for sale, etc.

Other signs are Ainu museums and exhibition halls, where Ainu material culture is displayed. In some villages people invite the public to take part in Ainu performances such as dances or celebrations. On such occasions we may find people dressed up in their Ainu-style garments. In other villages, people arrange Ainu-style field trips of various kinds. These include camping activities where the public can take part in Ainu-style hunting and gathering parties and field trips where the public is invited to areas which used to be powerful Ainu settlements.

This way of displaying one's culture has been classified as folklore by authorities and scholars. Yet, beneath the surface we find a network among contemporary Ainu communities which reveals itself, not in what we can see on the surface, but in the way in which individuals express various aspects of Ainu activities and practices in its contemporary guise. In this regard, the contemporary guise may or may not correspond to local customs and beliefs.

An example where they do not correspond to the local customs of former days, is an Ainu woman whom I met in one of the villages. She claims to be a shaman and as such she earns her living today. Yet, in this area it is said that shamans, whether men or women, were non-existent. Nevertheless she claims to heal people by driving evil spirits out of their bodies and she is very skilled at reciting the language of the elders, Ekashi Itak, which, as has been pointed out by Ohnuki-Tierney (1981: 102), quite unlike to Kamuy Itak, the language of the gods, is accessible to both sexes. Furthermore, this Ainu woman also functions as a fortune-teller and not so long ago she was a midwife, *Tusu* (information obtained in an interview with Kayano, 1988).

In addition we also find Ainu who view their situation as a challenge, and in going about their daily life reveal, when examined closely, the hidden face of a culture rich in tradition and with a great deal of potential.

Without further entering into a discussion about Ainu attitudes to their own cultural inheritance, at this stage, I will be content with presenting the following material from an interview with Utariyan Narita, an Ainu who sees his work as a *Kibori* man, wood carver, as a challenge and whose products are manufactured in a "traditional" Ainu way. The material speaks for itself and I will refrain from making any comments. Mr Utariyan Narita speaks English and the interview was conducted in English at his own request and he wrote it down himself. The following is his own writing:

The Ainu Way – Making Best of Green Woods
Carving green woods:
My interest in Ainu wood works began more than 30 years ago. In those days, the Ekashi of the Ainu in Kushiro region of Hokkaido took me to the mountains. There I learned to catch birds and animals with bow and arrow, and I also learned to dissect and cook the game with "tashiro", hatchet, or a "makiri", knife. Having spent such boyhood, the first thing that that drew my attraction was the cutlery. Especially, the attraction of makiri was the greatest. I used to watch the Ekashi making makiri at the fireside, or carving a tray with a new makiri for hours without ever getting tired. Slightly arched shape was appealing and the handling was exceptional. Especially, the device to hold the handle and press with a thumb when drawing from a case was just fantastic. From the first, woods were the center of Ainu's way of living, so I naturally became familiar with it, but I also started to make makiri from the necessity of covering the living....

Referring to old materials, I earnestly began making makiri in my twenties, when I got married and settled in Okayama. As I continued to make makiri, I rediscovered its attractiveness, the beauty of use or service. Later, through the guidance of Mr Yoshinosuke Sotomura, Mr Shoji Hamada, Mr Bernard Leach and others, I went on to produce vessels and trays....

There is a daily tool of Ainu called "nima", a vessel similar to present day bowl. This nima is deeply carved inside, with the edge of indescribable curve. I kept asking myself how were the Ainu of the old days able to create this shape with a single makiri. Without finding the solution, I kept carving with a chisel or a makiri, which I have modified the edge in hooked-shape. One day I got the clue from a TV program which I just happened to watch. It was a scene of the natives, living deep in the jungles of Amazon, making canoes with the arrival of rainy season. Chop a big tree with axes and let the tree float on water. Then, several men got on the log and began to carve the floating side. When carving was finished, branches were spread at the bottom and set on fire. Then ashes were raked out and the men began to scrape the internal with round-edged wooden rod. And so, a canoe with a capacity of about 10 persons were complete in a day. I thought that perhaps Ainu used green wood to carve nima....

Common sense in handling wood was that it should be dried before use, and that insufficiently dried wood will inevitably result in cracks or distortion. I immediately began trial production. Green wood was quickly and beautifully carved, like chopping a radish. But I had reservations. I had made more than 300 nima in 4 years, but nearly 30% were cracked by the time of coloring. Unlike a wooden bowl, nima is not a uniformly round vessel. Core side of a half log will be the bottom of the vessel. In shape, quality side is piled rather than grain side. So I attended to devise various forms. Some using the "shirata", external part of the wood, others removing the shirata. Also various thickness were tried. As a result, I found that nima made of green wood will not crack easily, regardless of shirata or thickness. Furthermore, I found out that conventionally dried material will rarely crack if shirata was used. After 10 years I finally mastered what I thought to be the old Ainu way of making nima of green wood....

Unique curve made by Nature:

By using green wood, I also learned many other things. As mentioned before, I had trouble because I could not get the curve unique to nima. So I decided to revisit museums with Ainu materials on display. I stared on the nima in the showcase. The only conclusion I got was that nima in the museum were thinner. So, my next challenge was to make thinner nima. I used green wood of "ityaya", apple, cherry, red pine and so forth. Then as the wood dried, the curve I dreamed, gradually showed up. Curved line born out of natural dying was just fantastic, impossible to be made by any man's intention. When the problem of curved line was solved, the wonder of surface treatment remained. Now, the surface can be finished smoothly, by paper file, but how did the Ainu finish in the old days? Then I remembered the time Ekashi was making makiri. He was scraping the makiri with hard wood and the same thing was done with bow. As I tried it, I learned that it was no good after carving or when it was dried. The most effective timing was when the surface was lightly dried, with some moisture remaining inside the wood. This method brought good results. Surface rubbing acts to crush the grain of wood as well as varnish. But, in this method, it is most important to repeat elaborately. The case of makiri which I had finished in this manner gave fabulous luster....

Polishing by burning the green wood:

Lastly, I would like to explain about the finishing method by burning the green wood. My nima or table, chairs are finished with this method. First burn the carved green wood with a torch lamp. At first, there will be some scorch, but water will start to come out. When burned until no water comes out, then the surface will start to be scorched. After scorching uniformly, quickly rub the surface with brush-like article. At this time, it is important to confirm the degree of scorch. The sap will harden in tar-form and will act as varnish, so by applying paper file and then polishing, the beauty of the grain will become alive....

Recently I finished a nima of paulownia with this method. I am most satisfied because it was much better than I had imagined. As above, my start in wood carving was triggered through my impression of daily tools made by my ancestors. And, searching to recreate them led me to discover the hidden truth of using green woods. I was also able to experience such techniques as rubbing trees together or burning the material of wide-leaf trees. Although I intend to pursue my own creation I can state with great enthusiasm that I would like to keep on working by conversing with green woods. I may be a little conceited, but as I enter my workshop every morning and touch my hand-made tools or machinery, greeting them with good morning, that is when I feel glad that I have continued this work (Utariyan Narita, 1988).

Today Utariyan Narita lives with his wife, who is of Wajin descent, and their two children in the Hidaka area in Hokkaido. I made the interview in Nibutani and Mr Utariyan came here on his own initiative to, as he told me "talk to me and give me some pieces of his mind". Both he and his wife are making a living from Kibori, wood-carving. Their works are highly appreciated and their products are shown at exhibitions not only in Nihon, but in the USA and Europe as well.

CHAPTER FIVE

The Ainu in prehistoric and historic time

This chapter is divided into two parts. In the first part I will concentrate on the Wajin means and strategies of classifying the Ainu in early historic time, and in the second part I will look at the historical period preceding the colonization of *Ezo*. My concern is not so much the actual results of previous investigations, but rather the way in which research material about the Ainu has been used.

The first part deals with questions about the origins of the Ainu and about the recognition or rejection of a joint Ainu-Wajin ethnic and territorial past. My intention is not to add yet another theory, only to present the existing ones. It could be argued that my ambition is set too low on this point, since I do not strive to present evidence that confirms or falsifies previous theoretical positions.

Instead I focus on the role that prominent authorities have taken when it comes to accepting and establishing "truths" about both the origins of the Ainu and a possible joint Ainu-Wajin ethnic and territorial past. My aim is to show that the conclusions arrived at are unsatisfactory in so far as there is a tendency to make the actual facts about the origins of the Ainu correspond to a picture outlined by these authorities, whose main concern seems to have been the differences rather than the similarities between the two ethnic groups.

A common feature of these writings is a Wajin attempt to present the *Yamato* people, the ancestors of the Wajin, as the conquerors and heroes of Nihon, and all other peoples (aliens) as either assimilated or driven away.

With their attempt to trace this image back as far as the "dim days of legend" (*Kojiki; Nihonshoki*), the Wajin have managed to lend an air of authenticity to their account. With such a strategy essential facts about the Ezo are lost, since we are deluded by the Wajin perception of history and legend.

The Wajin make us understand the course of history as they themselves believe it to have taken place. After all, their history is "written" and is preserved in a documentary form, whereas the history of the Ainu is "verbal" and lives in the minds of the Ainu. For the Ainu this has serious consequences, as the only way used hitherto to construct their own version of history is through Wajin eyes. Accordingly, there is a possibility that their (the Ainu) version has been used to complement the documented accounts. Or in other words, the Ainu verbal accounts can easily be moulded to fit the dominant ideology.

In the second part of this chapter I will deal with the historical period preceding the annexation of Ezo by Nihon proper. The material for the presentation of this period derives primarily from the documents of Wajin officials who were in charge of managing Ezo affairs during the period that preceded the end of Ezo as independent of Nihon proper (Takakura 1960: 82-89). Here my concern is to clarify certain aspects of the "backwardness" of the Ainu and the "successfulness" of the Wajin, and a principal ambition is to provide additional explanations for the initial enthusiasm of the Ainu when the Wajin invoked an official policy of assimilation in the *Hokkaido Kaitakushi*, the time of colonization.

AINU ORIGINS

The problems connected with the origins of the Ainu are considerable, and even though research into this has been a central part of the studies of the Ainu in general, their origins remain unsolved.

Ohnuki-Tierney (1981) thinks that the identity of the Ainu is not only intriguing in itself but according to her, it also holds one of the keys to a broader anthropological problem, namely that of the peopling of the Old and New Worlds. She points out that Ainu land is situated at a strategic location through which early migrants have passed from the Old to the New World. She writes:

> The cultural, biological and linguistic identity of the Ainu is not only intriguing in itself but also holds one of the keys to a broader anthropological problem – the peopling of the Old and New Worlds. The Ainu land is situated at a strategic location through which early migrants may have passed from the Old to the New World. Are the Ainu one of these peoples who stopped short of crossing the Bering Straits to the New World, when waves of big game hunters and gatherers were pushing their way through the Asian continent? Or do they represent a population that claimed the land before the ancestors of the native Americans passed through (1981: 21)?

The problem of Ainu identity can be studied in several different ways, and one approach, largely employed by early scholars, is to solve the problem from the standpoint of the relationship of the Ainu to the aboriginal populations of the Nihon archipelago. A main concern has been to prove that the Ainu are not identical to the aboriginal population of Nihon.

According to the reports of some of these scholars the original inhabitants of Nihon proper were not the Ainu but an ancient group known in Ainu legend as the *Koropok-un-guru* and it is believed that this population expanded to its greatest number about the year

3000 B. C. According to this theory the Koropok-un-guru were driven away by the Ainu (Levin 1958: 261; Kodama 1970: 263 ff.; Peng & Geiser 1977: 8; Ohnuki-Tierney 1981: 204 ff.). J. Milne (1882) was the first to claim that the Koropok-un-guru, and not the Ainu, was Nihon's aboriginal population and one of the theory's strongest supporters in Nihon was an archaeologist named *Tsuboi* (see Ohnuki-Tierney 1981: 204 ff.).

A rival view claims that the close resemblance of Nihon's Neolithic population and the Ainu must be seen as evidence that the Ainu were the aboriginal settlers of the Nihon islands. Scholars holding this view argue that, after the Neolithic period, a new type characterized by Mongoloid traits entered the islands from Korea and mixed its characteristics with the peoples already established here (Levin 1958: 262-3). *Koganei*, a Wajin archaeologist, advanced this theory forcefully and claimed that the Ainu were actually the true aborigines of Nihon. He based his claim on the similarity between the recent Ainu and the skeletal material of the *Jomon*, a Stone Age people, who are supposed to have inhabited the Nihon archipelago prior to the ancestors of the Yamato people.

His theory was however not generally accepted at the time when he presented it and it seemed as if scholars were reluctant to accept that the Ainu were actually identical to Nihon's aboriginal population. Yet in 1903 evidence was found by a scholar named *Torii* that made it hard to maintain that the Ainu and the aboriginal population of Nihon were not one and the same people, as Tsuboi claimed.

According to Tsuboi the strongest evidence for this view is that there was no evidence that the Ainu knew the technique of manufacturing pottery and stone implements, whereas the Koropok-un-guru knew this technique. His argument was that, since the Ainu did not know this technique, they were not identical to the Stone Age people of Nihon. Torii found evidence that until recently the Kurile Ainu had been using bone and stone implements and pottery and this was taken as evidence that the Ainu and the Koropok-un-guru were one and the same people.

Although this was evidence which worked in Koganei's favour, that is, supported the view that the Ainu were Nihon's aboriginal population, it was not used as proof that the Ainu were Nihon's earliest population, but instead it was used to propose yet another theory, and thus both Tsuboi's and Koganei's theories were challenged by Kiyono (1925: 5-11) who put forward a third theory.

Kiyono argued that the aborigines of Nihon were the population from which both recent Ainu and the historic Nihon population were derived. His position was that the Ainu were a result of a mixture of the aboriginal population of Nihon, of unknown origin, and the people who later migrated to the islands from the northeastern parts of Siberia. The historic Nihon population, on the other hand, was according to him a mixture of the aborigines and the people who later came from the south. According to this view the Ainu were not Nihon's aboriginal population; the aboriginal population of Nihon was of unknown origin.

A different opinion was supported by Haseba (1956: 101-5), who argued that the ancestors of the Ainu came from the north to Hokkaido, whereas the ancestors of the historic Nihon population came from the south of China to Kyushu and then moved north to the Nihon islands. He argued that there was no link at all between the Ainu and the aboriginal population of Nihon (Levin 1958: 261 ff.; Kodama 1970: 263 ff.; Peng & Geiser 1977: 8; Ohnuki-Tierney 1981: 204 ff.).

None of these theories has won over the other. Since the nineteenth century Tsuboi's and Koganei's theories of the nature of the aborigines in Nihon have been competing (Munro 1911, 1962; Kodama 1970).

According to Kodama (1970: 263), researchers dealing with the biological, cultural and linguistic identity of the Ainu represent five different theoretical positions: the Mongoloid theory, the Caucasoid theory, the Oceanic Race theory, the Palaeo-Asiatic Tribe theory and the Rasseninsel theory.

The Mongoloid, Caucasoid and Oceanic Race theories are based on conformities in material culture, customs, weapons, ornaments, utensils, similarities in ritual and ceremonial performances as well as correlations in word arrangements, that is, prefixes/suffixes, and place-names (Levin 1958; Kodama 1970; Peng & Geiser 1977; Ohnuki-Tierney 1981). According to an unsigned article called "the Mysterious Race: The Ainu" in *The East* (I.I. [Anon.] 1969), a monthly journal, four different theories of Mongoloid and Caucasoid origins with respect to correlations in word arrangements and place-names are put forth. These are:

> 1) The Ainu came from the continent to Korea and thence to Nihon. This theory is supported by Ainu words which resemble Korean and by place-names in Hakuriku district of Honshu's northeastern section which seems etymologically to be Ainu in origin. 2) That they came south through Karafutu (Sakhalin), from the Asian continent, finds support in the fact that Ainu place-names are found in Karafutu, as well as around the mouth of the Amur River in China. 3) The theory that they came from the continent via Chishima (Kurile) islands is based on the fact that Ainu place-names can even be found in southern Kamchatka. This theory would suggest that they have long been accustomed to the severities of northern ice and snow. 4) Soviet scholars insist that it was a drift from the South rather than a movement from the continent (1969: 64).

However, since the above correlations are linked to two different theories, the one cannot claim superiority over the other. In support of the Caucasoid theory, which maintains that the Ainu most certainly are a branch of the Aryan family and that their ancestors moved from their homes in central Asia to the Nihon islands (Levin 1958: 266), it is further claimed that the Ainu language, Ainu Itak, bears strong resemblance to the Indo-European language.

The Caucasoid theory found its strongest supporter in Naert (1958), who claimed that the Ainu Itak has its origin in an Indo-European language. His theory was, however, not unchallenged. Gjerdman (1926, 1959), a supporter of the Oceanic Race theory, which claims that the ancestors of the Ainu were members of an Oceanic race and belonged neither to the Caucasoid nor to the Mongolian race although they possess some characteristics of both (Levin 1958: 270), was one of Naert's most energetic critics. He claimed among other things that the linguistic material collected by Naert was insufficient in quantity. According to him there exist as many parallels between the Ainu Itak and the Malayo-Polynesian languages as there exist between the Ainu Itak and the Indo-European languages (1958: 93 ff.). Others, like Lindquist (1960), were relatively mild in their criticism. Lindquist wrote:

> If Pierre Naert's evidence holds good, the number will be increased by yet another, and a living language at that. This in itself is very remarkable, and is of great moment for us Indo-Europeans. But we must not find faults with those who demand unimpeachable evidence (1960: 3).

Although Lindquist's optimism about the possibility that the Ainu Itak had its roots in an Indo-European language is obvious, especially since the Ainu Itak is a living language, he has his doubts and he hesitates to fully accept it.

Although the Oceanic Race theory, at least according to Sternberg (1929) and Gjerdman (1926, 1959), did not lack similar correlations, and although this theory has the same claims as the Mongoloid and the Caucasoid theories, as far as folklore and ethnographic data are concerned (Dixon 1883; Tarentsky 1890; Pilsudski 1912; Sternberg 1929; Levin 1958; Peng & Geiser 1977), the general view is, according to Kodama (1970: 265), that the Mongoloid and Caucasoid theories appear to have the strongest claims.

Since the Mongoloid, Caucasoid and Oceanic Race theories seem to have been equally strong as far as folklore and ethnographic and linguistic data are concerned, these claims alone are not sufficient for a judgment of the true origins of the Ainu people, and it appears to have been racial aspects that have been decisive for the divergent positions.

Kodama (1970) provides us with a very thorough summary of the studies of the problem of racial classification of the Ainu. In his introduction to the subject he writes:

> The problem of racial classification of the Ainu has been discussed among scholars in the world for a hundred years. However the argument has not led to an agreement yet. The causes of the complicated discussions are due to the fact that the Ainu who settled down in one part of Asia a long time ago to get mixed with the neighbouring tribes, have lost most of their original characteristics. The writer will describe briefly the main points of the theories of the scholars in the world. However, most of them are limited to the description that the Ainu have resemblance to such-and-such race or tribe. The arguments concerning their origin or

racial classification are confined within the limits of hypothesis at present (1970: 263).

Kodama himself is of the opinion that "the characteristics of the full-blooded Ainu indicate that the Ainu are closer to Europeoids than to Mongoloids" (1970: 265). All he can do is base himself on "indications", since the problems connected with the origins of the Ainu are considerable, something which he connects with the fact that the Ainu who settled in Asia a long time ago got mixed with neighbouring tribes and as a result have lost their original characteristics.

Although Kodama stresses that "arguments concerning the origin of the Ainu are confined within the limits of hypothesis" his own position is rather clear. He enumerates the characteristics of the pure Ainu which, according to him, indicate that they are closer to the Europeoids than to the Mongoloids. The terminology he uses to prove this is highly specialized and one gets the impression that he is not dealing with humans at all. The terminology is, in fact, applicable both to invertebrates such as protozoa and insects, and to vertebrates such as mammals and humans:

> Dolichopcehaly: Larger diameter bizygomatic maximum with small facial height. Sharply depressed nasion. Chamaerhiny. No prognathism. Rocker mandible with broad ascending ramus. The orbit is spacious as its medial wall is less convex than that of Mongoloids. Deep-set eyes. Narrow superior palpebrae (Kodama 1970: 265).

However, in the conclusion to his standpoint he makes the following reservation: "In general the development indicates that the Ainu are much more primitive than the modern Europeoids" (1970: 265). This is a remark which he does not comment any further.

The Caucasoid theory was first proposed by Bickmore (1868), who argued that the Ainu belonged to the Caucasoid race on the basis of their distinctive physical characteristics such as widely separated eyes and small cheekbones. In addition Ainu blood types more resemble European types than Mongoloids. The so-called "Diego Factor", the Mongolian spot, is missing among the "pure" Ainu, a characteristic indicating an affinity closer to Europeoids than to Mongoloids.

Let us now consider the Oceanic Race theory which was first proposed by V. de Saint Martin (Kodama 1970: 265). According to this theory here existed in ancient times a special Oceanic race, ancestors of the Equatorial races, Australoids and Polynesians. This race once spread in two directions, one into Polynesia, the other from Formosa to the Nihon islands and further to Kamchatka. The Ainu belong to the latter branch (Kodama 1970: 265).

Supporters of the Oceanic Race theory point to the strong resemblance of the Ainu material culture, including clothing, handicraft, household implements, weapons, ornaments, religious ceremony and cult, to the peoples living in the Philippines, Indonesia and Melanesia (Levin 1958: 271-2).

Since the Mongoloid and the Caucasoid theory have the same claims such evidence is insufficient. In support of the Oceanic Race theory it is however argued that since the Ainu have an abundance of body hair and since the main characteristic of this race was an abundance of body hair, the Ainu belong to this race. Geiser, who is an advocate of this theory, states:

> A considerable weight of opinion supports the theory that the Ainu and the Polynesian had a common ancient history. Although a relatively late Mongolian admixture occurred, the Ainu have a marked physical resemblance to the Australoids (1977: 9).

In support of the Mongoloid theory it is argued that the physical differences between Ainu and neighbouring races are not remarkable and thus the Ainu can be included among them. Today this theory is the most favoured one and the argumentation that the Ainu have a closer phyletic affinity with their geographical neighbours in northeastern Asia than with the peoples of either Europe or Australasia is accepted among scholars of today (Ohnuki-Tierney 1981: 206).

Researchers who support the Rasseninsel and Palaeo-Asiatic Tribe theory are of the opinion that the Ainu do not belong to any race now living. This is based on the fact that there is not yet convincing evidence as regards the craniological, somatological and cultural material gathered in the studies of the Ainu and the Jomon age people, that is, the people who lived in the Nihon archipelago in prehistoric times (Kodama 1970: 278).

The Palaeo-Asiatic Tribe theory (Kopernicki 1883) concludes: "As the Ainu who lived since ancient times in the Asiatic continent do not belong to any other race of today, they must be called Palaeo-Asiatic" (quoted in Kodama 1970: 265). The Rasseninsel theory states: "The Ainu do not belong to any of the races in the world of today" (quoted in Kodama 1970: 265).

According to Kodama (1970), Koganei was a supporter of the Rasseninsel theory, but his position was not clearly expressed. On the one hand he claimed that the Ainu are prehistoric remnants preserved relatively pure, yet on the other hand he also suggested that the Ainu were "procreated by the mixture between the Stone Age people and the Mongoloid people from the Asiatic Continent". Kodama writes:

> According to Koganei [1903], the Stone Age people in Japan were the ancestors of the Ainu and the skeletons of the former were remarkable in the characteristics and those of the latter were less remarkable in them. According to him, the above fact may be caused by the admixture between the Stone Age people and the Mongoloid, namely the modern Japanese from the Asiatic Continent. On the other hand, however, he stated in the other part of the same paper that the Ainu were

the Stone Age people in Japan who were driven away northward as comparatively poor ones by the Japanese. In other words, he had the following two different opinions as to the provenance of the Ainu: 1. The Ainu were procreated by the mixture between the Stone Age people and the Mongoloid people from the Asiatic Continent. 2. The Ainu was the Stone Age people who were preserved comparatively pure (1970: 270).

Let us add here the Ainu views of their own origins, of which there are several. What unites them is that they claim to be the earliest settlers not only in Ezo but in Nihon as well.

According to Ainu myth they are of the same origin as the Koropok-un-guru, and the claim of the Ainu is that the Koropok-un-guru are the earliest settlers in Nihon. In this regard, their opinion corresponds to the theoretical position of Tsuboi. Nevertheless they have divergent positions as regards whether the Ainu are identical with this people. Koropok-un-guru has been translated "dwarfs" by Wajin interpreters (*The East*, I. I. [Anon.] 1969: 65) and this is essential to the whole theory.

However, according to Batchelor (1925) Koropok-un-guru means "people who dwell below" and does not mean dwarf in any context. The Ainu in fact lack this word in their vocabulary.[1] He further writes:

> There is the question of the ancient Japanese name Tsuchi-Gumi, Earth spiders, and Ko-Bito, little people.... Ko-Bito really means little people, dwarfs: but the Ainu when speaking of these so called dwarfs use the word Ko-Bito, which is purely Japanese.... I find no grounds for supposing that the Ainu would speak of a race of dwarfs at all ... but were the Koropok-un-guru here and does not that mean the people of the Petasites [butterbur] plant? Well: no it does not. Koropok-un-guru cannot mean Petasites: it can only be translated by "under, beneath", the 'un' being a locative particle (1925: 6-7).

---

1 Here it should be emphasized that Batchelor's work with the Ainu Itak (1938) is not held in high esteem by Wajin scholars succeeding him. Chiri Mashio (1956), an Ainu himself but trained in the Wajin school, writes:

"However, quite contrary to the trust which is generally placed in Batchelor's dictionary (1938) I must say that I have never in my life seen a dictionary with so many flaws" (Chiri 1956: 237 quoted in *Ainu Language*, Refsing 1987: 19).

Refsing further writes:

"Perhaps Batchelor's knowledge of Japanese was more at fault than his knowledge of Ainu, since in a number of instances one finds that while the Japanese translation is totally misleading, the English one is much closer to the point. Perhaps one may question whether Chiri actually bothered to read the English translation as well" (1987: 19).

FIGURE 5   Ekashi *(chief)*

Regardless of this piece of information and regardless of the fact that the *Petasites* plants have very big leaves which can easily shield grown-up persons, something which, apart from the fact that it is pointed out by Batchelor (1925: 7), is undisputable for everyone who has seen these leaves, Kodama makes the following statement:

> The Tsuboi's Koropok[un] guru theory was itself a good idea … but the use of Ainu folklore, especially as to dwarfs, for the explanation of his theory, caused misunderstanding among general critics and met with objections (1970: 268).

Further contribution to the study of the origins of the Ainu has been made by Ohnuki-Tierney (1981). It is important to note that although Ohnuki-Tierney in her writing presents us with a thorough summary she does not clarify her own position. She seems, however, to have rejected the Caucasoid theory and points out that recent investigators favour Ainu affinity with other Mongoloid peoples. She puts stress on the fact that "the Ainu culture is not monolithic but rich in intracultural variations" (1981: 21). Here she says that the use of a blanket term "Ainu" has largely overshadowed this aspect. She asserts that when dealing with questions about the origins of the Ainu we should focus on the fact that the blanket term Ainu actually stands for "Hokkaido Ainu", "Sakhalin Ainu" and "Kurile Ainu" (1981: 21).

This information is not remarkable as such – it has in fact been pointed out by everyone who has studied the origins of the Ainu. However, as she significantly points out, "this geographical location does not merely represent a mechanical division of the Ainu, but each of them reflects a distinctive way of life" (1981: 21), and this is interesting in so far as focus is on comparison between neighbouring Ainu tribes rather than comparison between the Ainu and neighbouring tribes of other cultures.

This view marks a departure from previous research where the Ainu relation to other neighbouring tribes has been made the prerequisite for the determination of their origins.

Apart from the fact that one gets an impression that previous researchers have been more concerned with falsifying each other's theories than with solving the problems of the origins of the Ainu, one also senses that there is a notable stress on differences.

But why is it that the differences rather than the similarities came to be of decisive importance for the positions adopted by early scholars and why is it that they tried to solve the problem of Ainu origins from the standpoint of the Ainu's relationship to the aboriginal populations of the Nihon archipelago?

Bearing in mind that the studies of the origins of the Ainu more or less coincided with the annexation of Ezo by Nihon proper, it is rather logical that focus was put on the Ainu relation to the peoples who occupied the Nihon archipelago in ancient time. Yet, this does not explain why differences rather than similarities came to be of decisive importance. Since it is the conqueror who writes history, we can connect the emphasis on the differences to a view of the Ainu as a "defeated" people, and there is a possibility that this view, in turn, has given preference to a view of the Ainu as an inferior people.

There is of course always a possibility to relate the emphasis on differences to politics, in the sense that if evidence was found that the Ainu were actually identical to Nihon's aboriginal population, the Ainu must then be recognized as the rightful owner of the land which the rulers of Nihon proper claimed as theirs. This could have had endangered the newly established Meiji regime.

ANCIENT AINU PEOPLE, TERRITORY AND HISTORY
AS DESCRIBED IN THE HISTORIOGRAPHY OF THE WAJIN

Let us now turn to the questions raised by the pictures constructed by the Wajin to depict the ancient Ainu people, their territory and history. Since the following sources – *The Account of the Three Kingdoms*, (*Chinese Records*) compiled before A. D. 297, *Records of Ancient Matters*, that is, *Kojiki*, A. D. 712 and *History of Nihon*, that is, *Nihonshoki* A. D. 720 – are the only existing ones, the picture presented derives from information obtained in these works. They give, however, only vague information and the pictures they paint are arbitrary to say the least, *Kojiki* and *Nihonshoki* in particular. As has been pointed out by Reischauer and Craig, the distinction between myths and facts is not clear:

> The authors of these works wove together often contradictory myths and tradition in an effort to enhance the prestige of the ruling family and create a picture of a long centralized rule and respectable antiquity to that of China (1973: 7).

In *The Account of the Three Kingdoms*, the Chinese records, the people(s) inhabiting Nihon proper are depicted as:

> law-abiding people, fond of drinking, concerned with divination and ritual purity, familiar with agriculture, expert at fishing and weaving and living in a society of strict social differences indicated by tattooing or other bodily markings. The land is described as divided into one hundred countries (Reischauer & Craig 1973: 6-7).

This description, which is very general and could be used to classify any people, does not make clear whether we are dealing with many "different" peoples. This may have been the case at least if we consider the following information: "A fifth-century Chinese history describes a Japanese ruler ... as having conquered fifty-five countries of hairy men to the east" (Reischauer & Craig 1973: 7).

In this description the Chinese sign *Toi* was used to describe "these hairy men and their countries". Toi is the common Chinese sign for barbarians or noncontinentals, that is, peoples who did not live in the Chinese mainland and may therefore depict any of the one hundred countries, provided of course that they were located in the eastern direction mentioned above.

However, since the Ainu at this time most likely inhabited the eastern parts of Honshu, it seems very possible that the "countries of hairy men to the east" refer to Ainu territories in Honshu. The emphasis should, however, be on "the east" rather than "hairy men" (Toi) since the term Toi merely indicates "outsiders". In addition, if we consider comparative material from other parts of the world we have evidence that "insiders" tend to regard "outsiders" as "non-humans" and "inferior", and thus "outsiders" are described in negative terms, such as barbarians. It therefore seems likely that the Ainu and their territories and the Wajin and their territories, in early historic time, were distinguished from others in the same way as they were from each other, since each "country" was a well-defined unit and the people outside its boundaries were defined as barbarians by the insiders. Nevertheless, the geographical location "the east", although extremely vague, is most certainly identical to Ainu territories at that particular time, at least as far as *Nihonshoki* records are concerned.

LOCATION OF AINU FORMER HONSHU TERRITORIES

To locate the Honshu territories of the Ainu in ancient times is indeed problematic. This is partly due to the inconsistency in the reports of territorial location in mythical (*Kojiki; Nihonshoki*) and historic times and partly to contradiction *in adjecto* in the classification of the Ainu.

According to Takakura (1960: 8), the Ainu were, in ancient times, referred to as *Koshi* or *Yumasa*. Yumasa refers to the great fighting qualities of these people, whereas Koshi refers to the location of their territories. However, according to Wajin legend (*Kojiki; Nihonshoki*), the territories of the Koshi were situated in a region called *Izumo*, with its geographical location in the southern part of Honshu. Since the location of the Koshi people's territory in mythical time is in the southern part of Honshu and not in the northern part where the Koshi region lies in historic time, we may assume that its location differs according to the kind of time we are dealing with – mythical or historical. This possibility Takakura labels an "interesting corruption" (1960: 8).

According to *Kojiki* and *Nihonshoki*, the Koshi people were partly assimilated by the Izumo people, who occupied the same territory as the Koshi, that is, the Izumo region in the southern part of Nihon, and partly driven to the east. This eastward-moving people came to be known as the *Koshi no Emishi*. Later this people came to occupy the contemporary Koshi region, which included the northern regions, *Echizen, Kaga, Noto, Etchu* and *Etchigo*. The remainder of northern Honshu was called *Ouu*, and here lived the *Kai* people.

Following Takakura (1960: 8) we learn that the word "Koshi" changed first to *Kushi* and then to *Kui* and later to *Kai*. It is noteworthy that the word "Kai", according to the Ainu has its origin in an Ainu word which means boy.[2] We are further informed that, "The fighting aborigines of the northeast [the territories of the Koshi], then were known interchangeably as the Kai or the Emishi" (Takakura 1960: 8).

This indicates that according to Wajin classification no differentiation was made between the Kai people and the Emishi, that is, the people referred to earlier as the Koshi no Emishi, since the concepts were used interchangeably. This is confusing in more than one way. First, according to Takakura (1960: 11) there existed in fact a number of different ways of identifying these peoples. He writes, "There are the Koshi, then later the Kai ... and finally the Ezo or Ainu of Hokkaido. But in the days of the Koshi and then the Kai there were further distinctions".

---

2   Information obtained at the Historical Museum at Shiraoi, 1988, further confirmed by interviews with Ainu in the Hidaka area, interview, 1988. Finally, the word can be found in *An Ainu Conversation Dictionary* (1987). According to Batchelor (1938: 222) Kai means "to carry".

Second, according to *Iroha Jirui Sho*, a Wajin dictionary compiled in the twelfth century, we learn that all aliens in Nihon were called *Ebizu*, which according to Kodama (1970: 270) is an early form of Emishi. This would indicate that no differentiation existed.

Calling all *non-Yamato* (alien groups) "Ebizu" is the most confusing point, since it has given rise to divergent opinions about the origins of the Emishi, that is, whether the Ainu and the Emishi are actually one and the same people. Kodama (1970), who is of the opinion that the Ainu and the aboriginal population of Nihon are not the same people, provides us with following view of this problem:

> Originally the word Ezo was a name given to the Ainu since around the 12th century, while the aboriginal Japanese were called Emishi or Ebizu. First these two tribes were distinguished, but later both of them were called Ezo in the common use and since then a confusion between them arose (1970: 270).

Kodama must thus be regarded as reluctant to ascribe an Ainu origin to the Emishi, since, when discussing the relationship between the Ainu and the aborigines in Nihon, he says: "It was concluded that the Japanese there [in Nihon proper] were not the Ainu, but the Emishi, the descendants of the Jomon age people" (1970: 270).

Takakura holds the opposite view but his discussion of certain linguistic problems (Koshi developing into Kai) adds confusion to his point, since we may be led to think that Koshi and Kai are one and the same people. Further confusion is added by the fact that Takakura and his co-writer, Harrison, seem to have divergent opinions about whether the Koshi territory and the Ou territory were actually populated by two different tribes or one and the same. Takakura writes: "Their [the Koshi] historical territory included Echizen, Etchu, Dewa [consisting of today's Akita and Yamagata Prefecture], Echigo, Tsugaru and Hokkaido, or all of Japan north of the Tokyo area" (1960: 8).

This would indicate that two different Ainu tribes, that is, one that inhabited the Koshi region, the Koshi no Emishi people, and one that inhabited the Ou region, the Kai people, did not exist. However according to Harrison in the "Translator's Preface" to Takakura's book there was a differentiation between the two regions, Koshi and Ou. Harrison states that, "The area which comprises modern Echizen, Kaga, Noto, Etch and Etchigo was called Koshi and the remainder of the northern Honshu was called Ou" (ibid: 6).

Because of the confusing picture of both the classification of the ancient Ainu population and the location of their former Honshu territories, the question of a possible joint Ainu-Wajin ethnic and territorial past remains. Nevertheless, we cannot exclude the possibiiity that we are in fact dealing with at least two different Ainu groups in the mainland – one with its origins in the south, that is, the Izumo region, the Koshi no Emishi people, and the other with its origins in the northern parts, that is, the Ou region, the Kai people.

It should be mentioned that the Ainu have an additional theory. In accordance with their own view of themselves as the earliest settlers in Nihon proper they claim that the peoples who in ancient times occupied the southern parts of Nihon, called the *Kumaso, Sobito* and *Hayato* people, are in fact of Ainu origin. Hence, their territories were in ancient times Ainu territories as well. Takakura and Munro have a different view. (For a lengthy discussion of their opinion see Munro [1911] and Takakura [1960].)

THE FATE OF THE HONSHU AINU

Since no conclusive evidence has been put forth, let us concentrate on the immediate fate of the peoples living in the northeastern and northern Honshu regions. Their fate was either assimilation or escape. According to Wajin historical writing, in the fourth century, when a border was established between these northern and northeastern territories, that is, Ou and Koshi, and the rest of Nihon proper, the peoples of the border territories are known to have moved around rather freely in each other's territories and intermarriages between the border populations are reported as frequent (Takakura 1960: 10).

According to Wajin records, *Kojiki* and *Nihonshoki*, the peoples who did not adopt the Yamato rule, soon became a minority and thus both intermarriages and the fact that people were allowed to move freely across borders worked to the advantage of the Yamato people, who according to the same records forced this people across the Tsugaru Strait to the Ezo territory (Takakura 1960: 11).

If we accept that the peoples living here were of Ezo origin we then find, when reconstructing the relationship between the Ezo and the Yamato descendants, that the latter succeeded in suppressing the Kai and the Koshi peoples, either by assimilation or by forcing them across the Tsugaru Straits. This circumstance may have influenced early scholars to present a dark and negative picture of the Ainu. In their works the "success of the Wajin" is seen as related to their racial superiority. Note for instance:

> from time immemorial the Japanese islands have been occupied by a population [the Ainu], carrying on that life cycle, which from its comparatively rudimentary nature has been called primitive (Munro 1911: 661).

> The hardy, tough, intelligent and industrious Japanese ... have driven these primitive, kindly, simple-minded, stupid, slothful, dirty people (the Ainu) before them less probably by the sword than simply by superiority of race (Kajima 1895: 1).

The Ainu, on the other hand, do not share this view but argue that it was their own choice (Kayano 1988b). Some of their people chose to stay and adapt to mainland conditions, whereas others chose to abandon their territories in Honshu. Those who chose to abandon their territories did so because the conditions in Nihon proper grew continually worse, due to such things as the escalation of feuds between feudal lords, and many of them left for Hokkaido.

In the next period, after the establishment of a border between Ezo (Hokkaido) and Nihon proper (Honshu) in the eighth century, the Ezo, that is, those who lived in Ezo, were distinguished from the people living in the northern and northeastern Honshu territories. The former were identified as the Ezo or Kai people, including the Koshi no Emishi, whereas the latter were identified as the Emishi.

According to these writers, the Ezo or Kai people are known to have preferred hunting and gathering activities to agriculture, whereas the Emishi took up agriculture. The ecological niche of the latter was thus converted into an agricultural one, while that of the former remained undisturbed. However, as there still exists a problem of identification I will in the following discussion refer to the Ezo natives as Ezo and the people who took up agricultural activities the northern and northeastern parts of Honshu as mainlanders or immigrants.

IMMIGRATION TO EZO, CAUSES AND EFFECTS

The mainlanders came to Ezo, as constant fighting made living in Nihon proper insecure and dangerous. Some of these immigrants were clearly distinguishable, since they maintained the lifestyle of the mainland. They built forts, *Tate*, similar to the forts, *Shiro*, that existed on the mainland, and ruled over the people living there.

However, as Takakura (1960: 11) puts it, "among them [the immigrants] there were a surprising number who left the mainland limits to accept Ezo life and rule". This attitude gives us reason to assume that the immigrants consisted of those who gave up their Wajin identity in favour of an Ezo identity and those who did not.

In Nihon proper, the constant fighting over land between different "domains", *Uji*, resulted both in increasing immigration to Ezo and a different type of immigrants. These later immigrants actually consisted of whole forts (Takakura 1960: 11). The lords and their subordinates established themselves in Ezo with the intention of eventually strengthening and/or regaining their position in Nihon proper.

In the mainland internal feuds weakened or strengthened the position of the domains, and since oligarchy was the dominant form of government the struggles were between oligarchy fractions. As Matsumoto writes:

> The particular group which formed the ruling few varied with time, but the pattern
> of political and military oligarchy remained the characteristic form of government.
> In drastic political changes, whether the Taika or Great Reform of the seventh

century, the displacement of the Heian court nobles, in the twelfth century, the hegemony of the Tokugawa Regime in the seventeenth century, or the Meiji Restoration in the mid-nineteenth century, the conflict were between one oligarchy fraction against another ... the struggles were never that of the ruled against the ruling (1960: 9).

The economic and political system that existed in the mainland had apparent difficulties within the mainland borders. Immigration from Honshu increased due both to famine and raging imperial warfare (Takakura 1960; Cornell 1964), and the system seems to have fed on feuds between rulers, which seems to have been an effect of scanty resources since land suitable for agricultural activities were sparse and the peasants weak (Cornell 1964; Baba 1980; Sanders 1985). For its survival it was forced to expand its borders on a large scale. Accordingly, the people in the mainland turned to Ezo with the intention of making its natural resources and land their own as well.

Since there seems to have been little hindrance to settling in the Ezo territory during the previous period the number of immigrants increased. Immigration on a large scale resulted, however, in conflicts between the two peoples, and the more immigrants, the more severe the conflicts. These resulted in the immigrants being defeated and driven out of their territories. Takakura writes:

> The natives were so powerful that settlement after settlement fell into their hands. The immigrants were driven out of their base... During these incidents Japanese forts were either lost or damaged (1960: 12).

Despite defeat, the immigrants were reluctant to give up their position in Ezo altogether. After all, they knew what they were losing. They had once been on friendly terms with the Ezo and apart from the fact that they had had the exclusive right to use the land resources within their own borders, they were also familiar with the location of profitable Ezo resources, such as fishing and hunting grounds which belonged to the Ezo but which the Ezo had allowed them to use.

The Ezo who feared that they would lose their resources altogether were determined to keep the immigrants out of Ezo. The immigrants were however determined to return and as a result the defeated immigrants turned to the mainland for support, which was also given them. The support was not sufficient and as a result the conflicts went on for a considerable amount of time, until the middle of the sixteenth century. When the Wajin changed their policy to one of reconciliation the fighting finally came to an end and in 1550 peace was made between the two peoples.

The Ezo were offered treasures such as lacquer ornaments and sake, which they held in great esteem, and the mainland people thus won their favour and were again allowed to settle in Ezo (Takakura 1960: 12).

TRADE

Theoretically, trade is a peaceful relation to the benefit of all parties participating in it, and trade between the Ezo and the people from the mainland was no exception. (Takakura 1960: 23). Both parties profited from it, at least initially. The traded items were fish and edible seaweed in large quantities, hawks and a number of rarities such as bear liver, seal skin and eagle feathers. These items came to serve as "tribute" to the imperial court. In return the Ezo were offered things like rice, sugar, sake, lacquer and cotton cloth.

Among the Ezo lacquer ornaments and sake were perceived as highly prestigious goods. These items were not entirely new to them, rather they represented "improvements" on the Ainu manufactured counterparts, since the lacquer ornaments were more shiny and the sake stronger. The Ezo used them when performing the *Iyomante* ceremony, a feast of celebration and reconciliation with Nature.

Since it was believed that the improved items would give the Ezo a favourable position in the eyes of the Kamuy they became desirable goods for every single Ezo unit, Kotan. Accordingly everybody became involved in the trade. The former saw possibilities to regain or strengthen their power both in Ezo and the mainland (Takakura 1960: 12), whereas the latter saw possibilities to offer the prestigious goods to gods, Kamuy, and thereby win their favour, and thus improve their situation in the Moshir (Kayano 1988a).

Later, however, the trade in Ezo came to resemble the fur trade that began in North America in the sixteenth century (Fagan 1983). Among other things, it came to involve not only competition between the various Uji powers in Nihon proper but between the Ezo powers as well.

It has often been assumed that no trade existed between the Ezo and the people from the mainland (Refsing 1980: 83) as the relationship should not be classified as trade at all but merely exploitation, since in the end the Ezo were deprived of both their land and their culture. This may be so if one chooses to take a retrospective view. However, in that particular period and under those particular circumstances, the Ezo chose to trade items which were not very easily manufactured. To put it any other way would be to deny the Ezo the ability to make profitable choices according to their own prevalent cultural concepts.

Those Ezo units, Kotan, with an abundance of desirable goods traded directly with people on the mainland, whereas those whose resources were in less demand used the former as middlemen. It was not long before the sociopolitical and economic structure of the Ezo was disrupted. Within the former groups, powerful chiefs, *Ekashi*, arose on whom the Ekashi of the latter groups came to be dependent. About this development Takakura writes:

However, it was but natural that the more powerful and wealthy of the chiefs ... should extend their power ... from which there arose chiefs of tremendous power among their people (1960: 23).

People from the mainland who saw the power of the Ekashi as a threat soon began to barter with anyone to keep prices down. Initially the Ezo chiefs, Ekashi, were the only ones with whom the people from the mainland were allowed to trade, but later mainland tradesmen appointed trading partners of their own. These were called *Otona* and were not chosen by the Ezo. Their qualifications as leaders did not correspond to Ezo demands, but rather to those of Nihon proper.

These leaders did not represent their units as a whole, whether politically autonomous or not, nor did they fulfil their obligations towards Nature and their subordinates. Under such conditions intergroup rivalry increased and territorial claims became insecure. The gap widened between both units and individuals. The various units were divided into those with an abundance of desirable goods and those without and so were the individuals (Kayano 1988b).

As a result, internal feuds between the various Ezo units increased and they were dissolved and reformed accordingly. This was the beginning of the end of the Ezo as independent of Nihon proper. According to Takakura the defeat of the Ezo was due to the insufficient economic power of the Ekashi, and from him we learn:

> because these chiefs did not have sufficient economic power and because the village groups were divided into small economic units owing to their small-scale hunting and fishing, coalitions found here died out once the chiefs who had united them lost their power (1960: 23).

Takakura's explanation reveals only part of the truth, and we have reason to assume that the prelude to Ezo defeat is not thoroughly accounted for. True enough, the Ezo units did not, at the time, have sufficient economic power, yet this may be due to external manipulation and interference, rather than to the structure of the "village groups" of the Ezo. Further, the way the Ezo looked upon the trade and its profits did not serve their case very well, especially with respect to the future. However at first the Ezo profited from the trade with the mainland. The traded goods, especially lacquer ornaments and sake, enriched their cultural and ceremonial life. The people from the mainland also profited from the trade and, as with the Ezo, it also enriched their cultural and ceremonial life. They used the traded goods to pay tribute to the court in *Edo* (today's Tokyo), while the Ezo used theirs to pay tribute to the Kamuy.

The people from the mainland used the goods to improve their situation as a whole, but this was also the intention of the Ezo, although for them it did not work in the intended way. Nevertheless, although there are similarities between the two groups' ways of dealing with the traded items, the Ezo were the most disadvantaged ones, as to them trade meant loss of land and natural resources. To the people from the mainland, on the other hand, the trade meant a gradual increase of their interference in Ezo affairs. What is important is that the trade between the two peoples initially strengthened the position of the mainland without improving that of the Ezo.

The impoverishment of the Ezo and its territory took place over a considerable period of time and involved other factors as well. Nevertheless, trade and the two cultures' different ways of interpreting its advantages must be regarded as the ultimate cause of the future development in Ezo.

When we, in retrospect, reconstruct what actually happened during the period discussed above, we find that the Ezo (*Ezo, Kai, Koshi*) were suppressed by the mainland people. Consequently, the latter were, in Wajin writings, the "most successful people". Yet, the exploitation of Ezo resources was, in fact, necessary for the continuation of the mainland system. After all, there was a shortage of arable land and there was also a weakened peasant group.

From this angle we find that the exploitation of Ezo, its natural resources as well as its land, not only satisfied the needs that existed in Nihon proper but that the exploitation of them also made it possible for the feudal system not only to survive but to expand as well.

The Ezo sociopolitical structure was relatively flexible: loosely organized units that could alter their organization, no absolute hereditary leadership and flexible marriage rules. Such arrangements fitted well the conditions of the Ezo. They gave room to explore the various ecological niches in accordance with their subsistence ability, but they also allowed a considerable number of immigrants to settle, including those who maintained the feudal system in Ezo.

On account of the dynamics of the Ezo economic and sociopolitical system, conditions in Ezo remained relatively stable for a considerable period of time. The inhabitants in Ezo, natives and immigrants alike, were thus able both to share and to use the resources as they saw fit. Apart from hunting and fishing activities, this also included agriculture, horticulture and trade with foreigners from Sakhalin and the Kurile islands, China, but also with Nihon proper. At the beginning of the sixteenth century, however, conditions in Ezo gradually changed. Now a period began which gradually transformed the Ezo into mainland subordinates and their territory, Moshir, into Nihon property.

THE HISTORICAL PERIOD PRECEDING THE COLONIZATION OF EZO: HOKKAIDO KAITAKUSHI

The prelude to *Hokkaido Kaitakushi* comprises a period of more than four hundred years, from the sixteenth to the nineteenth centuries. Speaking in general terms the period

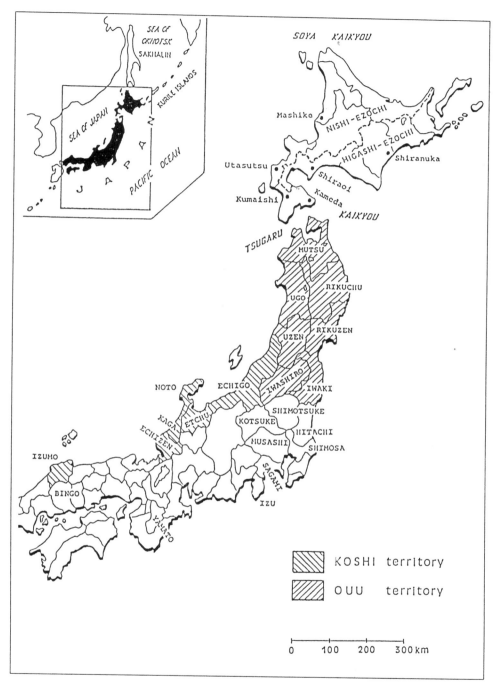

FIGURE 6   *Presumed Ainu territories in Honshu (i.e. Ouu and Koshi), Wajin territories mentioned in the text and Hokkaido in historic time, with sites of battles and historic sites mentioned in the text marked*

was as rich in positive consequences as regards the Wajin aims as it was in negative consequences for the Ezo.

To the latter, the period was to bring about a depletion of resources, a general reduction in the power of Ezo chiefs, a weakening of social and political bonds and the introduction of diseases to which the Ezo had no immunity. In other words, the period meant a decline as far as both cultural and social values, and population were concerned. During the period as a whole the position of the people from the mainland was strengthened whereas that of the Ezo was continually weakened.

On the mainland, the *Sengoku Jidai*, epoch of wars (1500-1600), when each fief was self-reliant and autonomous, was succeeded by the Edo period (1603-1867). In the Edo period the *Giri* psychology was rigidly fostered by the *Tokugawa* regime. Within the system, the lords were referred to as *Shujin*, masters, and their followers or subordinates as *Ienoko*, children (Matsumoto 1960: 9; Nakane 1970: 5; Smith 1983: 10). Matsumoto writes:

> The giri psychology was fostered in Tokugawa Japan. Its salient feature was its tranquility and peace following a full century of endemic wars and endless feuds between powerful daimyo (1960: 9).

> After Tokugawa Ieyasu vanquished all rivals by the decisive Battle of Sekigahara in 1600, the society was frozen into a legally immutable class structure (1960: 9).

To the people in the mainland, the period was a time of unification, during which those hierarchical and ascriptive values already prevalent in the previous mainland society became permanent and static.

Meanwhile, in Ezo it was a time of disunity. The continuing depletion of resources caused by, among other things, intensified hunting activities, the construction of fishing industries and gold prospecting, increased both rivalry between Ezo leaders and rebellion against intruders from the mainland.

The most notable battles were the battle of *Shakushain* in 1669 and the battle of *Kunashi Meanshi* in 1789. The first battle diminished the controlling influence of the *Matsumae Han*, a powerful Wajin Han who had settled in Ezo at the beginning of the sixteenth century. The second totally deprived the Matsumae Han of control (Takakura 1960: 25). But the most important consequence of these battles was that they gradually made the Ezo economically dependent on Nihon proper (Takakura 1960: 27).

THE PERIOD BEFORE EZO WAS ANNEXED TO NIHON PROPER

This period can be characterized as one of constant fighting between various Ezo units as well as between Ezo units and the immigrants. It was a time of endemic wars, similar to the Sengoku Jidai in the mainland, where the Ezo sociopolitical system was of more benefit to Nihon proper than to the Ezo.

The period is divided by Harrison (1960: 9) into the following five political periods:

a. *The early Matsumae Han period* (1514-1798), characterized by Matsumae monopolization of Ezo trade. Matsumae's reign came to an end in 1798, which is attributed to repeated Russian attempts to conquer Ezo and proclaim the island a Russian territory. The Matsumae were neither in a numerical (about 27,000) nor in a financial position to defend the mainland interests in Ezo. Besides, the Ainu had turned to people in Russia for assistance in times of hardship on several occasions.

b. *The early Bakufu period* of direct control from the central mainland government (1799-1821), characterized by an attempt to transform the Ainu into a peasant community. The Ainu were encouraged to take up mainland customs and traditions. The shift in reign of the Ezo this time was officially attributed to the fact that the agricultural experiments gave poor results, and also to the Ainu's interest in giving up their own culture in favour of the one represented by the Wajin. Unofficially, however the shift is attributed to a decline in the Russian threats.

c. *The later Matsumae Han period* (1821-1854) was largely identical to their first period in control.

d. *The later Bakufu period* of direct control (1854-1868) was a result of the Matsumae's inability to govern Ezo and to satisfy mainland claims and interests. But in reality it was the collapse of the Tokugawa regime in 1868 that made a continuation of their reign impossible.

e. *The San Ken Douchou period*, the Three-prefecture period, and the *Kaitakushi period*, the Colonization period (1868-1899), when a group of Shogunate soldiers, *Samurais*, occupied the Hakodate administrative office and declared Hokkaido independent from Nihon proper, an enterprise that ended with their defeat.

The first period involved a monopolization of Ezo trade, which was achieved through a policy of segregation. This policy included, apart from trade regulations, a prohibition on hunting and fishing in neighbouring territories. According to Takakura the policy was originally initiated to avoid conflicts between the immigrants and the Ezo:

> The Matsumae ... forbade Japanese to live in Ainu territory and also interdicted
> Japanese territory to the Ainu ... This system was introduced because intermin-
> gling of the two people had always led to trouble (1960: 23).

Trespass was severely punished and this was thought to discourage temptation to
break the laws (1960: 23). Although the main feature of this policy was to maintain
peaceful relations, the policy also worked to secure the controlling influence of the
Matsumae Han. This was primarily due to an edict made by Tokugawa in 1604, who, as
expressed in the letter, extended the power of the Matsumae Han in order to avoid racial
intermingling and eventual riots. It reads:

> It will be unlawful for those who come to Matsumae to trade with the Ezo without
> permission of the Lords of the island (the Matsumae). Those who do engage in
> trade without permission of the Lord of the island are to be reported at once
> (Takakura 1960: 25).

Originally, the basis of the Matsumae Han trading system was a group of
tradesmen, the *Chigyonushi*, with whom the Ezo were allowed to trade at special trade
centres within the borders of Matsumae's territory. In addition the Matsumae Han had
the rights, granted them by the *Bakufu* (central authorities) in 1516, to collect taxes from
mainland ships which came to Ezo to trade. Outside the sphere of the Matsumae Han
influence, Ezo settled down in as yet unoccupied areas (Takakura 1960: 27). Before the
Tokugawa edict in 1604, they were able to trade directly with merchants from Nihon
proper. In accordance with the edict, however, such trade relations became restricted.

For the immigrants in Ezo the segregation policy came, initially, to strengthen
their position in areas already conquered by them. These areas comprised at first the region
"within forty to fifty miles of the coast between Kameda and Kumaishi" (Takakura 1960:
23), and later, when the immigrants became powerful enough to expand both their
influence and their territory, they eventually came to include the southern and eastern
parts of Ezo, that is, *Nichi-Ezochi*.

However, to the Ezo the segregation policy worked in the opposite direction and
their ability to make barter into as profitable an enterprise as it was for the immigrants
was severely circumscribed. The measures proposed by the edict did not include trade
price regulations and the Ezo commercial inexperience worked in favour of the immigrants. As a result, "unjust profit gained by fraud and monopoly and the taking advantage
of the ignorance of the natives became more and more obvious" (Takakura 1960: 27).

Before long the regulations formerly established to avoid conflicts became in effect
one-sided and applicable to the Ezo only. The weakened trespass regulations were not
officially recognized. Offences were not reported to officials higher in rank, and were thus
"not provable" at the time (*Secret Records in the Development of Hokkaido*, Archival record
in Hokudai in Sapporo).

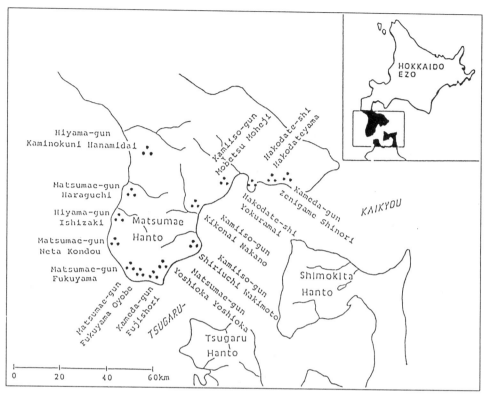

FIGURE 7   *Location of Wajin Han in Hokkaido*

Later, when Ezo came under Bakufu control, trespass came into the open. Nevertheless at the time when trespass was not reported to officers higher in rank, the immigrants took advantage of the situation and soon began to establish fishing and mining industries in Ezo territories. In addition, in 1631 gold was found in Ezo territories and the mainland intrusion was intensified.

In order to maintain its territorial rights intact, each Ezo unit began to act in its own interest, which endangered the sociopolitical alliances in the prevailing Ezo system and caused the first split in their *matri-patri alliances*.

Further, not every Ezo unit constituted a politically autonomous unit: there were those which were local and soon these had difficulties in maintaining territorial control (Kayano 1988b). Eventually, their dependence on the unit to which their leader belonged increased and their prospect of achieving political autonomy diminished. As a result, the act taken by the Ezo to regain territorial control also helped to wipe out prosperous local units, many of which were temporarily without a local leader, but where this temporary condition was made more or less permanent (Kayano 1988b).

To maintain order within his unit the leader strove to strengthen the position of the unit and inevitably also his own position, which to a considerable extent depended on his own generosity, that is, that he divided the goods among his subjects and the Kamuy instead of keeping them for himself. To maintain territorial control each unit thus became dependent on the skill of its leader in trading, which inevitably was connected with his ability both to provide a sufficient amount of products to bargain with and to make as profitable a bargain as possible with the Chigyonushi. According to the Ezo, the most important element in their trade relations as a whole was "Nature" as Nature provided them with their trade items. In order to prosper in trade their leaders had to return to Nature what Nature had provided. This was done with the help of religious items such as wood-carvings and lacquer ornaments but also sake, that is, barter items from the mainland, things which the Ainu offered to their gods in thanksgiving ceremonies.

The effects of an unfavourable trading position, a lack of enforced trade regulations, increased mainland intrusion, an exchange of manufactured goods for natural resources which was limited in quantity, soon became obvious for the Ezo. The production capacity of the parts of the island which belonged to them gradually failed to meet the demands. Such conditions helped to hasten both the depletion of natural resources and the decline in power of the Ezo units.

To the Ezo, and especially those in closest contact with the immigrants, the combined effects of increased demand for their goods and intrusion into their territories which were intensified in connection with the establishment of gold and fishing industries, was considerable. In addition, increased immigration caused a decline in the Ezo population. Such effects are not rare: they in fact are a common feature in periods of contacts (cf. Fagan 1985).

To meet the general trade increase, competition between Ezo units was intensified. To be able to meet changed conditions the split in Ainu alliances, caused in the initial phase of the contact period, widened. With such changes it became more difficult to take up residence in the territories belonging to one's *Matikir-Esap-Utar* relatives, previously a possibility in times of hardship. Marriage alliances were also affected. Previously, marriage had been restricted to the *Upshoro-Kut*, but now competition between patrilinies, *Shine-Ekashi-Ikir*, which were territorial corporate groups, added yet another regulation: it was no longer possible to marry someone belonging to a competing unit, *Kotan* (Kayano 1988b).

In its initial phase, competition favoured those territorial units which were located in areas with an abundance of desirable goods. The ones less favourably placed, from the mainland's point of view, were disadvantaged. Ezo leaders of the former units were able to negotiate with the Chigyonushi directly, whereas those of the latter had to rely on the former for their supply of valuables.

The leaders of the favourable areas soon demanded prices which, according to them, corresponded to the value of the items they offered. The Chigyonushi, who were less inclined to accede to their demands, found a solution to this new problem. They simply turned their backs on the demands of the Ezo leaders. They chose other leaders among the Ezo as their trading partners. These were, as mentioned previously, not an Ezo choice. As a result internal feuds increased and Ezo units were formed, dissolved and reformed accordingly.

Under such conditions many Ezo saw migration into the northern and north-eastern parts of Ezo as a possible alternative. Here game and fishing grounds were still available (Kayano 1988a, b). On account of the relatively isolated location of these areas they remained autonomous for a considerable period of time. The people here were in fact able to continue their lifestyle during this period and it was not until the colonization of Hokkaido, Kaitakushi, that an actual change of lifestyle began.

For those Ezo who chose to remain, the situation gradually worsened and in 1669 they revolted against the mainland intrusion. The direct cause of their reaction was the escalation of disputes over fishing rights and hunting grounds rather than unfair trade regulations. A Shizunai leader, Shakushain, was the appointed leader of the rebel forces. Shakushain succeeded in uniting all Ezo units from *Shiraoi* to *Shiranuka* on the east coast and all Ezo units from *Utasutu* to *Mashike* on the west coast. The revolt, which lasted from 1669 until 1672, ended in defeat for the Ezo. The Ezo were forced to surrender, pay compensation and sign a pledge of obedience and loyalty.

The defeat was, according to the Ainu, due to "lack of support from more remote Ezo units, a lack of modern weaponry and economic difficulties. Besides, the weapons of the Ainu were manufactured for obtaining food rather than for fighting. The Ainu never developed effective weapons to fight their enemies, primarily because they have no fighting tradition (Kayano 1988a, b). Their weapons, bow and arrow, used earlier when the immigrants were driven out of their territories, turned out to be inadequate in this battle (Tomi 1985; Davis 1987).

THE BASHO SYSTEM

During the rebellion years of 1669-1672 both Nihon proper and the immigrants in Ezo suffered losses in their Ezo trade, a factor that signified a change in the Matsumae Han Chigyonushi contract system, the Tokugawa edict from 1604. The losses in income from the Ezo trade during the years of rebellion made it obvious that the Matsumae was not powerful enough to guard the mainland trade interests in Ezo. The mainland merchants who had prospered during the peaceful Tokugawa regime, and the warriors, who had become superfluous, took control of the trade by force. As a result the Matsumae controlling influence diminished, not to the advantage of the Ezo, but of Nihon proper.

The new system was called the *Basho system* and meant that the Bakufu system in Nihon proper authorized mainland merchants to control the trade activities of the Ezo units. Eventually, as mainland capital investment rose, the equivalent of branch offices were opened in Ezo. With the help of the warriors and powerful mainland merchants they were able to establish trade regulations of their own and secure their own trade interests. As a result, trade slipped into the hands of uncontrolled and uncontrollable merchant profiteers.

The effects of intensified trade became obvious and soon trade was in decline. Meanwhile, since it was the Ezo who had the most unfavourable position they began to trade surplus to requirements. A credit system for trade evolved, and there were many Ezo who fell under contractor control as labourers.

With diminished profits in trade, compensation was sought and found in improved and diversified marine production methods, introduced by people from the mainland (Baba 1980: 65). Such enterprises offered a solution to the immediate inconveniences which came from trade in decline. Disadvantaged Ezo were found in occupations administered by people from the mainland and eventually they became more and more involved with the mainland system.

At the beginning, the Ezo working for the mainland interests thought of their present situation as temporary. Their intention was to regain their former position and control. This they thought possible by offering valuables, such as lacquer ornaments and sake, to Nature and thereby ultimately regaining what rightfully belonged to them.

To the Ezo the primary and accepted explanation of their situation was bad relations with Kamuy, the Ezo deities. Hardship or misfortune was not a new phenomenon in the lives of the Ezo, and as offerings to Kamuy were a way that corresponded to their cognitive model, they sought a solution within the framework of their cosmology. Their concern was to change their disadvantaged position, for which they had to transform bad relations with Nature into good relations. To achieve this, essential valuables, preferably those gained by barter, or at this time by working for the mainland, were necessary (Kayano 1988b).

However, the combined effect of endemic war, depletion of resources and weakened bonds between kin made their situation worse and permanent.

During the Matsumae Han period of control, conditions in Ezo deteriorated whereas those in Nihon proper improved. Ezo labour and Ezo resources complemented the exploitation of the mainland peasantry. In short, Ezo people and Ezo resources had become essential to the development and management of the economy in the mainland (Takakura 1960: 38-44). Since the Ezo during the latter part of Matsumae Han period of direct control became more and more economically involved with the mainland system, one would expect them to become culturally and socially involved too. This was not the case, however. This was to a considerable extent an effect of the policy of segregation maintained throughout the rule of the Matsumae Han (Kayano 1988b).

In the succeeding period, the early Bakufu period of direct control (1799-1821), there arose an immediate need to make the Ezo allies of the Wajin. Repeated Russian attempts to conquer the island and proclaim Ezo a Russian territory made for a change in policy, and according to *Ezo Shinkai Kikigai* (Records of newly opened areas in Hokkaido), to be found in Hokudai, Sapporo: "Fourteen or fifteen years ago [1785-86], the people in Moscow, with the intention of getting control of the island tried to win the favour of the people of Kunashiri ... using the Christian religion as a tool".

For fear of losing Ezo to the Russians the segregation policy was abandoned for a policy of assimilation. Officially the shift of both political authorities and policy relates to the fact that Ezo is underdeveloped and the Ezo poor, and the new authorities wish to change this condition:

> Ezo has been brought under the direct control of the central government because it is underdeveloped and its people are living in a poor condition.... Teach the Ezo, in due time, how to raise crops and live on cereals and to become used to our ways of life. Even before you teach them to cultivate the land, try to change their diet from meat to grain by telling them that cereals are much better than meat. Then when the time comes to teach them how to raise crops their progress will be much faster. Make the Ezo feel that this change in policy is a generous gesture of the government. It is important not only to tell them this but to be honest with them. It has been said that they are ignorant but innocent and if they receive the impression that we are not honest it will be a great obstacle in winning their loyalty (Instructions to officials in charge of the management of Ezo, February 10, 1799, archives at Hokudai, 1988)....
>
> The reason why the Bakufu has taken control is that the Ezo have a poor standard of living and know little of industry, so that if the fishing is bad they suffer extreme hardship. The Bakufu has great sympathy for these conditions and desires to show the natives new methods (Instruction to Ezo, June 15, 1799, Ohashi Zenshiro, Hokudai, 1988).

The "great sympathy" of the Bakufu for the conditions of Ezo natives may be a plausible explanation for a shift in policy. There is, however, also the question of whether their concern for the poor conditions of the Ezo merely was used as an excuse for their real interests in Ezo. Perhaps we should direct our attention to the increase in threats from Russia and question whether the shift of controlling influence merely coincided with these threats or whether they actually caused the change in the policy of the Nihon authorities. According to Takakura (1960: 51) the Matsumae Han could not defend the mainland interest in Ezo, being numerically weak (the number of his people is estimated to around 26,500) and in a poor financial position (he was in debt as a result of his diminished influence).

The new controlling authorities also formulated a kind of native policy that aimed at transforming Ezo into a peasant community, and their efforts were directed towards the encouragement of both farming and assimilation. In addition, immigration was actively encouraged. Yet the mainland system did not lend itself to the release of a labour force for the purpose of colonization. However, using the Ezo as the labour force in Ezo was seen by the Bakufu as a viable option. Other measures taken were to the use of Nihongo, the language of the Wajin, and allowing the Ezo so wishing to adopt mainland customs. Further, much effort was put into teaching the Ezo respect and loyalty to Bakufu authorities. The intention was that mainland law was to supersede Ezo customs regarding law and punishment. In addition intermarriage between Ezo and the immigrants was encouraged.

The assimilation policy invoked by the Bakufu met with obstacles from both sides. There were almost no intermarriages, primarily due to prejudices against the Ezo (Kayano 1988b). In addition, the static and hierarchical system in the mainland, where the population was divided into four social strata did not allow for transgressions, and since this system was as accepted among the mainland people in Ezo as it was in Nihon proper, the intermarriage policy was in fact doomed to fail, as were also the agricultural experiments. They gave poor results primarily because in Ezo there is a shortage of land suitable for agricultural activities (Kayano 1988b). Accordingly, the agricultural experiments were abandoned in 1802. The mainland interference with Ezo conceptions of law and order was also a failure, since their views on legal matters were too far apart. The mainland system was thus never properly introduced. The introduction of Wajin customs and language were other areas in which the assimilation policy met with obstacles.

Besides measures taken to promote the assimilation of the Ainu, the concern was also to stimulate migration to Hokkaido. People who were loyal to the lords of Nihon were an important asset, since a main concern was to ward off Russian invasion. In 1802, Buddhism was introduced and the first temples built. Their prime responsibility was to perform rituals and burials for Wajin officials and immigrants as well as to supervise religious activities (Takakura 1960: 52-75).

However, the building of these temples also provided an alternative to Christianity, formerly introduced by the Russians (Hokkaido Government 1821, 1981). During this period, in the event of rebellion and/or increased Russian competition for both land and souls, precautions were taken in the form of transportation facilities and the establishing of post houses.

The goodwill policy of the central government dissolved with the diminishing of the Russian threat, and the administrative controls were accordingly relaxed. The Bakufu control turned out to be an expensive enterprise. At that time income from Ezo covered less than fifty per cent of the costs of its administration. Eventually economic benefits were once again given priority.

Now, it could always be argued that since income from Ezo covered less than fifty per cent of its administration one should not describe this period as an exploitation. There is, however, no reason to refrain from this merely because the Bakufu miscalculated its profits. After all, there was more at stake than just money: there was the Russian threat, and as soon as this threat diminished the Bakufu disappeared from the scene.

Judging from the above, the conclusion arrived at in the various official documents is that there is little evidence that an actual improvement of the condition of the Ezo occurred during this period.

In the eyes of the Wajin, this lack of improvement was due to the Ezo people's inability to catch up with development. In the official documents of the Wajin we have, however, ample evidence that the policy of peaceful relations was primarily established with an eye toward mainland defence and mainland interests in Ezo, and had little to do with an actual wish to improve the conditions of the Ezo.

From an Ainu point of view, we may depict the measures taken to incorporate them as a special technique employed by the Wajin authorities to control both the land of Ezo and its people. After all, improvements such as the introduction of agriculture, the encouragement to teach the "natives" Nihongo, the introduction of mainland law and religion hardly bettered the lot of the Ezo but rather they improved conditions for the immigrants in the mainland, particularly.

In 1821, when the Matsumae Han was again in control, the position of the Ezo did not change, but remained much the same during their second period of control which lasted till 1854. By this time the Tokugawa regime in the mainland was in decline and feuds between powerful lords threatened once again to ruin the mainland system. Hence, when in 1854 the Bakufu again was given control over Ezo territory and its people, this has been viewed as the last effort of Tokugawa regime to unite the lords of Nihon proper.

The period was a relatively short one, lasting for only fourteen years. When it ended, in 1868, it was due to the collapse of the Tokugawa regime, which made a continuation of the Bakufu control impossible. The Bakufu was dismissed by force in 1868 when a group of Shogunate warriors occupied the Hakodate administrative office in Ezo and declared Ezo independent of the mainland, an enterprise that ended with their defeat.

Now a period of colonization, *Kaitakushi*, begun. This period runs parallel to the Meiji Restoration on the mainland. The new era was called the Meiji. With it Nihon was brought into the world market and rapid modernization begun. Baba writes, "the development of capitalism was urgent and ... the emergence of policy slogans like *fukoku kyohei* [enrich the country, strengthen the military] and *shokusan kogyo* [industrialization] reflected this urgency" (1980: 63).

Meiji officials were sent to Ezo to survey and map the island. The island was renamed Hokkaido, since a Nihon name was thought more appropriate than an Ainu one. Hokkaido was divided into fourteen districts or regions, which cross-cut the original Ezo settlements and consequently had little in common with former autonomous Ezo units. In order to keep track of the subjects of the nation, a register of the people living in Hokkaido was proposed. Immediate problems arose since the Ezo did not have family names. Hence it was decided that they were to be named after the place where they lived. For such reasons many Ainu have the same surnames, yet they are not related to each other in any other way.

In addition they were also to be registered by the name of *Kyuudojin*, aborigines, or *Dojin*, natives. This was to facilitate distribution of land grants initiated to encourage agricultural activities among the Ezo (5th article of *Hokkaido Hyuudojin Hogoho*, Utari Kyokai 1987b: 4).

In accordance with the wish of the newly established Meiji regime to have but one homogeneous population in the nation to be, the Ezo were formally and on equal terms to be integrated into the Nihon Minzoku. An official policy of assimilation was proposed. By this time the Ezo population had declined by almost seventy-five per cent (Registration office in Sapporo 1988) and was in a very poor condition. Despite "integration on equal terms", discrimination prevailed. Therefore, *Hokkaido Kyuudojin Hogoho*, came into being in 1899.

The act, which consists of thirteen articles, primarily treats the following subjects: (1) transfer of land to promote agriculture, (2) medical policies, (3) education policies, (4) housing policies and (5) the management of joint property (Utari Kyokai 1988: 7). The preface to the act reads:

> Since the beginning of the Meiji era, measures have been taken as to the protection of the indigenous people of Hokkaido in accordance with the Emperor's notion to love every one of his subjects equally, without discrimination. However, they have not been completely fruitful as yet. It is because the benevolent influence of the Emperor's fine government has not spread itself widely enough and also because the indigenous people were unenlightened. The natural blessings on which they have been living were taken away from them by the immigrants from the mainland little by little. As a result, they gradually lost their sources of livelihood and they were left in extreme poverty. It is an irresistible course of nature that the superior get the better of the inferior. Nevertheless, the indigenous people are the abandoned in their sufferings. It is the duty of the nation to cure their misfortune through remedial measures and secure their livelihood by means of the appropriate industries, which is believed to meet the Emperor's wishes also. This is the reason this bill shall be submitted.

The fact that the Ezo "were left in extreme poverty" seems to have been as obvious to the Emperor as it was to the Ezo. The cause of this condition was differently interpreted however. To the Emperor, the immigrants and the innocence of the Ezo had caused this problem, whereas to the Ezo, it was caused by bad relations with their own gods, Kamuy.

In the eyes of the Ezo their Kamuy had deserted them and their own explanation of this was that they had not fulfilled their obligations towards Nature.

Since, as it turned out, their own disgrace and the favourable position of the people from the mainland extended over a considerable period of time, the Ezo thought that the gods of the latter must be more powerful than those whom they themselves worshipped. They thus saw the mainland offer as a possible solution to their problem. In other words, they interpreted their situation in religious rather than in political terms and they saw the promise of an ideal life in the future if they abandoned their Ainu ceremonies and their way of life in favour of Nihon customs. Accordingly, when in *Hokkaido Kaitakushi*, the Wajin proposed an official policy of assimilation there was little resistance to change on the part of the Ezo, only initial enthusiasm as how to meet the changes. Little did they know that it was not possible for them to gain entrance to the Wajin arena, for no other reason than that they were not of Wajin origin.

CHAPTER SIX

The integration
of the Ainu People
and their land

In this chapter I will discuss the integration of the Ainu and their land
into the Nihon nation, *Nihon Minzoku*. When discussing integration it is essential to
distinguish between land and people. Generally speaking, the land and its exploitation
was a matter of utmost concern to the Nihon nation as a whole. As Baba puts it:

> Implemented with a considerably large investment, the development of Japan's
> large northern island had several objectives: First it was seen as a means to defend
> Japan from a rapidly developing and expansionist Russia. Second ... it offered a
> solution to unemployment for the former samurai class ... Finally, development
> promised to yield the needed natural resources for a growing capitalist economy
> (Baba 1980: 63).

With respect to its indigenous population, if we choose to look at their present
situation as it is now, there is reason to believe that issues concerning improvements for
them became a matter of secondary importance, and the argument that they merely "came
with the bargain" is hardly an understatement. The result is, that "the Ainu fall far behind,
economically, occupationally, educationally and also in terms of welfare" (Utari Kyokai
1987b). This is not a new problem. It is, in fact, a subject widely discussed among the
authorities in Nihon for a considerable period of time. This problem is discussed during
the annual *Diet Meetings of the Lower House Budget Committee Sessions*.

During these annual meetings the authorities come to an agreement that an
improvement of the natives' situation is urgent and the participants express a wish to help
raise the living standard of the Ainu and help improve welfare services for them.
Meanwhile, however, the situation of the Ainu remains very much the same. They are still
in the lowest income bracket, 60.9% (Wajin 21.9%) of them rely on social welfare for
their survival, unemployment is 15.1% (Wajin 8%) and only 8.1% (Wajin 27.4%) of
them have graduated from high school (*A Proposal for Legislation Concerning the Ainu*,
Hokkaido Government 1988).

THE MEIJI RESTORATION: HOKKAIDO

Hokkaido is located between 148° 53' and 139° 20' E longitude and 41° 21' and 45° 33' N latitude. It is the northernmost Nihon island and is separated by the *Tsugaru Kaikyou* from the main island of Honshu. It faces the Sea of Japan to the west, the Pacific Ocean to the south and the Sea of Okhotsk to the northeast. Sapporo is the "capital" of Hokkaido. Hokkaido covers an area of about 83,500 km, which is about 22% of the total land area of Nihon. About 53% of Hokkaido land area consists of mountains and forests. The climate of the island varies, from both sub-frigid zones in the north to temperate zones in the south.

The first people settled in Hokkaido more than twenty thousand years ago. In the *Kamakura* era, seven hundred years ago, the Wajin made their first migration from Honshu to the southern parts of Hokkaido, where there is a temperate climate.

The first year of the Meiji era saw Ezo annexed to Nihon and a colonization office, *Kaitakushi*, was established in Sapporo. (Other parts of Ainu domains, such as the islands of Sakhalin and Kurile were annexed, deannexed and reannexed in connection with treaties settled, revoked and resettled between Nihon and Russia, during the years 1875-1945.)

Ezo was renamed Hokkaido and Ainu places were given Nihon names. The island was divided into fourteen regions, which cross-cut formerly autonomous Ainu settlements or *Kotan*.

In 1868, when the Meiji government set up the Colonization Commissioner's Office in Sapporo, it was decided that foreign expertise was necessary to develop Hokkaido. Advice was sought from the U.S.A. Horace Capron, the commissioner of the U.S. Department of Agriculture, was invited as the supreme advisor.

In 1874 a colonial militia system, *Tonden-Hei*, was established to serve manifold purposes, such as supplying a military force to defend the northern frontier against Russia and to maintain domestic law and order in Hokkaido and to prevent rebellion by dissidents. In this period, which lasted until 1904, the foundation of Hokkaido's future development was established in a variety of fields. Government-managed farms introduced bullocks for plowing and reaping. In addition a number of factories such as flour mills and beer breweries led to the development of a road system. The *Horonai* main trunk railway line exploiting the Horonai coal mine was built and the Sapporo Agricultural College was founded.

In the early days of the Hokkaido Prefectural Government, which was established in 1886, government factories were sold to private companies, harbour facilities were consolidated, and the extension of roads and railway lines was supported. It was a period when the prefectural government focused its efforts on the establishment of an infrastructure, the introduction of enterprises and the promotion of development with private capital.

In 1910 *The First Development Plan* was introduced. Financial difficulties were an obstacle to the plan at the beginning, but it soon became successful. In 1926, 780,000 hectares of farmland were cultivated.

The Second Development Plan (1927-1946) included the exploitation of natural resources. The next plan, which was called *Urgent Development Period* (1947-1951), had as its goal an increase of food production, and a number of agrarian reforms were carried out.

The next development plan, called *The First Comprehensive Development Plan* (1952-1962), was divided into the first and the second five-year-plan. The first five-year plan stressed the necessity of establishing an infrastructure to promote industries, that is, developing electricity, maintaining and expanding roads and harbour facilities. The succeeding five-year plan included schemes to improve facilities for culture and welfare.

With *The Second Hokkaido Comprehensive Development Plan* (1963-1970), industrial advancement was furthered through the adoption of a policy to modernize agriculture, forestry and fishery (Matsumoto 1960; Takakura 1960; Cornell 1964; Baba 1980; Sander 1985; *Passport to Hokkaido*, Hokkaido Government 1988a).

Since its early days of colonization, Hokkaido has been developed to receive immigrants, to defend Nihon territory and to provide a base for food supplies, not only for Hokkaido but for the nation as a whole. Today Hokkaido represents the major part of rice production in Nihon.

RESEARCH INTO THE AINU
AND THEIR INTEGRATION
INTO THE LARGER SOCIETY

Research into the situation of the Ainu and their integration into the larger society has been done with the focus on the Wajin strategies of assimilating the Ainu. In this regard racial and cultural differences between the Wajin and the Ainu have been de-emphasized. After all, there is little interest in emphasizing them since, from the point of view of the authorities, there is only one ethnic group recognized as such in the Nihon nation. The Ainu were, in fact, ignored when, in 1968, the centenary of Hokkaido's incorporation into the Nihon nation was celebrated. Besides, as has been pointed out by Baba (1980), the standard position in Nihon, when talking and writing about its culture (and its people), is that it is homogeneous, despite the fact that there are actually a number of different cultures and peoples in Nihon:

This claim is made so often that one either slides into unthinking acceptance, or, begins to wonder why the refrain is still repeated despite the existence of several well-defined minorities in Japan (1980: 61).

This standard position has influenced researchers who study the situation of the Ainu to concentrate on factors that support or confirm the assumption that the policy of assimilation is a success (Naert 1960; Munro 1962; Cornell 1964; Hilger 1967; Kodama 1970; Newell 1967; Peng & Geiser 1977; Baba 1980). This type of research has been preoccupied with signs indicating that "racial and cultural assimilation" has been achieved.

Studies focusing on the Ainu in the interaction situation deal with the Ainu as an indigenous population (Cornell 1964; Hilger 1967; Newell 1967; Peng & Geiser 1977; Refsing 1980; Froome 1983; Sanders 1985; Tomi 1985; Davis 1987; Masler 1987). Of these studies a considerable number have been preoccupied with questions related to the consistent discriminatory treatment of the Ainu population by the Wajin majority. In their studies the prevailing discrimination has largely been viewed and interpreted in a situation where the established official ideology encourages the development of competing ideologies (Myrdal 1944; Lange & Westin 1981).

In the Ainu case there are two different approaches. One of these deals with what is termed ideological racism, a kind of racism that permeates administration and official-dom. According to this view there is nothing wrong with the established official ideology. Instead the cause of the discriminatory treatment is that administration and individuals do not live up to the officially established ideology. The other approach states that there must be something fundamentally wrong with the officially established ideology since it promotes discriminatory treatment.

The result of these studies varies and at best they oppose the prevailing discriminatory treatment, while at worst they admit that it once existed and deny that it still exists. Hilger (1967: 12), for example, points out such trivial facts as "today Ainu and Wajin are often seen working side by side".

Earlier explanations for the discriminatory treatment of the Ainu were sought in various racial factors, and emphasis was put on the "savage nature" of the Ainu or factors of "general degeneration" which were not specified. Compare:

The Ainu ... are altogether without the element that goes to make up what we call "modern civilization" and may be described as savage (Kajima 1895: 1).

The Ainu must be held to have undergone some degeneration.... Yet I am confident that they are capable of partaking in a higher culture.... The children are proving capable and industrious.... The Ainu seem to be on excellent terms with the Japanese peasantry, but a little official encouragement and sympathy would do much to elevate them (Munro 1911: 662).

Today, however, the explanations for the discriminatory treatment of the Ainu are sought in social factors, and now emphasis is put on the poor social conditions of the Ainu:

> The contemporary problem of the Ainu is structured in terms more relevant to social work than to anthropology. The living Ainu are regarded as one kind of "frontier poor" (Cornell 1964: 302).

Nevertheless, it appears to be difficult to isolate the social factors which differentiate the Ainu, and according to Peng and Geiser (1977: 20) this is due to the fact "that the Ainu and the Wajin have existed in an 'intimate' relationship for a long period and have adopted in addition to the language [Japanese] most of their customs and habits".

This emphasis on social aspects is related to the ideology of the Nihon nation, made obvious in Prime Minister Nakasone's speech in September 1986 where he unequivocally stated that Nihon's success on the world market is due to its homogeneous population. This speech had its roots in another statement made in 1976 in the Upper House when it was Prime Minister Miki who brought up the subject. In *Statement Submitted to the Fifth Session of the Working Group on Indigenous Population* we are informed that "Prime Minister Miki said Japan should become a model country for the world with her high standard of education and no problem of racial discrimination" (Utari Kyokai 1987b).

With this attitude it becomes extremely difficult to explain the unfavourable situation of the Ainu and the discriminatory treatment of them with the help of racial factors. Instead it is much more convenient to explain these things by social factors, "difficult to isolate and describe", to use the words of Peng and Geiser (1977). Discriminatory treatment and unfavourable conditions of other peoples in Nihon, such as the Burakumin and the Ryukyujin, are explained in the same way. In this way the Ainu and their situation is made similar to other minority peoples in Nihon, who jointly make up Nihon's lower stratum.

ACCULTURATION AS A FEATURE OF THE POLICY OF ASSIMILATION

With the restoration, vast social, political and economic changes occurred and foreign Western ideas, such as constitutional limitations on the power of the government and the rights of the governed, influenced the authorities (Cornell 1964: 295). Human rights in the form of the equality of citizenship rescued the Ainu from the Basho contracts and henceforth they had the right of private land ownership. The official status of the Ainu changed, at least theoretically.

From then onward the Ainu were no longer a distinct "cultural" group having racial (anthropomorphic), religious, linguistic and historical traits in common. As has been pointed out by Nakasone "they [the Ainu] like the rest of Nihon's population were a result of the mingling of indigenous groups in Nihon" (Prime Minister Nakasone, Upper House, Nov. 10, 1986, Utari Kyokai 1987b). In reality, however, they became one of the nation's many vaguely defined minority peoples.

A possible contributory factor to this development may be, as Baba (1980: 62) states, that the constitutional policy was immature and that feudal ideas still prevailed. Hence, when it came to classifying the Ainu they were given names chosen according to their place of birth.

Since Ainu place-names were changed after Nihon fashion, the authorities found it proper to insert Kyuudojin, former natives, before their "fictive" names given to then in order to facilitate registration. With such actions the Meiji restoration initiated the process of incorporating the Ainu into the political and administrative system of the Wajin, in whose eyes the Ainu had now gained the equality of citizenship.

The policy of assimilation as it was maintained by the Wajin included an acculturation of the Ainu. Acculturation as a concept refers to the processes and events which result from the act of joining together two or more formerly separate and autonomous cultures. In this situation it meant that the Ainu were forbidden to practise their own customs, to speak their own language, to dress in Ainu clothes, and so on. Instead they were to become Nihonjin, abide by new laws and adapt themselves to a life as farmers. At first this resulted in that they devoted much effort to forgetting about their Ainu inheritance and adapting to the new conditions. After some time, they found that their land and natural resources had been properly integrated, while they, as a people, had been excluded from the profits.

THE PROCESS OF ASSIMILATION: THE AGRARIAN FAILURE

To develop Hokkaido was indeed a difficult task. About fifty-three per cent of the Hokkaido land area is composed of mountains and forests. In addition, governmental investments were insufficient. Above all, lack of experienced farmers threatened to retard the development.

The Ainu, who at the time of the annexation were inexperienced as farmers, had difficulties in taking up agricultural activities. Yet they were not unwilling and as a result, agricultural specialists were sent to Hokkaido to train the Ainu as farmers and to supply seed and tools.

The Ainu willingness to adapt to the new conditions was not necessarily a choice of their own; when I discussed this topic with my Ainu informant he made it clear that it was actually a matter of survival:

> Hunting deer or fishing for salmon became poaching, while collecting firewood became theft. Meanwhile people from the mainland flooded the land and initiated destructive development (interview with Ainu male, aged 53, Hidaka, 1988).

The Ainu population was at this time decimated, mainly due to epidemics introduced by the Wajin. Their living conditions had begun to deteriorate, initially with the administrative attempts to agrarianize their land.

The attempts to transform the Ainu into farmers were, however, not successful, so, other recruits were sought and found in the former Samurai families and among farmers from the mainland. Baba informs us that:

> the primary source of labour for the development of Hokkaido were former "Shizoku" [samurai families] who lost their economic support after the decline of feudalism, and middle and lower class farmers who were impoverished during the early phase of industrial capitalism (1980: 64).

To stimulate immigration, the immigrants recruited by the Hokkaido Development Bureau were given land free of charge. If the property was not developed by the farmers within three years of settlement with their own labour, it was taken back. This was in accordance with *The Regulation of the Lease and Sale of Land.*

According to Kayano Hokkaido territory was now distributed as "plots" and took on a reservation-like pattern of settlements similar to those of the natives in the U.S.A. (see also Takakura 1960; Cornell 1964; Baba 1980; Sanders 1985).

Hokkaido, now formally part of the Nihon nation, was thus colonized by Wajin immigrants belonging either to the Samurai or to farmers who took advantage of the situation and claimed the best parts of the land in Hokkaido.

Meanwhile, however, the land distributed among the Ainu was, for the most part, of infertile soil and they had difficulties in supporting the needs of their families. The efforts of the Meiji government to develop Hokkaido came to serve the immigrants, whereas the same efforts created great hardship for the Ainu who, unable to cultivate their land, became engaged as part-time labourers or hired labour for the more fortunate immigrants. Many Ainu also sought their living as "surveyors" for the government. As such they were engaged as ditch-diggers, cable-layers or as pathfinders (Baba 1980: 65).

As regards the latter, in 1988, a book called *Kaneto: A Man of Burning Spirit* was published. This book is the result of a joint investigation made by a group of Wajin scholars who in cooperation with the Board of Education in Nihon took it upon themselves to present an Ainu view of their own contribution to the development of Hokkaido. The form of the book is that of a novel and the book's main character Kaneto is fictional.

The aim of the book is to give a picture of Ainu assistance in developing Hokkaido and the hardship that they suffered in those days. Here is an extract from the book:

> I began to work as a hand for surveying when I left elementary school. Surveying was impossible at that time without the help of Ainu, who were accustomed to walking in the mountains. We worked harder than ordinary Wajin workers, but our wages were only half of theirs.... It is a pity that I see that kind of injustice even now among some ignorant people. I made up my mind to be a surveying engineer. I studied very hard to achieve my purpose. Late at night, I got up and went to the river to wash my face with cold water. And then I read a textbook by candlelight while the other workers were sleeping (1988: 39).

From the above extract we get an Ainu view of their own indispensability. Yet in *Secret Records in the Development of Hokkaido, Hokkaido Kaitaku Hiroku* (Archival records, Hokudai, Sapporo 1869), minimal credit was given to their assistance in developing Hokkaido. Without suggesting that they did not participate, their help was described as dispensable, rather than indispensable (see also Takakura 1960; Cornell 1964; Newell 1967; Baba 1980).

It has been argued that the native policy, *Hokkaido Kyuudojin Hogoho*, initiated in 1899, was a sincere attempt to improve the situation of the Ainu in Hokkaido. Among other things it was supposed to have the following merits: reliance on agricultural skills would bring the Ainu out of extreme poverty, and Ainu labour could be utilized in the development of Hokkaido. The first four articles in this law read:

> 1) Those Hokkaido Former Natives who engage in agriculture or who wish to engage in agriculture will be given 15, 000 tsubo land per family free of charge....
>
> 2) The right of ownership given in article 1 shall be understood as follows: 1. No transfer of ownership other than succession is allowed. 2. No right of pawn, no mortgage rights, no surface right and no permanent tenant rights are allowed. 3. Without permission from the director of Hokkaido Agency, the right to use another man's land is not granted and 4. The right of lien and the right of priority are not allowed. Land which is given in article 1 shall not be taxed or registration fees collected within thirty years of lease. Those former natives who owned land previously cannot transfer or set up possessor rights mentioned in section 1, 2 and 3, except succession, without the permission of the director of the Hokkaido Agency....
>
> 3) If the land given by article 1 is not cultivated within fifteen years, it will be forfeited....
>
> 4) Those Hokkaido former natives who are poor will be given agricultural tools and seeds (Utari Kyokai 1987b).

FIGURE 8   Chikushi-un-guru *(pathfinder)*

Under the circumstances, this seems to be a fair offer, but most of the land divided among the Ainu tended to be infertile and could not support the subsistence needs of the Ainu families. Further, since the Wajin owned and controlled much of the best agricultural land, it became difficult for the Ainu to find suitable land near their original village sites, and they were thus forced to migrate to distant areas. Some of them managed to cope, but many did not. Considering the fact that the Hokkaido climate varies, containing both sub-frigid zones and temperate zones, it is possible to connect the frequent failures to this fact. Accordingly, most of the land became forfeited and fell under common property.

Another contributory factor to the failure of the introduction of agriculture among the Ainu was that, although alienation of land to non-Ainu was in principle prohibited, in practice this was actually done and, as has been pointed out by Cornell (1964: 300), "Most Ainu farmlands were not tilled by their owners but by Japanese on long-term lease arrangements".

Consequently, despite the fact that in *Hokkaido Kyuudojin Hogoho* emphasis was on both land tenure and land use by the Ainu, the law passed in 1899 to protect the interests of the Ainu, their land and people, did not live up to its promises. To the Ainu it proved to be not worth the paper it was written on.

The damage this law has done to the Ainu is discussed by Davis in an article in *Tokyo Journal*, October 1987, who points out that even its title is discriminatory. He writes:

> The most damaging law to the Ainu race was "The Law for the Protection of Native Hokkaido Aborigines" [Hokkaido Kyuudojin Hogoho] passed in 1899. Written unilaterally by the mainland Japanese, without any Ainu input, the original law was designed to "protect" the impoverished Ainu tribes by providing economic "support". The "land grant portion", which allowed mainlanders to take over Ainu-controlled land was rescinded in 1935 but the rest of the law is still on the books and most Japanese scholars agree that even its title is discriminatory. One article therein provided arrest if Ainu hunted or cut wood. Another stated that land not fully cultivated would be confiscated.... Most Ainu families' land was in fact confiscated, forcing these natives into becoming low-paid day workers in order to survive. Only Ainu were required to obtain the official permission of the governor to buy or sell land (Davis 1987: 9).

Judging from the above, the policy of agrarianization, as it was maintained by the Development Agencies in Hokkaido, did not serve to improve the situation of the Ainu, rather it worked to disintegrate their society and economy, and the practice behind the equality of citizenship and equal rights revealed that some people were more equal than others.

When I discussed the agrarian failure with one of the employees at the Development Agency in Sapporo, I learned that their position is that:

> The agrarian failure must be seen in its relation to the cultural differences between the two peoples. It is only natural that the Ainu failed in their agrarian attempts. After all, not very long ago they lived as hunters. It is however regrettable that this was overlooked when the articles of the law were formulated (interview in Sapporo, 1988).

From the viewpoint of the Ainu, as expressed by Kayano, "It is quite obvious that we should fail in our attempt to adapt to new conditions, since the land 'given' to us did not support our needs" (interview in Nibutani, 1988). Although the explanation put forth by Kayano is relevant, to say the least, we should not underestimate the role of cultural factors. Naturally, these factors played an essential part in the interaction as a whole. We have reason to believe, however, that the emphasis that has been put on these factors in explaining why the Ainu became a "marginal minority people on the outskirts of the larger society" has been much too strong. To claim, as the authorities and also Peng and Geiser (1977) do, that the fact that the Ainu who until recently had been hunters, had difficulties in adjusting to new conditions and use this as a plausible explanation for their failure as farmers, is not only insufficient but it might, for all we know, be completely wrong.

THE PROCESS OF ASSIMILATION: ACCULTURATION IN GENERAL

Following a course of acculturation, the Ainu were encouraged to abandon their customs and their language. In this way they were, as a government official in Sapporo told me, "knocked loose from conventional ideas and expectations" (interview in Sapporo, 1988). Further, intermarriages with Wajin were, of course, also seen to promote a rapid acculturation. And, if we are to believe Hilger (1967), the Ainu had no objection to that. On the contrary, they were enthusiastic. One of her informants gave her the following view:

> Ainu and Japanese should marry. The Ainu should be absorbed by the Japanese. Japanese and Ainu should be one people.... It is enough if old Ainu culture is preserved in literature and museums. In actual life, there should be assimilation. Then too, in many cases, children of such mixed marriages are more clever than are children of marriages between Ainu.... Yaeko, the adopted daughter of John Batchelor, was mixed Ainu and Japanese blood. Yaeko was intelligent enough to help Batchelor with his dictionary (1967: 161).

My own material indicates that the following attitude was common: "If it continues like this, our people marrying 'stupid Shamo', they are the only likely ones, we do not have much to offer in the future" (interview with Ainu in the Iburi area, 1988). It is thus obvious that according to them, only "stupid" Wajin are available marriage candidates.

More than two decades have past since Hilger (1967) did her research among the Ainu, which gives us reason to assume that the attitude that prevails among the Ainu is based on experience. One may of course also question whether Hilger's concern was actually to present the attitude of the Ainu. In the preface to her book we learn that her investigation was supported by the Nihon government. It reads:

> With the encouragement of Crown Princess Michiko and the help of the Japanese Ministry of Foreign Affairs ... Sister Inez [Hilger] was given the full support of the Japanese government in planning a modern intensive study of these interesting early inhabitants of Japan (1967: v).

Anyhow, intermarriages between Ainu and Wajin exist, but Wajin who marry Ainu are more or less forced to give up their Wajin identity. To some extent they become integrated into the Ainu way of life, yet they are not recognized as Ainu by the Ainu, that is, the Ainu do not identify intermarried Wajin as Ainu, because intermarried Wajin do not have any Ainu blood in their veins, which is judged to be the sole determinant for a claim to an Ainu identity.

My fieldwork observations reveal, however, that intermarried Wajin often work both to activate and stimulate Ainu activities and practices. This can be seen in their involvement in Ainu activities, such as wood-carving and cloth-making and also their participation in ceremonial performances, lessons in Ainu culture, history and language. Some of them are even regarded as experts in their fields by the Ainu. Yet, their work is sometimes looked upon with a great deal of scepticism by the Ainu. In one of the villages I met a Wajin woman who was very skilled in Ainu language, she was in fact an "Itak" authority. Nevertheless, when the Ainu of the village needed advice about language questions, they did not turn to her initially, rather turning to their own people who they knew were not as good as she was.

According to one of my informants, the unwillingness of the Ainu to turn to Wajin experts for advice is because they feel that Ainu "work" should be Ainu affairs and not Wajin. He continued: "You see, we feel threatened by the interference of the Shamo. We do not want them to be experts on our culture" (interview with Ainu male, aged 52, Asahikawa, 1988).

Under the guise of science the Ainu were subjected to humiliating research. Their culture and their language were scrutinized by researchers whose scientific credibility, in Ainu opinion, was dubious. The position of the Ainu is that studies of their race, culture and language were undertaken in order to determine their origins once and for all. One of my informants expressed this in the following words:

> It seems as if the Shamo cannot rest until they have solved the question of where we came from. Among ourselves we often discuss this and we ask ourselves, why is it that this is so important and if it is so important why do they not listen to our voices? We know where we come from. We know that we are the earliest settlers in Nihon. Why do they not accept this? I myself think that they already know this in their hearts but with their minds they cannot accept it. That is why they go on and on with this question and present "results" of which the one is more confusing than the other (interview with Ainu male aged 62, Chikabumi, 1988).

When discussing issues related to the acculturation of the Ainu, we must take into consideration that the Ainu in the initial phase of the Meiji Restoration willingly adapted themselves to the new rules and were more concerned with hiding their origin than emphasizing it.

When they were given what they judged the chance to alter the stereotype opinions about themselves and their culture they took it, even if it meant submission to humiliating tests. Before the introduction of compulsory education there were Wajin discussions about whether they were educable. According to an interview which Hilger did with an Ainu women we learn that:

the Japanese decided to do some test cases. In 1872, thirteen Ainu boys and five Ainu girls were selected ... and went to special schools established for them at Zojoji Temple in Shiba, Tokyo - Hokkaido had no schools for the Ainu at that time. They were to be there for several years (1967: 197-198).

Compulsory segregated education was formally introduced at the turn of the last century with separate schools set up to meet Ainu needs, which included compulsory education in Nihongo, the Japanese language, for Ainu children for three years beginning at the age of seven, and for four years beginning at the age of six for Wajin children. No less than twenty-one Ainu schools were built during the following eight years, none of which were used very frequently (Sanders 1985).

The cause of this can primarily be related to the fact that the Ainu needed their children for work. Each child that went to school made it harder to support the family. Another contributory factor was the lack of educated personnel willing to devote themselves to teaching the Ainu. This is a subject widely discussed among the Ainu, and a common reply among them is the following, "Uneducated Shamo teachers, sharing little or no interest in our matters, were not enough to motivate us to send our children to school" (interview, Iburi, 1988).

Other obviously discriminatory factors, such as the varying length of education and the use of separate schools for Ainu and Wajin children, contributed also to the lack of enthusiasm of Ainu parents for their children's future education. Consequently, the Wajin with no interest in and no understanding of the problem, were unable to find a suitable solution.

The Ainu children stayed at home. In spite of this the segregated, largely unattended school system survived until 1937. When the Ainu were to be educated in the same schools as the Wajin and for the same length of time, teaching was much the same. Ainu children were taught Wajin history and glory, while their own history was either neglected or described in the most negative way. Historical events of glory to the Ainu, such as the battle of *Koshamain* in 1457, the battle of *Shakushain* in 1669 and the battle at *Kunashiri Menashi* in 1789, were ignored. The Ainu were referred to either as an "inferior race" or as a "proto-Wajin type" (interview with Kayano, 1988, see also Tomi 1985).

In April 1947, educational authority was transferred from the federal to the prefectual and local levels. According to Kayano: "the principal aim of the shift was to meet educational needs on the local level. However, since the majority of our people are in the lowest income bracket we cannot afford to give our children higher education. We need financial support" (interview with Ekashi, Nibutani, 1988).

Wajin discrimination against the Ainu and the ongoing violation of the enactments taken to protect Ainu interests were issues carefully omitted. Today the segregated education system has a different form, yet it is still segregated, as can be seen by the low number of Ainu with higher education. When I discussed this with one of my Ainu informants in the Hidaka region, he provided me with the following information:

> I lost all interest in education. "Why?" You ask. The teachers did not treat us in the same way as they treated their Wajin pupils. For one thing we were excluded from taking part in domestic science for no other reason than the teacher's fear of eating food which we had touched. It was humiliating. Further, in junior high, subjects such as physics and mathematics, which were compulsory to Wajin scholars, were voluntary to us. At first we thought this good, most children would, do you not agree? Later, as an adult I attended night classes to be able to take in what was denied me in my school days (interview with Ainu male, aged 53, 1988).

Little or no encouragement to go to secondary school resulted in a poorly educated Ainu population and the stereotype picture of them as racially and culturally inferior became as accepted by the Ainu as it was by the Wajin. Many Ainu gave up in their struggle for equal rights. Some of them sought consolation in sake, others sought to escape their stigma by migrating to the cities, where they became absorbed in the jungle of the unemployed. Still others began an irksome way to seek redress.

UTARI KYOKAI

In 1930, due to continuing poor living conditions among the Ainu, the Utari Kyokai was established by the Wajin authorities. According to the Ainu: "this was a measure taken because the authorities in Nihon were afraid of being accused of ethnocide" (interview with Ainu male, aged 49, Akan, 1988).

According to a spokesman of the Kyokai: "the Kyokai was established to prevent a further exploitation of the Ainu by unscrupulous mainland profiteers who were numerous at that time" (interview in Sapporo, 1988). According to him the Kyokai's main purpose was to make sure that the regulations and restrictions of *Hokkaido Kyuudojin Hogoho* were not violated (see also Cornell 1964; Baba 1980; Sanders 1985).

However, according to the Ainu, its greatest efforts were given to the establishment of welfare services for the Ainu (Utari Kyokai 1984: 1). Hence, Ainu efforts to alter a stereotype picture of their own condition became a matter taken care of by the Wajin authorities.

Since the start, the Kyokai has been preoccupied with the tasks of helping the Ainu to adjust to new conditions, such as finding jobs for them. A considerable portion of this work has been devoted to help raise Ainu living standards and in 1974 the *Hokkaido Utari Welfare Policy* was initiated. This policy has no legal relationship with *Hokkaido Kyuudojin*

Hogoho, and it does not come under the category of ethnic policy but rather general welfare policy (Utari Kyokai 1988).

This policy's lack of emphasis on ethnic issues is of course related to the official policy of assimilating the Ainu, aimed at transforming the Ainu into "self-awakened" Nihonjin. This subject was discussed in 1976 when State Minister Ueki brought it up in connection with the 77th Lower House Account Committee Session:

> Both the government and the local organization have been making efforts for them (the Ainu) to be self-awakened as Japanese. But it seems true that the Ainu people are so called natives who have been living in the Hokkaido and the Sakhalin regions from early days, and that they have been considering themselves as a separate, small ethnic group calling the non-Ainu people Wajin or Shamo. Nevertheless, we now hope that the Ainu people will be self-awakened as Japanese people (State Minister Ueki, Draft from the 77th Lower House Account Committee Session May, 20 1976, Utari Kyokai 1987b).

It is rather obvious that the official attitude towards minority people and the questions relating to them is biased. Douglas Sanders, a lawyer working for the rights of indigenous peoples, presented his view in an article in the *International Work Group for Indigenous Affairs* (IWGIA) where he points out the following:

> Minority questions have not been linked in Japan. There is no pattern of minorities forming political alliances with each other. There are no governmental programmes aimed at minorities in general. The special programmes for the Burakumin and the Ainu are similar, but they are officially and institutionally separate (1985: 123).

Despite preoccupation with social work, the living standards of the Ainu remain far below those of the Wajin. In the *Report on Actual Conditions of the Ainu People in Hokkaido* made by Hokkaido Local Government and published in November 1986, we find that 60.9% of the Ainu and only 21.9% of the non-Ainu receive public assistance in Hokkaido (Utari Kyokai 1987b).

The opinion of the Ainu is that the Kyokai's emphasis on social work has made them passive, undermined their self-esteem and prevented them from taking actions by themselves. Their position is that:

> The protectionist policy, "Hokkaido Kyuudojin Hogoho", does not exclude work with the restoring of ethnic rights and work to give us a cultural definition. If the Kyokai had been more sensitive about these issues we would have been far better off. As it is now we find ourselves with a segregated welfare system, consisting of the building of houses and money to pay the rent (interview with Ainu male, aged 51, Kushiro, 1988).

The Kyokai, initiated by Wajin authorities and provided with funds from the national budget, organized in 1930, named in 1946 (*Hokkaido Ainu Kyokai*) and renamed in 1961 (*Hokkaido Utari Kyokai*), is today, quite understandably, looked upon with a great deal of scepticism by the Ainu. After all, the authorities did not bother to give the Kyokai a name until sixteen years later and when they did so it was chosen by the Wajin and not by the Ainu. It took another fifteen years to change the name into one which the Ainu approved of.

The Kyokai does not have the confidence of the majority of the Ainu. Today the Kyokai has 15,500 Ainu members. This may seem to be a high number, if we consider that their official total is only 24,381 (*Hokkaido Registration Office* in Sapporo and Utari Kyokai 1988). Yet not even the Kyokai itself agrees to this, but states that the unofficial figure is "several times higher" (interview with Kyokai spokesman, 1988). According to Davis (1987: 18): "the Kyokai estimates that some 50-60,000 Ainu live in Nihon proper under various names and identities".

The Kyokai admits that the proportion of Ainu members is low and their explanation is the following:

> Many Ainu do not recognize themselves as Ainu descendants. This in turn has to do with the fact that the situation among the Ainu has improved. Further, the Ainu take advantage of the Kyokai as long as it serves their purposes, such as provided by organizations for health and welfare, where the Kyokai intervenes. When their goals are fulfilled, they resign. This indicates that the majority of the Ainu people are content with their situation. That the low figure could be linked to a distrust in the work done by the Kyokai is not likely (interview with Utari Kyokai spokesman, 1988).

The Ainu argue that the total figure presented by the Kyokai is as fictitious as the official one. In their opinion 250,000- 300,000 is a more realistic figure. The discrepancy in numbers is explained by them in the following way:

> As we see it, all those who have Ainu blood in their veins are Ainu. They must be, since they cannot be "Shamo" [Wajin], at least not if we consider the discriminatory rules that are practiced on this particular point (interview with Ainu male, aged 53, Hidaka, 1988).

Further, the Ainu have a somewhat different explanation for their low representation in the Kyokai and say:

> If the Ainu are poorly represented, it is because the Kyokai do not live up to the expectations of our people. Our people is of the opinion that the Kyokai should concentrate their efforts on the abolition of "Hokkaido Kyuudojin Hogoho", instead of working with "Counter Plans to a Proposal for Legislation Concerning the Ainu". These are nothing but half hearted attempts. In our opinion, the most

efficient way if one wants to improve our situation is to abolish this law. The only reason why this cannot be done is the fact that the Kyokai is dependent on the Wajin state, and since the ratio to which we Ainu rely on social welfare is so high, the Wajin state cannot justify its abolition, at least not as long we are perceived as a social unit. The only way to show our disapproval of the Kyokai is to resign, if registered, or not join if not (interview with Ainu male, aged 53, Hidaka, 1988).

The Ainu who are represented in the Kyokai agree with those who are not on the main issue, that is, the harm inflicted upon them by giving priority to welfare policy. When it comes to the criticism of *The Counter Plans*, they argue:

Since the Wajin does not approve of withdrawal, there is no prospect of getting rid of it [the law]. Presenting a counter plan is better than just accepting. Insisting on abolition does not help our case. Further, resigning from the Kyokai is foolish. Resigning does not solve our problems, rather the opposite. There must be more efficient methods to induce the Kyokai to serve our purposes. If we show our discontent by resigning, the existing dialogue – however one-sided it may appear at present – between ourselves and the Wajin will cease. If it is the opinion of the Kyokai that the low representation is due to improved conditions among our people, why not join by the thousand? After all, the Kyokai is the only institution-alized link between ourselves and the Wajin authorities (interview with Ainu male, aged 45, Chikabumi, 1988).

Compare also the following reply by Mr Saito, State Minister, to Mr Okada, an Ainu representative:

As you pointed out, "Hokkaido Kyuudojin Hogoho" has turned out a dead letter. I agree with you. At the same time I understand that some people are afraid of the government's possible indifference towards the welfare of the Ainu, when this Act is abolished. Also I think it reasonable to argue that such an Act should contradict with equality of all the people as prescribed under the present constitution (Utari Kyokai 1987b).

To demonstrate their disapproval of the Kyokai and the way it works, the Ainu have made several attempts to establish Kyokais of their own. Most have proved to be failures (Refsing 1980; Froome 1983; Sanders 1985). One exception is Ainu Kyokai in Asahikawa, Kamikawa province, established in 1973. The position of its initiator is:

Our members are experiencing antagonism to the Utari Kyokai administration. We are not satisfied with a Nihon organization of our own cultural values. Besides, as it is now, our people have the impression that the Kyokai work in the interest of the Kyokai and not in the interest of their own members (interview with one of the initiators, Chikabumi Kotan, 1985).

Today only fifty Ainu households are represented in this Kyokai, and about half of them are also Utari Kyokai members (information obtained in an interview with Utari Kyokai and Ainu Kyokai chairmen, 1988).

The Utari Kyokai's work with social issues and their efforts to help to transform the Ainu into self-awakened Nihonjin were, contrary to the prevalent expectations, to reveal a picture of an Ainu population objecting to the scientific interpretations of their own culture. Today the Ainu are critically studying foreign as well as Wajin writings about them:

> [Question, Mr Okada] Another point I would like to ask you for your view about their [Ainu] culture. The Ainu people have a very rich culture. One example of this is "Yukar", their oral tradition .... They now try to transcribe it for preservation purposes. "Uwepeker" [history] is another example.... [Answer, Mr Kuranai] As for Uwepeker I understand that 50 volumes had been completed .... by professor Mashiho Chiri. [Answer, Mr Okada] I am afraid that you have misunderstood. They have not yet been completed. With Professor Chiri it is a different matter. What I am talking about now is a complete new work ... Mr Kayano has been working with it. It is completely different from the work that was previously done (Dialogue between Mr Okada, Ainu representative, and Mr Kuranai, State Minister, March 5, 1973, Utari Kyokai 1987b).

Their main criticism is directed against the absence of an Ainu view of their own culture and customs. Such neglect of an internal view, they argue, leads to misreadings of the cultural tradition of the Ainu and to a historical perspective where the Ainu are used in contradistinction to the Wajin, in terms of uncivilized versus civilized.

TOURISM

Ironically, Ainu tourist centres came to constitute the basis for their cultural redress. The irony in this lies in the fact that these centres, in their initial shape, were more in accordance with commercial Nihonjin interests than with the interests of the Ainu. In the *Taisho* era, succeeding the *Meiji* and preceding the *Showa* era, the Ainu were described in the following way in a tourist guide:

> The Ainu people is now passing through the course its forefathers trod more than a century ago... The young Ainu people of today think it most humiliating to have any sightseeing to come to their villages. So the tourists are requested when going there to take this feeling into consideration. Under the circumstances there are little or no things in most of the villages that may smack of their tradition. The people have striven with one another in casting off their old customs and manners.

It is too late now to see the Ainu in their primitive state of life. We are sorry to have to say so....

Shiraoi and Tikabumi [old spelling for Chikabumi] are the only two Ainu tourist villages where sightseeing strangers are welcomed. Shiraoi has a railway station. If you alight there you will find some Ainu boys waiting for you. They will take you to one of their chieftain's houses to rest for some time and he expects some fee for his services. One yen will be enough....

There are three chieftain houses at Shiraoi. It is prearranged that sightseers who alight at the station could go to such a chieftain. Accordingly if you engage a guide you must follow his prearrangements. Excellent photos and postcards are on sale at shops and some kind of Ainu manufactures are also obtained....

Tikabumi, the outskirts of Asahikawa. The bus from the station will take you there. At Tikabumi an Ainu has been accustomed to receive sightseeing visitors for whose inspection he has built some old- fashioned houses. At Tikabumi an Ainu has built an Ainu Museum at his own expense for sightseeing visitors. Here is also an Ainu house of the antiquated style in which an old man and his wife are seen to live....

If you are prepared to pay money, you may perhaps be able to see a number of Ainu people dance and sing. But in the summer time most people are busy working, so you must be ready, if you want to see them dance and sing, to give them sake....

Many thoughtful Ainu people are ashamed to perform the old manners of their ancestors for money amidst the laughter of spectators. They consider it disrespectful to their forefathers. You are therefore requested, while looking at them to refrain from laughing without any reason, or assuming an attitude of mockery (*Tourist Guide to the Ainu Life*, Hokkaido Government 1927: 12 ff.).

Apart from the fact that the Ainu felt humiliated by the way in which their culture was exposed in these centres, which proves that they were not an Ainu initiative, there is no doubt that the main function of the centres was to increase the profit from tourism.

It was not until after the Second World War (Hilger 1967; Sanders 1985) that a large-scale Ainu participation in the tourist industry became a reality. The Ainu were encouraged by the Wajin authorities to reconstruct the villages of their formerly autonomous settlements, Kotan, and to reintroduce the Iyomante performances. At the time, former Ainu chiefs, Ekashi, were consulted. The Ekashi were given the title of Otona, introduced in the days of the Matsumae Han (Takakura 1960; Hilger 1967).

At this time Ainu Kotan were arranged according to a pattern that was supposed to have existed at the dawn of history, and this was presented "as the contemporary Ainu way of life". The way in which their culture was presented in these centres came to the Ainu to symbolize the final blow to the true essence of their cultural tradition. Not only did the centres present a static and ahistorical picture of the Ainu way of life, but the people who joined the centres did so for the sake of earning a living rather than for the sake of presenting a true picture of themselves and their culture.

On the surface, there still is much of this pattern that remains, and the tourist centres appear, at first glance, to be more oriented towards commercial Nihonjin interests. "Wajin and Ainu are in fact working side by side", as Hilger (1967) expressed it. Some of the Wajin who are working here are married to Ainu, others are Wajin who for some reason have difficulties in finding another type of job or else these Wajin have a genuine interest in Ainu culture and thus seek a living in the Ainu tourist centres.

From this angle the tourist centres as well as the high percentage (70%) of Ainu involved in agricultural activities seem to support a view of the assimilation as a success. At the most, the high percentage of Ainu relying on social welfare and the likewise high percentage of unemployed Ainu disturb the picture, but this, as a government official in Sapporo told me: "is due to the difficulty they have had in being able to catch up with development within a century" (interview, 1988).

If we accept the surface view and the explanation given to us by officials without further question, there seems to be little more to add. If we do not, we soon find tendencies pointing to the opposite direction. If we ask questions like: "What would you prefer to do for a living?" we find that in nine cases out of ten Ainu engaged in agricultural activities would have preferred to work with something else.

Furthermore, the majority of the children do not see agriculture as a preferable option in their future choice of occupation, nor do they think of working in the fishing and mining industries, driving trucks, digging ditches, and the like, as attractive alternatives. Instead many of them see a future for themselves in activities such as teaching Ainu history, language and culture.

For such reasons we may question "the picture of a successful assimilation" and start to look at the tourist centres from another angle. My study reveals a shift both in purpose and in attitude and I found that the people who work in these centres do not look upon their work here as just another job, nor do they agree that the main purpose of the tourist centre is still to present a folkloristic picture of Ainu practices and activities to tourists.

The change of the profile of the tourists centres took place when Wajin "intellectuals" (journalists and students), in connection with the centenary of Hokkaido's incorporation into the Nihon nation, initiated several destructive acts such as the bombing of historical Wajin monuments, the attempted murder of the Wajin mayor of Shiraoi and setting of fire to a tourist bureau. All this was done in professed sympathy with the Ainu (Refsing 1980; Sanders 1985).

It was, however, obvious that the Ainu had nothing to do with these acts, because those Ainu who were blamed at first and sent to prison were in fact soon released. This obviously unfair treatment affected the Ainu in several ways, apparent in the way in which the Ainu now took a stand against both "misguided sympathy", as it was expressed by the Wajin in the acts of violence, and against Wajin involvement and handling of Ainu affairs in general. Hence, after the violence conducted by misguided sympathizers, the tourist centres come to play another – and for the survival of Ainu culture – a more important role than before. The most apparent sign was the way Ainu now began organizing studies for Ainu interested in understanding their own culture. The movement took up studies of former places-names, oral literature and recitations, the teaching of "traditional" knowledge of Nature, the manufacturing of Ainu culture items, and the like. Equipped with this knowledge, the people working in the tourist centres began to present a different picture of their culture to the public. Hence, they and the people who work here are now looked upon, by Ainu, from a different angle than before.

Today the centres also function as places where Ainu feelings of common understanding and mutual belonging can be displayed. During one of my visits to the Akan tourist centre I overheard the following conversation between two Ainu women:

> Can you imagine, the other day a Shamo [Ainu word for Wajin] asked me if the "chise" [pointing at the house where she works, which consists of one big room with a fireplace at its centre] was my dwelling house. I said: "Yes me and my family and our six children live here" [the women has two grown up daughters]. Thinking of it I should have added our grandparents. How come the Shamo are so ignorant? We thought they were smart. "Wen guru" [stupid people]" (Akan tourist centre, 1988).

The main purposes of the tourist centres today, although the commercial aspects cannot be ignored, are to foster an awareness of Ainu idenity and to function as information centres. If we consider the time and effort that the Ainu spend on increasing their knowledge about their own culture we will also realize its contribution to an increased knowledge of the cultural tradition of the Ainu.

Those Ainu who work in the tourist centres are not only local people, but Ainu from all over Hokkaido. The tourist centres offer a manifold picture, because the Ainu who work here add local and regional variants of Ainu language and culture. Ainu who visit the centres recognize products coming from their own areas and they discuss and compare with those of other areas:

> What do you call this [pointing at some of the products]? Oh! where I come from we call it something else. Why do you call by that name? What kind of material do you use? Where I come from we use another type of material. Imagine, I did not know that we Ainu used different materials and called the products by different names (Shiraoi tourist centre, 1988).

Another example:

> I see you are using the same technique as a person from our village. Did she teach you how to weave "Saranip" [a kind of bag]? [Answer] No, I was taught this technique by one of her pupils. My mother and the person you are referring to

came from the same village. It took a great deal of time to learn, but now I am glad I did not give up. You are not the first person to ask me this question (Shiraoi tourist centre, 1988).

The manifold quality of Ainu activities and practices reveals itself in the different ways in which the Ainu at present approach their own culture. This in turn makes up the network among contemporary Ainu communities. The basis of knowledge obtained in this way allows for the assignment of specific tasks and activities.

These purposes are orchestrated in various ways. In some Ainu areas the emphasis is put on the natural environment and therefore these areas may function as national parks where local flora and fauna can be preserved. Areas where powerful Ainu Ekashi once lived may serve as "historical" meeting places. One example of this is Shizunai, the village where Shakushain, a powerful Ainu leader, once lived. In Shizunai Ainu from all over Nihon have gathered once a year since 1976 to take part in the celebration of Shakushain. Other areas may still function as "knowledge centres". An example of this is Nibutani in the Hidaka area. Nibutani is perhaps the best-known Ainu village in Hokkaido. John Batchelor, the missionary from Great Britain, lived there once, as did also Neil Munro, the doctor and archaeologist from the U.S.A. Pierre Naert, the French linguist, came here in 1960 and stayed for several months.

The violent Wajin "sympathy acts" resulted in the Ainu altering their own situation and henceforth the emphasis was put on ethnic issues. As they are different and feel that they are different, they also express a wish about how their problems, in their opinion, should best be treated. This was expressed by their Kyokai representative in the following way:

Their problems should be treated as the ethnic problems of ethnic minorities. This viewpoint must be firmly established and efforts must be directed in such a way that their ethnic uniqueness and potentials will be exercised to the full (Utari Kyokai 1987b).

Therefore their criticism addresses the assimilation policy of the government:

The government policy has been an assimilation policy. This policy was aimed to extinguish the Ainu, under the pretext of equality under the law (Utari Kyokai 1987b).

In conformity with the government policy, the official stance of the Nihon government is exemplified by its declaration to the United Nations in 1980. It reads:

There are no minorities in Nihon to which article 27 of section III [the article which defines minorities and guarantees them freedom to practice their own religion and speak their own language] of the international Covenant on Human rights refers (Utari Kyokai 1987b).

According to Davis: "not recognizing Article 27 of Section III is more of political concern than of cultural and the real problem is money", and he continues:

> if the Japanese government recognize the Ainu as a people, then it will have to come up with a cultural definition which would mean a doubling or tripling of the financial support it would have to pay to these people. Instead, the Japanese government would rather ignore the Ainu hoping they'll be culturally assimilated (1987: 19).

The Ainu also relate their own unfavourable position to politics, which they claim is rooted in the Wajin belief in the political and economic power of a homogeneous population which they term Nihonjin and who according to them is the "result of the intermingling of various indigenous groups". With a non-existent cultural definition of the Ainu, their distinct culture is recognized as a variant of the Wajin culture and it is from this starting point that their situation has been analysed.

Today the Ainu not only question "scientific" works about themselves, but they present their own version. Further, they devote a considerable amount of their time and effort to coming to terms with the ignorance, not only of their own people but also of the Wajin. In 1973 they edited a monthly journal called *Anutari Ainu*. This journal was edited by a prominent Ainu representative and its main purpose was, according to the initiator himself: "to raise the public opinion in favour of the Ainu people" (interview, 1985):

> In the journal it was strongly stressed, month after month, that the Ainu are against the continuation of the protection law, a proposition supported by Hokkaido Utari Kyokai. However this plea, along with others, such as the abandonment of a segregated registration system, was in vain (interview with the initiator, 1985).

At the beginning of 1976 *Anutari Ainu* was declared to have been not as successful as expected and distribution stopped. According to the editor himself: "distribution stopped because of lack of both Nihon approvement and support" (interview, 1985). He continues:

> Attempts to try and alter conditions did not stop with this defeat. On the contrary, it helped increase our resistance against the governmental policy of maintaining the protection law in their own interest....
>
> Unfortunately these aims, although shared by all, turned out to divide our people into groups and factions, due to different views of how to achieve these ends. It frequently turned out that these often small and short-lived groups were established in an initial state of optimism about the future. They often existed side by side, the one unaware of the aims of the others, which by the way often

coincided. They emerged and reemerged according to the shifts in the profiles of the different groups, all because the sensitivity of the Nihon establishment towards world opinion....

I would stress, however, that the opinions differ among our people as to whether these differences are a negative factor. They can also, according to some of us, be seen as signs of real strength which in the long run could contribute to enabling a united Ainu people to receive strong support on specific issues as well as the more general ones. Until now, the majority of our people tend to have relied on Nihon "good-will" and hope for equal rights in a foreseeable future....

Some of our people also stress that it might be positive to deal with Ainu affairs in a more "individually specific" way. By individualizing our problem, it may in the long term contribute to a neutralization of our lower status vs. the Wajin. This would be an internalization of our culture which we would then continue to maintain "in private"....

However, some of our people are uncertain of this ever becoming a reality and are not in agreement. For them the only solution is to unite our people so that strong and united we can put sufficient pressure behind our claims. The most important issue is to achieve equal rights and equal opportunities and to realize these aims in a society which is dominated by an ethnic group other than the one to which we belong....

We do not want, and most important we do not need a segregated welfare system, which divides us into classes and status groups (interview, 1985).

The situation of the Ainu in Nihon is apparently somewhat different from that of other indigenous peoples and, as has been pointed out by Cornell (1964: 296): "the colonization of Hokkaido had little in common with for instance the European colonization of America". After all, Hokkaido was not an unknown country to the Wajin. On the contrary, interaction between the Wajin and the Ainu had been frequent for several hundred years.

THE AINU AS AN INTERNATIONAL ENTITY

Nihon is a signatory to one and has ratified four of the twenty-one instruments of which the United Nations' Human Rights International Instruments is composed. Those ratified are: (1) the International Covenant on Economic, Social and Cultural Rights (E.S.C.R), (2) the International Covenant on Civil and Political Rights (C.P.R.), (3) the Convention on Political Rights of Women and (4) the Convention for the Suppression of the Traffic in Persons and of the Exploitation of the Prostitution of Others. The one to which Nihon is a signatory is the Convention on the Elimination of all Forms of Discrimination against Women (*Human Rights International Instruments*, United Nations 1981: 8-9).

The Universal Declaration of Human Rights deals with civil, political, social and economic rights and it asserts that:

> All Human beings are born free and equal in dignity and rights... and that everyone is entitled to all the rights and freedoms set forth in the Declaration without distinction of any kind such as race, color, sex, language, religion, political or other option, national or social origin, property, birth or other status. Furthermore, it states that no distinction is to be based on the international status of the country or territory to which the persons belong, thus making it clear that the Declaration applies to all non-self-governing territories (Goodrich 1974: 165-166).

As a member of the UN, Nihon agrees to abide by the Universal Declaration of Human Rights, and membership in the UN implies that Nihon must ensure such basic rights as life, liberty, equal protection under the law, freedom from slavery, freedom of thought, freedom from arbitrary arrest, freedom of religion, employment, social security, the right to own property, equal pay for equal work and education (*International Bill of Human Rights*, United Nations 1978: 4-9).

Such basic rights as described above are applicable to all people living in Nihon, the Ainu included. In the Ainu case there is a problem since the covenants can only be as effective as the member states permit. In theory, if the E.S.C.R. and the C.P.R. were strictly and seriously enforced, it could lead both to a re-examination of the status of the Ainu as Nihon nationals, whose social and cultural development has included the deterioration of "traditional" customs and beliefs and to a return to tribal or village autonomy for the Ainu:

> All people have the right to self-determination, by virtue of this right they freely determine their political status and freely pursue their economic, social and cultural development (*International Bill of Human Rights*, United Nations 1978: 10-11).

> All people may, for their own ends, freely dispose of the natural wealth and resources without prejudice to any obligations arising out of international economic co-operation, based on the principle of mutual benefit, and international law. In no case may a people be deprived of its means of subsistence (ibid: 22).

However the covenants do not deal with the rights of a group of people, their main emphasis being individual rights and in the Ainu case the rights of the individual do not necessarily assure the rights of a group with its own needs, especially since the Ainu are not officially recognized as a distinct group by the authorities in Nihon.

The Convention on the Prevention and Punishment of the Crime of Genocide (1948), has not been ratified by the Nihon authorities although Article II of this convention is applicable to the Ainu. According to Brownlie's definition of this article:

In the present Convention, genocide means any of the following acts committed with intent to destroy, in whole or in part, a national ethnic, racial or religious group, such as: a) Killing members of the group: b) Causing serious bodily or mental harm to members of the group: c) Deliberately inflicting on the group conditions of life calculated to bring about its physical destruction in whole or in part: d) Imposing measures intended to prevent births within the group: e) Forcibly transferring children of the group to another group (1971: 117).

Although Nihon may not physically be killing the Ainu, assimilation policies in general tend to cause an erosion of customs and values that belong to indigenous peoples. The Ainu are no exception. On the contrary following Refsing we learn that:

The Japanization of the Ainu has not brought racial equality – neither economic nor social. The racial prejudice of the Japanese is still strong enough to keep the Ainu people in an inferior position.... Poverty is still a basic feature.... Unemployment is the fate for the majority of those Ainu who are not permanently engaged in farming or fishing.... Almost no Ainu are employed in the liberal professions (1980: 87).

This negative and dark picture has not worked to convince the authorities in Nihon of the necessity to ratify the Convention on the Prevention and Punishment of the Crime of Genocide. The reason why they have not done this can only be explained by the fact the authorities in Nihon deny that there is a native problem. If a native problem is non-existent in Nihon, one could always argue as Froome does:

If there is not a native problem in Japan, what would be lost by ratifying this Convention? Surely ratification would be a constructive diplomatic and political maneuver. Lack of ratification of the Genocide Convention, coupled with the non-ratification of numerous other UN instruments,[1] indicate that there exist "ethnical, racial and religious problems" with which the Japanese government refuses to come to terms (1983: 84).

Although a ratification of this convention according to Froome would be "a constructive diplomatic and political maneouver" the authorities in Nihon obviously do not share this view. In Ainu opinion this has to do with the fact that the position of the authorities in Nihon is that the disadvantages of doing so do not outweigh the advantages.

---

1   Such as: Optional Protocol to the International Covenant on Civil and Political Rights, The International Covenant on the Elimination of All Forms of Racial Discrimination (Froome 1983: 63).

Today the Ainu have only individual rights. Their rights as a people are non-existent, simply because the authorities in Nihon do not recognize distinct ethnic groups within their national context.

For the same reasons Ainu plans to establish national parks, education centres, and the like, have been reduced to a means of fulfilling personal commercial interests. According to this view their attempts to improve their situation are recognized as small-scale enterprises, disguised in the shape of charismatic leaders who are liable to put forth "personal" interpretations of the Ainu language, history and culture, obtained either through personal experiences or through interviews with local Ainu people and presented in the form of novels rather than scientific works. Nevertheless, unofficially such measures can be taken, although they cannot be given official recognition. The possibility that the Ainu actually use their knowledge and skills as an instrument or a means to gain recognition as a people cannot be dismissed simply because this does not fit the official ideology in Nihon.

With respect to the minorities in Nihon, if the authorities had it their way, they would be non-existent. In an article in the *Tokyo Journal*, October 1987, Masler provides us with the following information:

> Even the beginning student of Japanese is regularly instructed that "Japan is an island country inhabited by a homogeneous population". This geographic myth portrays a distant, isolated people of unique characteristics. Free of the racial conflicts of U.S. or the Fremdarbeiter deluge of West Germany, the newly industrialized giant of the Far East is represented as a quiet land of mutual acceptance. A phenomenally low rate in violent crime is often cited as evidence of the nation's unity and the absence of prejudice. In truth, from 3%-6% of Japan's population consists of minorities. Though these groups may not be forced to ride in the backs of buses, segregation and discrimination here exist in a quiet, yet pervasive form (Masler 1987: 14).

Utari Kyokai is not unaware of this and their efforts to alter the situation are expressed in *The Proposed Ainu Law* (1988). It reads:

> The Ainu problem is a by-product of the modernization process underway in Japan. It challenges the basic human rights guaranteed under the Japanese Constitution. The government should bear the responsibility to solve the problem by abolishing the discriminatory Law for the Protection of Native Hokkaido Aborigines of 1899 (LPNHA) and establishing a new law, which should contain the following basic provisions....
>
> 1. *Basic Human Rights:* Ainu have suffered for many years explicit racial discrimination and as a result, have suffered great setbacks in education, social and economic activities. The purpose of the new law should therefore be the abolition of all forms of discrimination against Ainu....

2. *Rights of Participation:* Even since the Meiji Restoration, the Ainu have been officially called "Aborigine" or "Former Aborigine", and thus discriminated against. There is no need to mention the discrimination prior to the Meiji Restoration. In order to restore Ainu dignity, the needs of the Ainu population must be represented in national and local parliaments....

3. *Education and Culture:* The national policy of discrimination based upon LPNHA not only directly infringes upon the Ainu's basic rights but also promotes discriminating behavior by the general public and, in doing so, discourages the young Ainu's attempt to educate themselves and to learn about their own culture, thus keeping them in a socially and economically inferior state. Therefore the government should: a) Implement a general policy for the education of the Ainu youth; b) Formulate a plan, as a part of the above policy, to teach the Ainu youth the Ainu language; c) Abolish discrimination against Ainu in school and social education; d) Establish university courses in the Ainu language, culture and history, employing capable Ainu people as professors, associate professors and instructors. They should be unhampered by existing codes and given special assistance in encouraging Ainu youth to take these courses; e) Establish a national institute, actively participated in by the Ainu scholars, to study and support the Ainu language and culture ['Ainu studies so far have been carried on unilaterally by non-Ainu scholars and do not reflect Ainu thinking, rendering Ainu into mere objects of study']; f) Re-evaluate and correct the method used to transmit and preserve Ainu culture....

4. *Agriculture, Forestry, Fishery, Commerce and Industry:* The LPNHA originally set aside approximately five hectares of land for every Ainu family willing to cultivate it. However, discriminatory articles exist which make it hard for the Ainu to carry on farming. A lack of understanding for Ainu living conditions prevents the government from developing a coherent policy for fishery, forestry, commerce and industry. A policy more suited to present-day reality must be established by first abolishing LPNHA (Utari Kyokai 1988).

The Ainu are not content with this new law. Their position is "a special law for us, no matter what it says, singles us out and makes us more vulnerable to discriminatory acts."

With this general background I will, in the next chapter, proceed to examine the present-day situation of the Ainu and consider the strategies they use in order to come to terms with it.

CHAPTER SEVEN

Mr Ainu

In this chapter I focus particularly on the strategies used by the Ainu in coming to terms with their present-day situation. Emphasis will be placed on their attempts to be recognized as an ethnic entity by attaching a face to their culture. The title "Mr Ainu" is chosen to illustrate that the effort to gain cultural recognition in general is used to gain recognition as a people in particular. In order to comprehend this I have chosen to relate Ainu methods to the larger context within which they live and operate.

To understand their efforts to gain equal opportunities and equal rights in Nihon, I have incorporated the viewpoint of both the ordinary man or woman in the street and those Wajin who are engaged in matters concerning the Ainu, that is, scholars and authorities, because their viewpoints reflect the premises that govern the context of the larger society.

This chapter is divided into three parts. In the first part, Wajin attitudes to the situation of the Ainu and the cultural mobilization that takes place among them will be presented. The main concern here is to show that their attitudes correspond to a reality that exists among themselves. In the second part of this chapter I deal with statistics about the Ainu. My concern is to show that official statistics on the Ainu serve to depict an ideal situation and that the actual conditions of the Ainu are somewhat different. In the third part I will present the ways in which the Ainu practise their ethnicity in Nibutani, my fieldwork base. Here my concern is to show that for the Ainu the act of putting emphasis on cultural artifacts creates an image of themselves as an ethnic entity.

WAJIN ATTITUDES

To most people in Nihon, the Ainu are largely unknown. They have only vague ideas about who the Ainu are or what the concept Ainu stands for. This became obvious when I tried to get a comment from the man or woman in the street.

In my material, representatives of this category include friends and fellow workers of my Wajin assistant. When asked for a comment about the situation of the Ainu and their present interest in ethnic features, they were indifferent and answered that they had never given the Ainu a thought. Some of them did not even know who the Ainu are. When I explained that the Ainu are a people who have lived in Hokkaido since ancient

FIGURE 9   *Learning Ainu dance in the city of Asahikawa*

times they said: "Oh! you mean those 'bear people'. They used to catch bears and such things. I do hope they are more civilized now".

Such attitudes in combination with the attitudes of the Wajin who are involved in Ainu matters, such as scholars, researchers, authorities and the like, reflect that their views of the Ainu and their situation correspond to a picture of a successful Ainu assimilation of them. At worst, people deny that there is a change in Ainu attitudes to the policy of assimilation, at best this change is recognized but ascribed minor importance. There is also a tendency to interpret their current interest in values and beliefs rooted in their culture as folklore.

Speaking in general terms, their position is that: "nowadays the Ainu and the Wajin think in the same way, that the Ainu have come to accept that they belong to the same cultural tradition as the Wajin and that Ainu leaders, or spokesmen, have taken upon themselves to work for an improvement of the conditions of their people that corresponds to the official view", and further: "that present-day emphasis on themselves as a distinct ethnic group and the attendant claims of ethnic status are trends that will blow over". In addition, according to them, "the low percentage of Ainu who register as Ainu shows that the majority of them have accepted the non-ethnic premises of state ideology as described by the highest authority".

To give a general overview of how the Wajin see the situation of the Ainu today, I have chosen to present their views with the help of representative extracts from interviews. My main concern is to show that their position reflects a picture of the reality that exists among the Ainu which is far removed from the reality in which they actually live. The interviews are unstructured, which means that I did not comment, interrupt or insert additional questions.

A Wajin scholar, female, aged 43, doing research on the Ainu oral tradition:

You say you are going to stay in Nibutani. Then there are a couple of things useful for you to know. First, since Nibutani is located in the southeast, the Ainu people living here have been in contact with our people for a very long time and therefore the Wajin influence is strong. For such reasons these people are closer to our way of thinking than to the Ainu way. Besides, the people living here are more concerned with fulfilling their own personal interests than fulfilling the interests of their own people....

Ainu people from the south/southeastern regions, the regions you have chosen, are those who have leading position in Utari Kyokai. Mr Nomura comes from Shiraoi and he is the chief of Utari Kyokai in Sapporo. Mr Kaizawa comes from Nibutani and he is the deputy chief. Finally, Mr Kayano also comes from Nibutani. He is very influential in the Kyokai, although he does not have an official status within it. He is what we call an "honourable member", which means that he has, in fact, the most power. These people are "Wajin-friendly" and their efforts to improve things for the Ainu people in general are their own professional myth. What they actually do is to improve the situation of their own people in their own regions, Iburi and Hidaka, in general and their own situation in particular. You see these people are not only advisers to the Utari Kyokai but they also have the power to take decisions. The board of the Kyokai decides on what purposes the funds they have received are to be spent. For such reasons the funds go to whatever purposes the board decides. For the most part the funds are spent on Ainu tourist centres. Remember all three of the board members are involved in tourism. This is considered unfair by those Ainu people who are not engaged in tourism and who, as you know, are in the majority. This is not coincidental, I mean that the majority of the Ainu are engaged in other occupations. The majority of the Ainu do not approve of the way these centres display the traditional values of Ainu customs and beliefs. It is their belief that the Ainu people who work here do so because there are no other jobs available for them. We usually say if you get involved in Ainu tourism once, there are no other choices for the future. People will not hire you. Consequently, because the board members are involved in tourism, the money which could be spent on valuating and dating the culture items, exhibited in the various exhibition halls throughout Hokkaido, so these halls could be given an official status, goes to tourism....

Take Nibutani. In the 1970s it was decided that Nibutani should become a tourist centre. It was a decision taken above many people's heads and therefore the village people were divided into those for and those against. This division remains. In Nibutani today there is one group consisting of people engaged in the rural sector and one group consisting of people engaged in tourism. As you know, Nibutani tourism did not turn out a success and now there are plans to make Nibutani an "Ainu Knowledge Centre". My personal opinion is that this is Utopia, because the people living here have, as I told you, more in common with our way of life than with the Ainu way of life. The things they know they have read in some book. As a result they can only give you information about things they have obtained through books (interview in Sapporo, 1988).

Another Wajin scholar, male, aged 53, involved in the present Ainu situation:

It is very hard to obtain information from the Ainu. The Ainu do not like to be studied. One of our people, a researcher from the Chiba University in Tokyo, went to Nibutani to do research about the material culture of the Ainu. She was unable to finish her studies because of her Wajin origin. The Ainu people in Nibutani are very hostile to researchers of Wajin descent. This is because their studies mostly give a very negative picture of the Ainu, that is, depict them as "hairy apes" [Kodama] or else as a "proto-Wajin" type [Tsuboi, Koganei etc.]. Since not only Wajin people have – or should I say present – this picture, the Ainu, unfortunately for yourself, do not like foreigners either. Their experiences with foreigners are much the same as their experiences with our own people. Take for instance Hilger [1967], Landor [1893] and Munro [1962]. Their studies have inflicted much harm on the Ainu. Further, and this may not be easy to take seriously, but you'd better, at least for your own sake. Some Ainu people think that USSR are sending spies to Hokkaido, there are some unclear threats. The Ainu think that these spies pose as researchers but in reality they are spying. In Nibutani in particular people are sensitive, because here some of the Ainu have spent many years in Russian captivity. This was in connection with the Second World War....

My personal advice to you is that you try to obtain as much information as you can from our people. Museums and universities are open to you and we will do our utmost to answer your questions. There is no need to "go out in the bush". Besides, the people in Nibutani are divided into two groups. The one, consisting of young people, are for Mr Kayano and his efforts to turn Nibutani into a "Knowledge Center", a fancy word, tourist centre is more appropriate. The other group, consisting of elderly people, are against this development. What you have is one group of pro Mr Kayano people and one group of anti Mr Kayano people.

FIGURE 10   *The celebration of Shakushain*

No matter how eagerly you try you are bound to have about half of the Nibutani people against you. As a result your presence will disturb the order and you may be thrown out of the village. If you are thinking of leaning on Mr Kayano's shoulder, you should know that he is not very popular outside his own circle and this may create hardship for you not only in Nibutani but also in Shiraoi and Akan. As you know, the Ainu people will answer your question with this knowledge in their minds. People who are anti Mr Kayano will either not speak to you or they will give you wrong, misleading, information on purpose. It is very difficult indeed. Mr Kayano likes to think of himself as a modern Ainu hero, like Shakushain, and he often speaks about how much effort he himself expends on uniting the Ainu people, making them feel proud of their Ainu origins etc. This is not a lie, he has. However, what worries people is that he seems to be more concerned with gaining personal power than with gaining power for his own people. We tend to say that Mr Kayano is world famous in Nibutani. Nevertheless my personal opinion is that Mr Kayano, if anyone, has the power to come up with some real changes with respect to the present discriminatory Wajin attitude against the Ainu and this is very important, since, as you know, the Ainu are not just seeking recognition as a distinct ethnic group, but they are also striving to gain equal status with the Wajin. In order to achieve this, the Ainu have to convince the Wajin that their culture is not just a primitive variant of our culture. This is not very easily done and that is why few of our people think it is possible. Our people are very proud of their Wajin origin. But this is not the only reason. You see, in Japan people feel uncomfortable if they are not included in a group. Today they belong to companies of different types, previously they belonged to Daiymou or Shogun. The Meiji restoration is a change of name actually, not a change of system. We work in the same company all our lives. We belong to the company. Furthermore we do, in fact, have the same position all our lives. I mean it is not very easy to climb or advance. I am not saying that it is impossible but that it is hard. Often we have contracts which state that if we want to advance we also have to change our residence. You know what that means. It means you have to move to another district, maybe you have children who are attending school, they do not want to move. Many people do not move but stay for the rest of their lives in the same branch office (interview in Hakodate, 1988).

Government official, male, aged 34:

I hear you are studying the present-day Ainu situation. I am proud to say that things have changed for them. Our figures show that Ainu choose anonymity. This is good. It reveals that there is little need for special treatment. For a long time now we have suspected that the Ainu made use of their Kyuudojin status only to gain special rights, such as funds for their children for higher education, welfare money for themselves, and so on and so forth. Since the majority of the Ainu now choose anonymity this is a step in the right direction. As a representative of the government I think I am entitled to flatter myself. Things have changed, and I wonder if there actually is "an Ainu problem" anymore. Discrimination is practically non-existent these days. In an area such as Nibutani in Hidaka region there is according to recent statistics no discrimination at all....

We do have some minor problems, of course. I will give you one example. In Hokkaido there are as you know 212 cho. The Ainu register in at least 70 of these but they have representatives in 9 only. The Ainu want, however, to have representatives in the chos where they live but this is very hard to implement. Our constitution has to be altered in such a case and the government is not willing to take such a step and select or give Ainu special rights in this matter. In my opinion this is also an unrealistic claim and my job is to convince the Ainu that it is not possible to take such a step. After all, in a couple of years there is no need for such a claim. By then, the Ainu problem will be solved. You asked me if the Ainu problem was not actually a Wajin problem, not the other way round. Well I do not know if I follow you. If you mean that we are the trouble-makers, I must correct you. We have done our utmost for the Ainu, you see, and it speaks for itself that this unfavourable situation of theirs is due to the difficulty they have had in only being able to catch up with development within a century. We are well aware of that, and our responsibility is that of 'giving a helping hand'. For one thing, they have a special welfare organization dealing with their problems exclusively. If there is no problem, then we would not establish this organization for them. Besides, it is thanks to such measures that we actually can state that there are practically no problems anymore. Now, let me think what other problems do we have with them. I cannot think of any for the moment. You see, most Ainu people want to be left alone. They are not interested in other people prying into their life. I hope you excuse me. You asked me about their employment situation, right? Of course we have a high rate of unemployed Ainu, 15 per cent at the moment. But mind you, our people also have difficulties in finding jobs. It is hard times for all of us. The Ainu are no exception to the rule. Besides, the Ainu have the protection law to take care of their interests, our people do not have such special treatment. I do not say that we should abolish this law, how could we, they are our responsibility. The intention of the law is to protect them. Even Mr Kayano agrees with this. Without the law things would be bad indeed. Mind you, I know of the alteration proposed by him in cooperation with Utari Kyokai. Well for the moment we are biding our time. We must wait and see. Besides, I am not convinced that his ambition is to have the Ainu separated from our people. They are a variant of our people, culturally there are many similarities. Surely you know that, and we are hoping that Mr Kayano's work will help Ainu people realize this connection. For the moment it may seem as if his efforts actually work in the opposite direction. I am convinced this is widely exaggerated. It is simply a trend which will blow over in no time. I mean, as it is now Mr Kayano's attempt, if understood as efforts for the Ainu people to be recognized as a distinct entity, can hardly be taken seriously, considering the fact that the majority of our Ainu population actually are engaged in the rural sector. I, and many Ainu people with me, agree with this. You have to look at his work for what it actually is. His work is nothing but a folkloristic enterprise on a rather small scale (interview in Sapporo, 1988).

Before discussing what these interviews actually reveal some comments are required about the negative attitude to my planned stay among the Ainu and also the advice that "I should concentrate on information obtained from 'our people'", as one of my informants expressed himself.

With respect to this, one gets the impression that there is a wish, if not to control, then at least to influence my investigation. This may indicate that there is a certain ambiguity about their own investigations into the situation of the Ainu – as if they are uncertain of the result of my study if I pay too much attention to the Ainu view. After all, their own investigations take little consideration of the view of the Ainu. Not only are they aware of this, they even think that an incorporation of the view of the Ainu is superfluous.

There is, of course, also the possibility that they are expressing the views of the authorities and officials, rather than their own. Anyhow, the attitudes expressed in the interviews are those which they choose to present, whatever their intention or aim might have been.

Now, what do these interviews actually reveal? In a way the message is fairly clear. The development that is occurring among the Ainu is at the most a "trend that will blow over" and there seems to be little evidence of an opposing view worth bothering about. In short, the essence of the cultural mobilization is recognized as folklore. Above all, the interviews reveal an obvious lack of "Ainu input", in the sense that the way in which the Ainu use their skills and knowledge is depicted, or understood, as means to advance (or gain a position) on terms stated or dictated by the majority population. The interests of the Ainu are thus not seen to go against the interests of the nation as a whole and the Ainu are understood to be acting for mutual national interests. Consequently the ambition of Ainu spokesmen like Kayano is to point out similarities between the Ainu culture and the dominant culture in Nihon.

This view is of course related to the official ideology in Nihon. Bearing in mind that homogeneity is considered to be of the utmost importance for the prosperity of the nation and the well-being of its subjects there is neither room for ethnic claims, such as ethnic status for the Ainu, nor for alternative land use, such as the replacement of imported economies with economies tied to values and ideologies rooted in the Ainu culture. According to this view the Ainu are properly assimilated and their situation is improved. The Ainu have the same rights as everybody else and they do not arm themselves to rebel against the system. Above all, the majority of the Ainu are engaged in agricultural activities – they no longer practise their former lifestyles so the possibility that they may actually revert altogether is minimal. Ainu attempts to improve their situation are understood and analized with the help of explanatory tools belonging to a model where the focus is on mutual national interests. Consequently, the measures taken by the Ainu to attain the rights of a people can be neither understood nor recognized as such. The perspective of the Wajin is one that sees the situation of the Ainu as a more or less unproblematic fusion of assimilation and maintenance of the values of the Ainu. It reveals an obvious lack of focus on the situation of the Ainu as it actually is and it overlooks the possibility that the actions taken by the Ainu may correspond to premises that govern the reality of the Ainu. After all, the rights the Ainu are fighting for are not recognized in the larger context. This gives us reason to believe that the measures taken by the Ainu do not correspond to the premises that govern the larger context, especially since the Ainu are against these premises and work to alter them.

By using an approach where the focus is on the reality that exists among the Ainu and by using explanatory tools that belong to their reality, we shift focus from the Wajin to the Ainu. Such a shift of focus is highly relevant, especially when considering official statistics on the Ainu and how they are used. At present, official statistics serve to depict a more or less ideal situation, rather than the situation as it actually is to the Ainu.

Since "an ideal picture", that is, a successful assimilation, finds its strongest support in (a) the low percentage of Ainu registered as Ainu and (b) the fact that the majority of the Ainu at present are engaged in the rural sector, I will focus on these two issues.

STATISTICS

Official statistics on the Ainu population in Hokkaido are based on free choice, that is, the Ainu can choose whether they want to register as Ainu or not. The official definition is consanguinity, or by marriage, including adopted children.

Today the Ainu people who choose to register as Ainu amount to 24,381. Of these 42.6% live in the Hidaka region, 27.0% in the Iburi region, 8.6% in the Kushiro region, 7.9% in the Ishikari region, 4.8% in the Nemuro region, 4.0% in the Tokachi region, 2.4% in the Oshima region, 1.5% in the Kamikawa region and finally 0.1% in the Sorachi, Rumoi and Souya regions. Hence, Ainu people live in twelve of the fourteen regions of which Hokkaido is made up and we find the highest percentage of Ainu in the Hidaka, Iburi and Kushiro regions.

Among the Ainu people of today 60.9% rely on welfare for their survival (Wajin 21.9%), 85.2% of them feel that they are discriminated against (marriages, society, job and education) (44.8% of the Wajin think that the Ainu are discriminated against) 78.4% have graduated from junior high (six years) (Wajin 94.0%), 8.1% have graduated from high school (nine years) (Wajin 27.4%). Only 2.0% of the Ainu have attended university.

The percentage of Ainu who are engaged in agricultural activities, including the industrial sector and construction, amounts to 71.9%. (In the statistics there is no differentiation between the sectors, that is, agriculture, industry and construction. All are included under the heading "Agriculture", which makes it impossible to find out the percentage belonging to each of the different sectors. The explanation seems to be that the Ainu under this heading alternate between the three sectors, which according to a government representative makes registration difficult.) Ainu people who find a living in the tourist industry or service amount to 29.1%. Unemployment is 15.2% (Seminar in Ainosato,[1] Mr Tsunemoto, Professor of Law, 1988; see also *A Proposal for Legislation Concerning the Ainu*, Hokkaido Government 188: 4 ff.).

Since the statistics are based on an Ainu population of 24,381, a figure which according to the Ainu ought to be around 300,000 they are, in Ainu opinion, hardly worth bothering about. Furthermore, the Ainu say that their unwillingness to register as Ainu reflects their disapproval of the ways in which their situation is officially handed.

Since there are two different ways of looking at the situation of the Ainu, (a) from the point of view of the Ainu and (b) from the point of view of the Wajin, there are also two different pictures of their actual situation. In case (a) it is the conditions in which the Ainu live that create difficulties for them. The nation to which they belong is an artificial

---

1   The name Ainosato has no connection with Ainu.

fusion of different cultures and peoples and the terms on which it is founded derive from the assumption that there is only one ethnic group in the nation as a whole. The Ainu do not approve of this. They are not willing to give up their own cultural uniqueness, nor are they content that their land and natural resources are used for corn, rice and bean cultivation, cattle and racehorse breeding or other crops and economies introduced from Nihon proper.

Their strategy for an alteration of their situation comprises attempts to getting to know their own history and culture. This includes attempts to revive old-time ideologies and values. This is achieved by reorganizing Ainu tourist villages – a change in the profile of these, so that they function as information centres for Ainu with an interest in their own culture, that is, places where not only material needs are fulfilled but also social and cultural ones. Here Ainu feelings of common understanding and mutual belonging are displayed. In these villages the Ainu are given opportunities to participate in lessons about Ainu history, language and culture, learn about Ainu dances and Ainu wood-carving techniques, how to prepare Ainu dishes, how to manufacture Ainu-style garments and the like. Knowledge obtained in this way, allows, in turn, for the assignment of specific tasks and activities tied to the culture of the Ainu, like the establishment of national parks and the introduction of Ainu crops and vegetables. All this is done in correspondence with a view of themselves as a distinct ethnic group. The strategy is used to separate themselves from other cultures that exist within the larger context.

In the other case (b) it is the premisses that governed the context of what is defined as their "traditional" way of life that create difficulties for them making it hard for them to adjust themselves to the new conditions.

The strategy of the authorities is one of assimilation. Hence, the values that belong to the Ainu are de-emphasized. The low percentage of Ainu actually registered is regarded as a sign that the policy of assimilation is a success. Another sign interpreted thus is the way the Ainu exploit their land and natural resources today. In this way the functions of the Ainu are seen as fundamentally adaptive to the national reproductive process.

According to statistics, the majority of the Ainu have deserted activities and practices that existed prior to the annexation of their land and adapted themselves to a model introduced by the authorities in Nihon. Statistics have been used as an indicator of the fact that the majority of them are fulfilling the interests of the nation, since the ambition of the authorities in Nihon was, and still is, to transform the Ainu into farmers.

However, statistics on their occupational situation only reveal that those Ainu who are engaged in the rural sector have adapted themselves occupationally. They do not reveal whether this is by choice or a necessity, nor do they reveal whether the Ainu, if given an opportunity, would actually use their land and natural resources in the same way. The possibility that Ainu and Wajin opinions differ on these matters remains and therefore there is also a possibility that their occupational adaption is a necessity rather than a choice of their own. According to a representative of the government, "the high percentage of Ainu engaged in the rural sector does not contradict the possibility of choice. Besides 'choice' is a luxury very few of us enjoy" (interview in Sapporo, 1988).

From this point of view, there is little evidence that the Ainu who are engaged in the rural sector are likely to use their skills and knowledge as means to exploit Hokkaido land and natural resources in other interests than those of the nation. Within the same perspective it seems relatively safe to assume that, henceforth, tourist centres, museums, exhibition halls and the like, will actually remain the only possible forum for the survival of the Ainu culture.

From an Ainu point of view we have reason to believe that this is not the case. After all, the majority of the Ainu engaged in the rural sector do not own the land themselves. It is owned either by Honshu companies or else it comes under common property. The Ainu only work on it.

This is a factor that requires some of our attention, especially if we consider the different suggestions made by them in *A Counter Plan to a Proposal for Legislation Concerning the Ainu People* (Utari Kyokai 1984, 1987a). One proposal is directed towards a change of the management of common property and seeks the permission of the Hokkaido governor to sell granted land, that is, land "returned" to the Ainu with the annexation of Hokkaido in 1868.

In the proposals the Ainu express wishes to use part of Hokkaido land in other ways, such as national parks and knowledge centres and for different purposes, that is, cultural, instead of purely commercial ones as is the case today. Since the guidelines for the proposals presented in the plans are the work of Kayano, a presentation of this man and his work is required.

MR SHIGERU KAYANO

Mr Shigeru Kayano's interest in his own Ainu inheritance, his concern for, and his work with the values and beliefs of the Ainu, have inspired many Ainu to follow his example. Today we find Ainu all over Hokkaido who are helping to create a manifold picture of the values and ideologies of the Ainu. Today Kayano is not only commonly accepted as a virtual authority on Ainu matters, but he is also the embodiment of the entire Ainu culture, that is, "Ainu personified".

This is an image created as much by his interest and work with Ainu matters as by his frequent appearances on television and radio where he acts as an official representative of the Ainu people. This combination will possibly serve to replace previous stereotyped opinions about the people he represents with more accurate ones.

To the Ainu the combination has already served similar purposes, in the sense that many of them now take both pride and interest in their own cultural inheritance, something which was unthinkable some decades ago, when the majority of the Ainu spent most of their time and effort in hiding their Ainu origins.

PERSONAL HISTORY[2]

In 1953, due to the loss of the family treasure *Ikupasuy* – his father gave it to a foreign scholar in return for sake – Kayano's interest in his own culture took a concrete form. Since then he has devoted his life to the preservation of Ainu culture items and to transmitting the spirit of the lifestyle of the Ainu to posterity.

He started to work with the construction of an "Ainu Culture Exhibition Hall", *Shiryoka*, which was completed in 1972. The work with the Shiryoka was started in 1939 when Kayano worked as a ditch digger at Sapporo Regional Forest Office. The Shiryoka is built on Nibutani land donated by him. He was appointed deputy chief and in charge of the exhibition section to which he donated 140 items, such as hunting and fishing utensils, including arrows, bows, quivers, knives, gathering bags, food preparation utensils, weaving and sewing utensils, cloth and dresses and trinkets and ornaments of various types, all from his private collection. To compensate for the lack of items and to replace old ones Kayano, who is a skilled craftsman, carves new ones himself. He takes an active part in exhibiting the items to visitors and as a result it has become very popular, as Kayano is now a famous man.

Kayano's contribution of culture items to other exhibition halls and museums all over Nihon includes about 580 items. The exhibition halls and museums to which he has donated his items are the following: *Noboribetsu Yukara no Sato Exhibition Hall,* 150 items; *Hokudai,* the State University of Hokkaido, 180 items; *Osaka National Anthropological Museum,* 250 items. In addition Kayano has been consulted as supervisor of the construction of various *Ainu Chise* in *Osaka, Nuyama* (Honshu) and *Chibetsu* (Hokkaido).

In 1960, Kayano started to interview and record old Ainu with a knowledge of *Uwepeker: Kamuy Yukar* (Ainu folk tales) and *Yukar Upopo* (Ainu legends). Today there are about 500 hours of recordings.

Kayano is married to an Ainu woman. They have three children – one girl and two boys. His two boys are married to Wajin and his daughter is unmarried. They all live in Nibutani and they take an active part in Ainu matters. Kayano has two sisters and three younger brothers. His elder sister and two of his brothers are married to Ainu. His younger

---

2   See Appendix B.

sister and one of his brothers are married to Wajin. All of them, except the youngest sister who lives in Honshu, live in Nibutani and are involved in Ainu matters.

NIBUTANI

In the paragraphs that follow below I will first present some data on Nibutani's Ainu population. This is required, because the development that is taking place here has inspired Ainu in other Hokkaido areas to follow Nibutani's example. In this regard Nibutani functions as a model village, that is, a centre for Ainu activities and practices, and a source of inspiration for the future.

This is followed by a general overview of Nibutani's environment, its land use and its profile. After that I focus on the activities that are taking place in Nibutani village, with special reference to the elementary school, *Sho-gakko*, the nursery school, *Kodomo-beya*, the exhibition hall, *Shiryoka* the library, *Tosho-kan*, Ainu-style houses, *Chise*, the boarding-house, *Geshuku-ya* and the tourist shops, *Mise*.

DATA ABOUT NIBUTANI'S AINU POPULATION

The data presented below derive from my own census and aim primarily to give a general overview of the occupational situation of the Ainu and their participation in the various Ainu activities.

Nibutani has a population of 414 people or 164 households and 80% of its population are of Ainu descent. Of Nibutani's Ainu population 67% are tied to and find an income in the tourist sector. Of the Ainu people belonging to this category 45% are engaged in this full-time. The remaining 55% are only loosely connected to this sector – they may help out in the tourist shops, contribute by providing raw material for the items manufactured or else they may manufacture items themselves and then sell them to the shopkeepers.

The people belonging to this category find their main source of income in the rural sector and of these 25.3% own the land they are cultivating or using for cattle-breeding activities, 50.6% work as hired hands to Honshu companies and 24.1% lease the land either from Honshu companies or else from the government.

Of Nibutani's Ainu population 72% have lived here all their lives. Intermarriage with Wajin is close to 20% and of these the majority are females – there are only three Wajin males. Only 4% of the intermarried Wajin come from Honshu, the majority come from either the same or neighbouring Hokkaido regions.

Of the intermarried females 81% are linked to or find an income in the tourist industry. The intermarried males come from Honshu. They are military men who are stationed at the army base in Hidaka. None of the men are connected to tourism.

Of Nibutani's total Ainu population 78% take an interest in Ainu activities of the village, they attend lessons and take part in Ainu ceremonies of different types. Of

Nibutani's total Wajin population this figure amounts to 65% (my census in Nibutani, 1988).

As shown above, the majority of the Ainu in Nibutani are, in one way or another, engaged in matters concerning their own cultural inheritance, although a relatively high percentage of them find a main source of income in the rural sector. This reflects that, while the history of the Ainu relation to Nihon is one of increasing economic and political integration, they have not only been able to preserve their own cultural uniqueness, but they are also strengthening it in various ways.

The change from a subsistence to a market-oriented economy has, quite contrary to what was generally assumed, thus not worked to alienate them from their own cultural inheritance. Their interest in values that are rooted in their own culture remains, in spite of efforts from the highest authority, with the aid of a policy of assimilation, to deprive them of this.

In addition, this interest has also stimulated a relatively high percentage of the Wajin who live here to a commitment to Ainu activities and practices, something which promotes, rather than hinders, a development that is in line with the visions the Ainu have of their future.

NIBUTANI VILLAGE AND ITS ENVIRONMENT

The journey from Sapporo to Nibutani takes about four hours by bus and we have to cross the Ishikari and Iburi regions before we arrive in Hidaka, where Nibutani village, Mura, is situated.

Most of the land in and around Nibutani is used for cattle breeding, racehorse breeding, rice and corn cultivation or other economies introduced from Honshu, such as the cultivation of white and red beans. The majority of the land used for these activities is either owned by Honshu companies or else the land comes under common property. To the population in Nihon, of whom a great percentage are Shintoists, the red and white beans are highly revered, and used in various dishes in connection with various Shinto celebrations.

Close to Nibutani, several acres of the land are used to cultivate lily-of-the-valley. This lily is the emblem of Nibutani village and the area used for its cultivation is the biggest in Hokkaido. Not far from the lily-of-the-valley plantation there is a recreation place called "Kentucky Farm". Here one can rent horses and go for a ride in the surrounding countryside. It resembles a Texas (Kentucky) -style ranch, and the people who work here, the majority of whom come from Honshu – although they also hire local people to do some carving for them – are dressed up as cowboys. The farm is owned by a private Honshu company. The owner of the company thinks it will turn out a great success, at least if one is to believe his employees:

In Nihon people are getting more and more spare time and they have to fill it with
something. We think this is a great idea, especially in this area where there are a
lot of race horses (interview with Wajin male, aged 26, Kentucky Farm, 1988).

Another recreation centre is the golf course. Golf is a very popular sport throughout
Nihon and in the big cities one often sees golf enthusiasts practising their skill in special
golf boxes, the size of ordinary telephone boxes, where they play a kind of computerized
golf. In the countryside there is at least space enough for these people to practise the sport
in a more realistic way. In Nibutani there are several people who play golf and some of
Nibutani's women (two of them are Wajin married to Ainu, while the rest of them are
Ainu by descent) work as caddies on the golf course.

NIBUTANI'S PROFILE

Nibutani is located in a valley surrounded by high mountains embedded in the
forests. The village is cross-cut by the the Saru River, *Saru Kawa* in Nihongo and *Saru
Pet* in Ainu language.[3]

This river originally provided the main source of food for the Ainu living here.
They used to catch various kinds of fish, such as *Cep* which is an Ainu word for salmon,
meaning fish as well as "main food", (the Nihongo word is "Sakana") *Cicira* (loach), *Esoka*
(bullhead), *Kirepo* and *Sakipe* (different types of trout) and *Nuira* (dace). Today the people

---

3   The Ainu word for river is "Pet". Some Wajin and some Ainu people pronounce this word
     "Betsu". This is due to the fact that "Pet" is difficult to write in Nihongo. The Nihongo
     "alphabet" consists of syllables instead of isolated letters and only vowels and the consonant
     "n" appear in isolation. This problem affects of course a great number of Ainu words, such
     as "Set", "Reyep" and "Ikir" to name but a few, and scholars and Ainu are in disagreement
     about how to transcribe the Ainu language. Of late Wajin scholars have come to use Roman
     letters when they transcribe Ainu words. Nevertheless, in the Ainu opinion this is a bad
     choice, since many Ainu are not accustomed to Roman letters. Instead they suggest that
     one should not depart from Nihongo. To indicate deviations, they propose that "small"
     signs are used. Shigeru Kayano also agrees that this is the best solution. Yet by using this
     technique there is a danger that people will not pronounce the words in the correct way.
     According to Kayano, this is, however, a minor problem, the important thing is the meaning
     of the word and not its pronunciation. However, in the case of "Betsu" the meanings are
     quite different. "Betsu" is Nihongo and means "different", whereas "Pet" is Ainu and means
     "river". (When I use Ainu words I use the pronunciation that my Ainu friends have taught
     me. In the event of uncertainty I have turned to Batchelor [1938]. This is not a random
     choice. Batchelor's work with the Ainu language is highly appreciated among the Ainu,
     who say: "he could make himself understood among our people, which is more than one
     can say of linguists of today". For more specialized terminology, that is, Ainu alliances and
     kinship organization I have turned to Seligman [1960].)

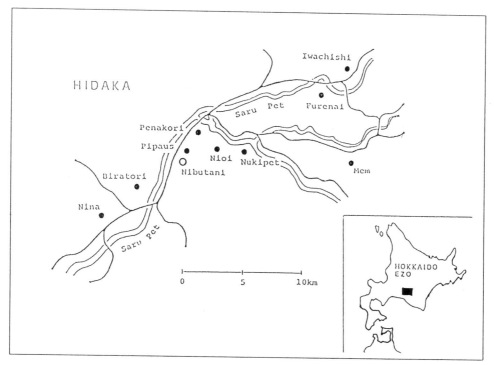

FIGURE 11   *Nibutani and adjacent areas*

are not allowed to fish here without a special licence. Saru Pet is very famous and there is, at least to my knowledge, no work written about the Ainu in which the Saru Pet is not mentioned. This may be related to the fact that Nibutani is the most researched Ainu settlement.

Parallel to the river there is the main road. Nowadays this road is heavily trafficked, because the railroad which used to serve these parts of the Hidaka region is out of use. The road is lined with two or one-floor Nihonjin-style houses. Each house has an Ainu dog, *Seta* or *Reyep*, to guard it. The dogs are kept in kennels and they are not allowed to enter the house. In front of each house there is a small ornamental garden or *Niwa* and at the back there is a kitchen garden, *Yasaibatake*.

In the kitchen garden the people grow various Ainu vegetables such as *Eha*, a kind of bean which they mix with rice; *Korokomi*, a sort of rhubarb which they eat with herring and dried fish; *Kina*, lily roots which they mix with cereal to make porridge and *Soroma*, wood anemone.

The front garden, the Niwa,they decorate with stones and ornamental flowers of different kinds. The Niwa, is a Wajin introduction.

The village has two Nihonjin-style boarding-houses, *Geshuku-ya*, each with a capacity to lodge about twenty people at a time.

One may think that there is no need for two boarding-houses in a village of Nibutani's size. However, in Nibutani there seems to be a need, not least during the tourist invasion, which starts in May and lasts until October. In the tourist season the boarding-houses cannot provide accommodation for all of the tourists. On such occasions the villagers lodge the tourists. During winter the boarding-houses are closed for the most part, but since Nibutani is the most famous Ainu village in all Hokkaido, visitors are never lacking, not even in the winter season. In the village there is also an elementary school, *Sho-gakko*. At present sixty-seven children from Nibutani are attending the school.

At the village centre we find one of the two boarding-houses in the village, *Geshuku-ya*; the tourists shops, *Mise*; the exhibition hall, *Shiryoka*; the library, *Tosho-kan*; the nursery school, *Kodomo-beya*, with twenty-two children; various Ainu-style houses, *Chise*, twelve in all; the post office; and finally the village's country shop, which is owned by a Wajin.

THE SHO-GAKKO

Nibutani elementary school, *Sho-gakko*, follows the educational guidelines stated by the highest authority and there is thus no special programme for Nibutani pupils that relates to ethnic issues, nor are they encouraged to take a special interest in them.

A possible explanation for the latter can, of course, be that the school personnel are of Wajin descent and not Ainu, and the main purpose of education seems to be to give the children a basic knowledge of Nihongo, Nihon history and culture.

For obvious reasons the Ainu are not content with this form of education, and demand a special programme for their children teaching their native language, *Ainu Itak*, and the values and beliefs of their own culture. This is a request which they have made in *A Counter Plan for the Legislation Concerning the Ainu People* (Utari Kyokai 1984, 1987a).

This year the school has its centenary. During these hundred years, 764 people have graduated from the school. In connection with the anniversary the Ainu people here are issuing a special book, *Nibutani Elementary School Centenary*, which is supposed to give a general overview of its history. In order to make the book as complete as possible all the villagers are asked to contribute in some way or another. Among other things they are asked to do research work by themselves, such as to find "prominent" pupils, provide pictures or write some essays. The expenses for the book are met with private funds from the villagers.

THE KODOMO-BEYA

The nursery school, *Kodomo-beya* (the proper name in Nihongo is *Yoichen* meaning "nursery school", but the Ainu call their nursery school Kodomo-beya which also is Nihongo meaning "children's room" [in a home]), is located in a Nihonjin-style house and at the time of my stay in Nibutani twenty-two children, the majority of them Ainu but with some Wajin, were attending the nursery school regularly.

The school personnel, four in all, are either married to Ainu or else they are of Ainu descent and they live in Nibutani. According to the personnel the main ambition of the school is to give the children a basic knowledge of their Ainu inheritance. Accordingly, much time is spent training them in their own language and giving them information about Ainu history and culture. They often arrange field trips in the surrounding countryside and during these the children are taught how to deal with Nature, that is, Ainu names for the Kamuy who live here, how to approach them, Ainu names for wild plants and roots, how to prepare them, and so forth.

On some occasions they invite Ainu from other areas, preferably from the Iburi and Kushiro regions, to take part in these field trips. During the school holidays, the schoolchildren from the elementary school are invited to take part in these field trips. In addition the children also take an active part in the building or restoration of Ainu-style houses, *Chise.*

CHISE, AINU-STYLE HOUSES

These houses are made of oak and linden pillars and have thatched roofs. The houses in Nibutani are built by local people but the funds to build them come from Biratori cho, the administrative unit to which Nibutani belongs. Each house consists of an entrance hall and one big room with a central fireplace. At the eastern corner of the fireplace there are two offering sticks, *Inau,* one male and one female, and the fire itself is guarded by the fire goddess, *Huchi Kamuy.*

The walls are decorated with mats made of sea grass, *Tatami,* to keep warm, and wood shavings, *Kike,* to ward off evil deities, *Wen Kamuy.* Alongside the walls there are various receptacles for Ainu treasures, *Kema-us-sintoko,* which contain trinkets, such as earrings, *Nikari;* chest trinkets, *Shitoki;* and *Imukusai,* necklaces; but also knives and quivers, *Makiri;* arrows, *Ya;* and offering sticks, *Ikupasuy.* The receptacles are lined up in rows along the walls.

Food preparation utensils are placed above the fireplace, where they hang down from the ceiling. They hang their garments in rows on the walls. The floor, which is made of mud, is covered with Tatami, similar to those covering the walls.

There is no exact rule about how many windows an Ainu house should have, so the number varies.

The most important window is the eastern one, which, according to the beliefs of the Ainu, is considered holy. It is believed that the gods, Kamuy entered the house through this window, called *Kamuy-Kus-Puyuara.* (According to my informants, originally the Chise had Kamuy-Kus-Puyuara only.) The Chise does not have any window facing the west. Here they have the entrance, where they keep cereal for immediate use.

FIGURE 12   *Inside the Chise*

The entrance is considered a profane place. Immediately connected to the entrance there is a youth and female place. Originally this space was reserved for youths and females, who had their beds and working places here while the men and elder women had theirs in the eastern part of the house.

Outside the house, to the west, there are two toilets, one for the men and one for the women, and in close vicinity to the toilets are the storehouses, where cereal is kept.

Outside the house, to the east, there is the *Nusa*, a gathering place for holy things, where *Inau* with animal sculls on top of them are kept in a row. In front of the Nusa they have the *Set*, a wooden bear cage.

In the old days there used to be a bear cub, *Heper*, in the Set, but nowadays it is empty. The bears which the Ainu have now are adult ones which are kept in iron cages. In Nibutani there are two caged bears whose main function today is to attract tourists. One of the bears belongs to the boarding-house which is located on the outskirts of the village.

The Ainu people do not live in Chise nowadays, they live in Nihonjin-style houses. The Chise function as workshops, where the Ainu manufacture various culture items in Ainu style, such as *Saranip*, gathering bags, *Attus*, cloth made of bark, wooden things, such as *Inau* or *Ikupasuy*, offerings to their gods, *Hashi* chopsticks, wooden bears and various other wooden things.

FIGURE 13   *Chise under construction*

The wood-carving profession, Kibori, was a highly revered occupation among Ainu males in the old days. In those days the items were traded among their people, whereas today they are mainly sold at tourist shops, but some of the items are sold to museums or exhibition halls all over Nihon.

The Chise are also used as venues for special Ainu activities and celebrations. The village people gather here to attend lessons in Ainu dances, weaving and wood-carving techniques, but also to learn about their history and language.

On some occasions they invite both researchers and Ainu from other areas in Hokkaido, on others they practise their skills among themselves. Such activities take place at least once a week and for the most part there are at least forty participants. It frequently occurs that outside Ainu specialists are invited, and then the local specialists and the outside ones discuss variants in method, practice and use of the various activities that are taking place here.

At the time of Ainu ceremonies such as *Cipsanke Matsuri*, a ceremony held when launching canoes, and *Chise Nomi*, a celebration of the building of a new house, people also get together here. To inform Hokkaido people about the activities taking place the Ainu advertise in regional and local papers. The newspaper sends a journalist who reports what happened during the events.

THE SHIRYOKA AND THE TOSHO-KAN

The *Shiryoka*, the exhibition hall, consists of three exhibition rooms, a small video room and an entrance hall. In the video room one can watch Kayano's films about "How to Build a Chise" (*Chise Akara*) "Ainu Wedding Ceremony" (*Ainu no Kekkon-shiki*) "The Bear Festival" (*Iyomante*) "The Games of Saru River Ainu children" (*Saru-Kawa Ainu Kodomo no Asobi*) "How to Build an Ainu Canoe" (*Fune Sukari*) and finally "Lectures in Ainu Language and Conversation" (*Ainu Itak to Kaiwa*). At the time of my stay, tourists came here to watch almost every day.

In the entrance hall one can buy books about Ainu history and cultural tradition, and among these we also find Kayano's own works, seventeen books in all. Since Kayano's books are in great demand it happens that the exhibition hall cannot guarantee to stock them at the time of one's stay. If the books are not available one can, however, order them and during my stay many people, tourists as well as researchers, did this.

Since the items exhibited in the Shiryoka never underwent scientific evaluations, the hall does not enjoy the status of a museum.

Close to the exhibition hall there is the library, *Tosho-kan*. It is a Canadian-style log house and it belongs to Nibutani village with Kayano in charge. The library is also used to lodge guests from far away, mostly researchers and students. Kayano's radio programmes, in which he teaches Ainu Itak, are broadcast from the library and also it is here that he receives journalists coming to interview him.

The library is well equipped and receives books from private donors and institutions, as well as from the state. Ainu books which could be hard to find elsewhere are available here and people who study Ainu matters often return to keep their material up to date.

THE GESHUKU-YA

One of the boarding-houses, *Geshuku-ya* or *Minshuku*, the one located on the outskirts of the village, also has a tourist shop, and an Ainu-style house. In both the Mise and the Chise, Ainu souvenirs are on sale, but the Chise also functions as a place where visitors, guests, researchers, students and tourists are entertained.

The landlord, who is an Ainu, invites people to have a look at the Chise and on such occasions he talks about old times and explains the advantages of the Chise (warm in wintertime and cool in summertime) compared to the Nihonjin-style houses in which the Ainu now live. He gives a detailed description of the building of the house, including ceremonies, the building material and how to find a proper place to build it:

> The proper month to start building a Chise we call the long month [April or May] and the day we start we call the long day. We ask our friends and brothers to help us find the proper place and according to our tradition the Chise has to be built where there is good water. We men go out in the forests and there we gather timber, oak for the framework and linden, for the roof. Then the man whose future house it is to be goes out and finds a measuring stick, mostly linden and he uses this stick to measure. Next he makes a three-headed gable frame, "Chehorokakep", and he places it where the heart of the Chise is to be. The men who are helping him in his work gather around it and perform the purification ceremony, "Ketuni". We sit down on the ground, with legs crossed in front of us and worship the Ketuni, offer sake to it and ask it to take good care of its lodgers. We strew it with grain and the Kamuy of the Chehorokakep divides this grain among all creatures who have lived and died here. Then we proceed with the work. To build the framework of the Chise is men's work but to help with the roof is women's work. Oak pillars are strong as a man should be, linden are soft and pliable as a woman should be. To construct the fireplace we dig a hole in the ground at the centre of the Chise and we fill it with pebbles and volcanic ashes. We place two "Inau" in the eastern corner of the fireplace. These are "Abe Huchi", and "Abe Chise", the house mother and father. The work with the Chise takes about fifty days and then we can all rejoice. We gather in the house and shoot arrows in the four corners of the Chise. This is to chase evil Kamuy away. You never know when some evil Kamuy may linger in the Chise. The shooting will chase them away and leave the good or benevolent Kamuy (Nibutani, 1988).

In the Chise the landlord keeps Ainu culture items of various kinds, some of which have been in his family for generations. He shows these items to the visitors and explains the history of each of them. Replicas of these items, manufactured by the landlord himself or his wife (who is also of Ainu descent), are for sale and are often bought by visitors. He also has Ainu-style *Kimonos* – they differ from the Nihonjin-style in material and decoration. The visitors are asked to put them on and then they are shown how to sit in an Ainu manner, on a cushion, legs crossed in front of you – the Wajin way is legs placed under you. Having taken this pose the visitors are photographed and the photos developed on the spot.

Afterwards the guests are offered *O-cha*, Nihon tea, and then the conversation begins. The landlord teaches the visitors Ainu greetings, *Iyraykere*, in words and demonstrations and then they might talk about the visitors' whereabouts, their families, work and business in Nibutani. If the visitor comes from abroad the landlord asks him to explain about greeting rituals in his own country. His interest in this is explained in the following way:

> Greeting rituals teach you a lot about other people's traditions. Take for instance the Shamo way, here you bow. The deeper you bow the more inferior you are. The bow in itself is an expression of "obedience". The people adhering to a tradition where you bow, at least in the way the Shamo do, tell you that the people are not equal. The way the Ainu people greet each other, on the other hand, tells you that we treat people in an equal way. Our gesture is an expression of love, with our hand pointing at our hearts we welcome each other (Nibutani, 1988).

The landlord also takes the opportunity to inform the visitors about Nibutani. He might talk about famous persons who used to stay here, such as Munro, Batchelor and Naert, and their work in the village:

> We are very proud that they honoured our village with their presence. Munro who was a doctor helped us a great deal, especially during World War II. He gave us medical treatment, free of charge. He knew we were poor so he did not want us to pay. Munro and Batchelor were friends. Batchelor came here to to teach us about Jesus, to convert us to Christianity. Some of our people even had themselves baptized. He also helped to educate our children, teach them to read and write. Both of them took a great interest in our culture, our life and tradition. They took notes and later they have written many a learned book about our ways. Naert, I think he came from some European country, was interested in our "Ainu Itak". Did you know when he came here he could speak our language better than we could? He did not know Nihongo so we had to speak with him in Ainu Itak. He stayed at Kayano's place and helped him with the harvest, he came in the middle of it. They said to him, we do not have any spare time. If you are interested in our language you have to come out with us in the fields. He did. Rumour says that he, Naert that is, never used any vehicle when he traveled in Hokkaido. He walked. "That is the way the Ainu do, I will do the same", he said (Nibutani, 1988).

FIGURE 14   *Tourist shop*

If time permits, the landlord takes the visitors to the places where Batchelor and Munro used to stay and shows them places such as Munro's home, or Batchelor's nursery school, which are in the vicinity. During the tourist season his sister-in-law, who is of Wajin descent, works as a helper. Out of the tourist season the landlord works for the Kentucky farm. He is a Kibori man, wood-carver, so he manufactures wooden Ainu souvenirs for the company but also Indian-style totem poles with Ainu motifs.

The other boarding-house, located in the centre of the village, also belongs to an Ainu. Because of its central position, there are no tourist shops in its yard – they are across the main road. Instead of a Chise it has a Canadian-style log house as its meeting place. Apart from the boarding-house the landlord also owns a stone garden. The stones are used to decorate the Niwa, a tradition with roots in Shinto beliefs, and selling stones is a very profitable occupation.

THE MISE

The size of the tourist shops, *Mise,* varies. For the most part they are relatively small – only one room – and the people who work here do not live there, although they or their family own the place.

Around thirty-five per cent of the family members migrate to Akan or Shiraoi during the tourist season and work in the tourist shops there. Most of the things for sale in the shops they have manufactured themselves, other items are made by Ainu people in the vicinity who do carving in their spare time and take this opportunity to earn some extra money, or as they themselves prefer to express it: "Every Ainu man is a 'Kibori man', we make carvings because we cannot stop. It is in our blood. If we can make a profit, well we do not think there is anything wrong with this".

The starting material for the products is taken from the surrounding forests. On such occasions they all join in, but every shopkeeper has his or her special "gathering place". Intrusion is not looked upon kindly, but it hardly ever occurs. The villagers could not recall one single intrusion during the last twenty years.

In the shops there are also imported things for sale. The imported souvenirs come from Honshu, mostly Tokyo. As in the workshops, the people working in these shops manufacture the items. In summer when it is very hot, people prefer to stay indoors, but in the spring or early autumn people work in front of their shops. The tourist shops are open every day during the season and it is only the village's country shop and the post office that keep regular hours.

The customers are greeted in an Ainu fashion and the shopkeepers take great pleasure in explaining every single detail of their activities. If you ask, you are allowed to try weaving or carving for yourself. They tell you from whom they learnt their special technique and they also give you information about local and regional variants. Often you

FIGURE 15   *A kibori man*

are asked what you know about them and their culture. If you do not know very much you may stay for hours.

The Ainu are very skilled story-tellers, an art with roots in their oral tradition, and they practise it with great success in their salesman's occupation, since the tourists seldom leave empty-handed. They carefully avoid speaking of delicate matters, such as discrimination, welfare allowances or other things which would disturb business.

Mostly they talk about their culture items, and the skill one has to have to be able to manufacture even the simplest objects. They seldom talk about personal matters. If they do you soon find out that their life histories are in fact invented. You get the same life history from every one:

> My grandfather was a very powerful "Ekashi". He was the ruler of this village. He was very well liked by the Shamo and the whole village profited from this. We were given land to cultivate and the authorities in this region gave us tools and seed. He was the first person who adapted himself to the new way of life. Since my grandfather was a powerful man he influenced the villagers to follow his example. They did, because they could see for themselves that he had made a good choice. We still have some land left but we do not cultivate it anymore on a large scale as we used to. We like this way better, and besides in this way it is possible for us to combine work and pleasure.

If you stay in Nibutani for an extended period (most people stay for a day or two), you are invited to take part in Ainu activities of different kinds. You may be invited to join when they are harvesting *Inakibi*, a kind of Ainu cereal. They may take you to the forest and the mountains and here they show you the places where they gather material for the items manufactured in the tourist and working shops.

They take great interest in informing you about the raw material and where the best places are to find it. You are also invited to take part in their lectures about their culture and language. If you are lucky your stay in Nibutani may coincide with an Ainu ceremony, and you are not only invited to participate but you are also appointed "honourable member".

For the most part the celebration of an Ainu ceremony is advertised beforehand in the local or regional newspapers or in tourist guides, and tourists arrive *en masse*. The celebration of Ainu ceremonies coincides with the national holidays in Nihon, which is a Wajin innovation, so there are usually quite a lot of "honourable members".

If you have a special interest in the carving and weaving techniques they introduce you to the expert in the field. He or she gives you detailed information about the profession. In addition you are told the whereabouts of other experts and if you wish and if it is possible they arrange for you to meet them. In Nibutani they frequently refer to Utariyan Narita, who lives in the vicinity. He is a famous Kibori man and he also has a thorough knowledge of the cultural tradition of the Ainu.

FIGURE 16   *Harvesting* inakibi *while photographed by tourists*

If Kayano is in town a meeting with him is high priority. Lately he has been difficult to reach because of his many appointments abroad, in Honshu or in Hokkaido, where he gives seminars, arranges meetings or else attends to Ainu matters, contacts Utari Kyokai, visits the Hokkaido governor and so forth. If he cannot be reached you may talk to his youngest son who is his deputy or Mr and Mrs Yoneda who work as assistants to him – they are of Wajin descent. These three persons make up Kayano's local personnel and they are paid with local funds (from Biratori cho).

Judging from the above, Nibutani's profile relies heavily on the figure (present or not) of Kayano which is to be expected, since he is the instigator of the many Ainu activities taking place here. He is also, as mentioned above, the initiator of *A Counter Plan to a Proposal for Legislation Concerning the Ainu People* (Utari Kyokai 1984, 1987a), proposals in which the guidelines of the future of the Ainu are laid down.

Before discussing the vision the Ainu have of the future as proposed in their counter plans, some information about the attitude of Nibutani's Ainu population to the discrimination against them will be provided.

DISCRIMINATION AGAINST NIBUTANI'S AINU POPULATION

The general view of discrimination is that the Ainu living in Nibutani village consider themselves privileged, because in this village discrimination is extremely rare. It is commonly believed that discrimination in and around Nibutani is non-existent. This was confirmed in an investigation initiated by government authorities in 1986 (Utari Kyokai 1987b).

Discrimination in Nibutani does exist; however, the form it takes is often the reverse, which reflects that discriminatory attitudes are neither supported nor accepted by the authorities and individuals in this area. This in turn serves to keep discriminatory treatment of the Ainu in Nibutani at a low rate:

> We do not have many Shamo here, but among them there are some who tell their children not to play with Ainu children. This is absurd, because their children will be harmed, not ours. You see, it is an isolated case so the child had no comrades, because other Shamo children refused to play with him since they were afraid to lose their comrades. The child got ill and the headmaster went to talk to his parents. I do not know what he said but since that day the child is playing with our children but in secret. Everybody knows about it except his own parents (Ainu female, aged 45, Nibutani, 1988).

Another example:

> A couple of years ago we had a teacher who did not like Ainu children. He gave them bad grades and complained about their smell. We, the parents, were of course very upset so we complained to the headmaster. He said that he could not believe it but he promised to keep his eyes wide open....
>
> Since the headmaster is a very fair person he had to admit that it was true and before long the teacher who had treated our children in such a bad way was forced to give up his teaching at our school (Ainu male, aged 55, Nibutani, 1988).

We may conclude that the kind of discrimination taking place in Nibutani does not permeate administration and officialdom and accordingly there is nothing wrong with the officially established ideology, since administration and individuals live up to this ideology.

However, when it comes to discrimination against Nibutani's Ainu inhabitants outside Nibutani, the pattern is different from the above. The form it takes reflects that discriminatory attitudes are even commonly accepted in these areas. In a situation where authorities and individuals approve of discriminatory treatment the Ainu feel strongly that they are not treated as equals to the Wajin. The expression it takes and the way it is interpreted by the Ainu is exemplified in the following statements:

> A couple of years ago one of the villagers fell in love with a girl who is not an Ainu. She lived in Tomikawa, two miles from here. They were very much in love so the man soon asked her to marry him. She told her parents that she had fallen in love with a wealthy man. He is, you know, very wealthy indeed. The parents were very happy, they were very poor and they liked to see their daughter well off and soon they were introduced to him. As soon as they saw him they recognized that he was

an Ainu so they said no to the wedding. The couple were in tears and they did not know what to do. The man asked his father for advice, so he went to see the girl's parents. He said: "Why do you refuse to allow your daughter to marry my son? We are well off so the girl will be well taken care of". They [the parents] said that they just decided that he was not the right kind of person for their daughter. Then they bade farewell....

To make a long story short, the young couple decided to elope. Today they live here in Nibutani and they have three children and they are very happy. Their only shadow is the girl's parents. They declared the daughter dead and had a death certificate arranged (Ainu male aged 62, Nibutani, 1988).

Another statement made by an Ainu woman, aged 58:

My son went to Sapporo to find himself a job. He was good at school so his grades were all right. He was called to several interviews, but there it stopped. My son's looks are Ainu looks, round eyes and his beard grows fast, so they turned him down. He stayed in Sapporo for about three months! He lived at my cousin's place, he does not look so much Ainu so he has got himself a job. He works as a truck driver. My son had to give up and now he is back again. He tries to find a job around here, but this is also very difficult. Nibutani is a small village, you know. For the time being he does a little bit of this and a little bit of that, whatever comes his way. He is no exception to the rule. We have several more cases similar to the fate of my son (Nibutani, 1988).

With respect to discrimination of Ainu from Nibutani when outside Nibutani, we may conclude that there must be something fundamentally wrong with the official ideology since, evidently, it works to promote discrimination, in the sense that discriminatory attitudes permeate administration and officialdom in such a way that authorities and individuals do not think it necessary to live up to this ideology.

Ethnic discrimination as manifested in Wajin reluctance to marry and employ people of Ainu descent is a serious problem. The solution the Ainu have to this problem, especially the Nibutani Ainu, focuses on cultural redress, and it is based on a conviction that their own values, if displayed in a proper way, will eventually change this situation. To achieve this goal, they advocate educational programmes for pupils of Ainu descent and alternative land use. This is how they view the future and their children:

Our children, who have spent the most vulnerable time of their whole lives in this place, have an advantage. In Nibutani they learn about their culture from elderly people whom they admire. The "Ekashi" take them to the forests and mountains and teach them all they know about Nature. They teach them about the "Kamuy" who live here, the way they take care of us humans and how we in turn must repay them. They also teach the children about which roots and plants are edible or which roots and plants they can use for medical purposes. They teach them to be proud of their origins and they also teach them how to counteract discrimination. If you do not accept that you are inferior you are practically immune to discrimination. When our children grow up they will be strong and proud and the Shamo will have to face a generation of Ainu people who do not buy their stories about inferior race and culture. They will say this is a fairy tale, which you have made up all by yourself and then they will refer to errors in the history books and they will have no trouble in finding them, there are many. Mr Kayano is working with our history, the true one. Our people think that his work will finally give us redress. We have waited a long time. The future will be ours, you just wait. It is his and our wish that Ainu people will regain their pride, and they will. Once they have regained this there will be nothing to stop them from fighting for their Ainu rights in general. You know, our people have to be proud of their cultural tradition, otherwise there will be no point in fighting for recognition as a unique cultural group (Ainu female, aged 71, Nibutani, 1988).

This attitude to their future is of course necessary as an important component for the success of the development as put forth in their proposal in *The Counter Plans.*

STRATEGIES OF ETHNICITY

In *A Proposal for Legislation Concerning the Ainu People* (Utari Kyokai 1984, 1987a) there are advanced plans to make Nibutani a centre for the study of the cultural tradition of the Ainu on a large scale. At present it is private individual commitment that constitutes the basis for the continuation of the activities taking place here. However, since Nibutani already functions as a centre, and since the village has also gained quite a reputation on this point, in the sense that studies of Ainu matters are not taken seriously if one does not visit Nibutani and take part in at least some of the various activities that occur here. The work with the centre has been going on for about two decades and is far advanced. For support and information on a national and regional level the Utari Kyokai in Sapporo is an important asset.

The vision is to have a historical museum, *The Saru Kawa Ainu Historical Museum,* constructed on Nibutani ground, more specifically, near the Shiryoka. This museum is to be surrounded by Chise, Ainu-style dwelling houses, in which Ainu products will be manufactured in an Ainu-style way. It is proposed to make a national park of the forests and the mountains. This is to preserve the flora and fauna of the once most powerful Ainu territory in Hokkaido. Part of Nibutani land will be used to grow Ainu crops and vegetables. This to preserve Ainu cooking tradition and to be able to serve Ainu dishes to visitors. Finally, the plan is to establish a centre for the study of Ainu history, culture and language. Lectures will be given by the Ainu themselves.

According to Kayano, Nibutani is to become a model tourist village that may function as a source of inspiration for other Ainu tourist villages, notably Shiraoi and Akan, whose chief curators coöperate with Kayano. Their plans are as follows:

That the tourist villages henceforth shall function as research centres for the investigation of local Ainu customs, language and beliefs. The vision is that the villages shall serve as information centres, with possibilities to give lessons in various culturally based activities (interview with Nomura, chief director of Shiraoi Historical Ainu Museum and Utari Kyokai chief curator, 1988).

Kayano is very optimistic, an optimism which, according to him, is not unfounded. He says:

For many years I have been the sole Ainu contributor to transmit the spirit of Ainu "genuine" traditional lifestyle to posterity. In recent years, however, other Ainu people have also taken an interest in these matters and they are now contributing in many ways, especially in Akan and Shiraoi. People here are turning to Nibutani for advice. They record old people's Ainu Itak, they are investigating our ceremonies and our cultural tradition. In Akan, one of our people has started a private video company. "The Turano production". They make their own video tapes about the traditional Ainu way of life....

Previously, our people were simply not interested in their own culture. They were thinking: "The Ainu culture is no good. We better hurry to forget it. Mr Kayano must be foolish. Does he think our traditional lifestyle will be appreciated, just because he cannot forget it himself?" Such thinking occupied their minds. I did not mind because I knew their feelings. I am an Ainu and I know what our people think, but nevertheless I simply could not forget my own ways. I thought, what harm can there be in saving the things I find when I work as a ditch digger, what harm can there be in trying to find out their use, what material they were made of and try to make duplicates myself. So I continued. And now so many years have passed and at last people are beginning to understand the value of it....

My personal opinion is that the Ainu people have come to realize that in order to become a complete human being, an "Ainu", one cannot repress one's origin. Instead one has to let it come into the open and that is exactly what is happening among our people today. They are eager to know about old times, values, things, everything. They have been starving, mentally, so many years now. There is nothing to stop their enthusiasm now....

They are arranging Ainu food festivals, where people can taste our food. We have our own specialities, you know. The food is cooked in a traditional way and the people use traditional cooking utensils when they prepare the food. Now, to be able to eat Ainu food we cannot use our land to cultivate imported crops only. We have to have areas where we can cultivate our own cereal. It is important. Further, if we wish to present it, the food I mean, as traditional dishes we have to prepare the dishes in a traditional way, otherwise it would not be traditional. We have to have material for the food-preparing utensils too. The material we find in the forest. These things are made of wood, you see. People have to provide them. They find the wood in the forest and then they go home and manufacture the food-preparing utensils. That is the way to manage. Our food festivals are very popular and people come from all over Nihon to visit and eat. They say our food is very tasty and they will recommend their friends to come here and eat. As a matter of fact, we do already have restaurants in Sapporo, Asahikawa and Hakodate....

Recently Ainu people have begun to revive old Ainu ceremonies and dances, such as the "Iyomante" and the "Chip Sanke" ceremony, the crane dance, etc. They attend lectures in traditional matters, or else they arrange lectures in areas were there are as yet no such activities. They invite Wajin authorities to join field trips and investigate traditional Ainu place-names. They also arrange for people to camp, and for a day or two live traditional Ainu lives. Utaryian Narita, whom you know, was the first person to initiate this. There are so many different activities I cannot recall them. As a result, the authorities in Nihon are doing some rethinking themselves....

Many things have changed lately. They, the authorities that is, have come to realize that we are not merely a burden, someone who relies on welfare for their survival. My ambition is to convince them, the authorities, that we can manage by ourselves. Now, we are actually taking things in our own hands, whether they approve or not. They, the authorities, will not deliver anything free of charge, except welfare money, but that is because their conscience is tormenting them. If we come up with some good ideas they will not turn them down. I am positive that the way things are working out in Nibutani has given them something to think about, not once but twice. For one thing they are taking our ideas seriously....

Through Utari Kyokai we receive funds to carry our plans through, such as field trips to former powerful Ainu settlements, but also to finance various lectures. Today we even get funds from private funds of various kinds. This was unthinkable a decade ago. Now they can see with their own eyes that other tourist villages are following our example and cooperating with us. I realize, of course, that there will be some difficulties about some of our issues. I mean our intention to make national parks of mountains and forests and use part of our land to cultivate our own crops, but if we can convince the authorities of the different "chos" [administrative units] that it will be profitable in the end, they will give us permission, I am positive. If they give us money, the government has to approve and if we have the approval of the government, there will be no problems. You see we are thinking: Traditionally the Ainu people love and revere Nature. Pollution is a serious problem in Nihon, especially in Honshu, but also here in Hokkaido. Many people from Honshu come to Hokkaido "to get some fresh air". We, the Ainu people will fight for the rights to have fresh air and our arrangements for our people are in line with such a development. Our people will be the perfect specialists, it is our cultural inheritance. We have great plans and the authorities are beginning to take our views seriously. Pollution is as delicate a problem as it is serious, but we think we can help out (Nibutani, 1988).

According to Kayano there are several things indicating a change in attitude both to the way the Ainu look upon their situation and the way the authorities look upon it.

According to Kayano, it is above all their renewed interest in their own cultural tradition and the ways in which they show that it is possible to incorporate values and ideologies that belong to it into the "rational" larger society, that have influenced this change. He has shown that these values and ideologies do not necessarily manifest themselves in isolation from the larger society.

His intention is to convince the authorities that the strategies the Ainu employ do not mean that they seek to leave the nation of which they are part, or that they strive to exist between two sectors, a "traditional" and a modern.

THE OPINION OF KAYANO'S AINU ANTAGONISTS

The position of Kayano's antagonists is that his commitment to matters concerning the Ainu, the culture has contributed to a renewed interest in their Ainu inheritance on a large scale and that this interest in turn may serve to improve their situation in several ways.

However, they are afraid that the present image of Kayano as an Ainu specialist, where he functions as the embodiment of the entire Ainu culture, may, eventually, circumscribe their freedom of choice with respect to how to improve their situation. They fear that their situation may be the subject of an exchange of one authority for another – Kayano instead of Wajin authorities. In this situation there is also, they fear, a possibility that a shift of authority may turn out to replace the current problems with different problems. Their main criticism concerns the fact that he makes his own ambitions their ambitions as well. According to one of my Ainu informants in Nibutani:

> Maybe we are not interested in being singled out. I mean, there is no saying that we cannot be proud of our own culture without stressing how unique we are, all the time. Maybe we are content with the way things have turned out around here. I lead a good life, I do not think of myself as different from the Shamo. I am a farmer and I like it. Some of us like to be left alone. Nowadays, we must avoid telling people where we come from. If we say we are from Nibutani, other people will assume that we share Mr Kayano's views. If they do not like him and his views they will not speak to us. Personally I think this is very bad. In the end it may even harm our case. Some people say it already has. It seems as if nowadays you cannot start a conversation without first stating what view you have on these matters (Ainu male, aged 35, Nibutani, 1988).

Other Ainu oppose Kayano because they think of him and his work as highly commercialized. "He is now, thanks to his involvement in Ainu matters, both a wealthy and famous man, but he is not 'devoted' anymore". Further:

If people have a different view they cannot make their voices heard. Mr Kayano and his associates have their plans and since they are rather powerful they will have it their way. The authorities are very sensitive to criticism, especially from other countries, and they have received a lot of criticism recently. They feel they have to do something for the Ainu people, so naturally they listen to Mr Kayano. He is famous, you know. But the authorities do not know very much about our people. They never took any interest in us. Now they think Mr Kayano represents our people as a whole. This is not true. Some of our people prefer to be left alone. However, Mr Kayano cannot understand that because he himself likes to be "a sensation". He thinks that his work with the Ainu culture will give him the Nobel Prize. He thinks if he gets this prize the Ainu people will be very proud of their own culture. Besides, the way he exposes our culture is not always the right way. His knowledge is too limited. He knows about Nibutani and the vicinity but he does not know about other places. Many Ainu people I know of think that his way of displaying the Ainu culture will be as biased as the one presented by the Shamo. Recently, I have heard that he has taken this criticism seriously. Now he is cooperating with Ainu people in Akan, Shiraoi and the metropolis. Ainu people from these areas join together and discuss Ainu matters specific to their own areas. They compare and discuss how to go about different problems. In this way they get to know each other and each other's people. I think that is good, but I am not sure that the Ainu people in Akan, Shiraoi and the metropolis agree. As far as Akan and Shiraoi are concerned their Ainu profile is limited to the tourist season. Therefore to say that the Ainu people who live here take a pride in their Ainu origin is greatly exaggerated. It is a standpoint which is linked to tourism and the profit from it. Naturally the Ainu are interested in getting to know their culture properly, but their primary concern is the profit, not the culture. There is, of course, no harm in such thoughts. They lead to a better material life. Further, once the basic material needs are solved there might be opportunities to fulfill other needs, ethnic needs. In Nibutani this is what is happening actually. If people take the development here as a model there might be a great change, at least in the long run. I think that the majority of our people are interested in a change. I mean, today most Ainu people are in the lowest income bracket and that does not make us very proud, only poor. That is why we choose anonymity. The Ainu people are a proud people. We do not like other people to know about our situation. We'd rather starve. The Shamo doors are closed to us. We have to open other doors. It is possible that the door which Mr Kayano has opened may lead us to the door that once and for all will improve our situation even give us an ethnic status, you know recognition as a people. That is our wish, but we have to be proud of the culture to which we belong, otherwise there would be no point in seeking recognition. Do you not agree (Ainu male, aged 29, living in Sapporo, 1988).

The criticism, as expressed above, reflects a disapproval that the measures taken by the Ainu are understood following Kayano's model, regardless of whether they are actually in line with his model or not.

The model constructed by Kayano is based on a conviction that emphasis on cultural factors will eventually give the Ainu status as equals to the Wajin. In this model there is a stress on cultural factors that unite the Ainu and distinguish them from the Wajin. According to the antagonists, however, this stress singles them out as much as the existing *Hokkaido Kyuudojin Hogoho* singles them out.

After all, a main concern among their people is to be accepted as Nihonjin on the same terms as the Wajin are accepted as Nihonjin. The position of the antagonists is that it is debatable whether emphasis on cultural factors actually serves this purpose.

The problem for the Ainu today is that the two concepts "Nihonjin" and "Wajin" have an identical status and in practice these two concepts are interchangeable. Of these two concepts Wajin is strictly ethnic, whereas the Nihonjin concept is not. The latter is used to denote all the subjects of the Nihon nation, that is, Burakumin, Ryukyujin, Ainu, Wajin and so forth.

At the time of the annexation of Hokkaido the concepts "Kyuudojin" and "Dojin" were used by the authorities to denote a people whose culture was perceived as a variant of the dominant culture. In the colloquial language, however, these concepts were replaced by "Ainu".

According to the model outlined by Kayano, it is no longer possible for the Ainu to accept that their culture is a variant of the dominant culture in Nihon. The principal ambition, if their hope is to become accepted as Nihonjin on the same terms as the Wajin, must be to educate their own people in values and beliefs that are rooted in their own culture – to foster an awareness of Ainu idenity and to establish a network of Ainu people skilled and trained in the beliefs and customs that belong to the Ainu. In this way the Ainu will, according to Kayano, be able to replace the present picture of themselves and their culture with one where they recognize themselves.

This in turn will, eventually, change the present stereotype opinions the Wajin have of the Ainu and it will possibly also work in favour of a shift in the Wajin attitudes to the present discriminatory treatment of them. For such reasons it is necessary for the Ainu, Kayano argues, to concentrate their efforts on establishing "Ainu" as a strictly ethnic concept.

The strategy used by Kayano can be said to stand in direct contradiction to the non-ethnic premisses of state ideology. It challenges the pe-established social context governed by these rules. Yet, according to his antagonists, such emphasis on ethnic factors may eventually harm their case. The wish of the Ainu, they argue, is to be accepted as Nihonjin on the same terms as the Wajin. This in turn does not necessarily imply that they are willing to go against the premisses of state ideology.

If one consistently confronts the values and ideologies the Ainu have with those of the Wajin, the result may be a widened gap between the two groups, and this may harm both the nation and its subjects. Besides, there are Ainu, who neither register nor identify themselves as Ainu and this, they argue, may be used in support of a view that the concern of the Ainu is actually to adapt themselves to the premisses of state ideology.

According to Kayano, however, this relates not so much to the fact that these people actually have given up their cultural tradition or claims of ethnic status. Instead, according to him, their indifferent attitudes to their Ainu inheritance are a consequence of their inferior social position in the environment where they live, rather than a carefully planned acculturation strategy, based on a rejection of their ethnic affiliation.

Although Kayano and his methods do not go unchallenged, his aim is to improve the situation of the Ainu. The principal concern here is to prevent the state, *Kokka*, taking over and controlling Ainu land and natural resources altogether. Included here is an ambition that the Ainu eventually may take over positions in the various Ainu museums – at present it is Wajin who occupy these. In this way the work with Ainu beliefs and customs will be more prestigious. This in turn will serve as a source of inspiration for the Ainu in their attempts to establish knowledge centres, national parks and the like. It will also encourage the Ainu to take up occupations that are related to ideologies and value rooted in their own culture. To achieve this an ethnic status is an absolute necessity. Their concern must be to clearly distinguish their own culture from the Wajin culture. Yet, it must be done in such a way so that the Wajin recognize it as equal to their own. In a society where the national identity is both holistic and hierarchical it is not very likely that the Wajin would work for something that contravenes their acceptable principle of reasoning. For such reasons the revitalization of the values and ideologies that belong to the Ainu must be achieved through the efforts of the Ainu. Only through their own efforts will it be possible for them to become accepted as Nihonjin and Ainu on the same terms as Nihonjin and Wajin are accepted today.

CHAPTER EIGHT

Summary and Conclusion

The principal concern of this work has been to understand the relation between cultural change and cultural mobilization as it is occurring among the Ainu. In order to do this fieldwork was conducted in Hokkaido, the main territory of the Ainu today. In my work I do not deal with the entire Ainu population as such, but with the cultural mobilization and those mechanisms and practices that have led to a situation where ethnic factors are emphasized.

My field research concentrates on two principal areas, one that deals with the complexity of factors involved in personal engagement in the cultural mobilization and the other that deals with the Ainu views of the way they have been identified in historical and ethnographic writings. In practice this implied that I did not settle for one area but alternated between several and that I used my field material to incorporate the Ainu views, comments, and criticism of the picture as they are "written" in the texts produced about them.

In order to grasp the special kind of cultural change that is occurring among the Ainu their culture must not be seen as self-contained, but rather as an outcome of the multiplex interaction between the Ainu, the larger society and its authorities. To grasp the phenomenon I have focused on the encounter between strategies of the state and local strategies which has proven ideal since we do not find any Ainu society in the general sense. What we have instead are Ainu individuals who employ different strategies of adaptation to larger Nihon society. A perspective that focuses on strategies rather than structure best suits the analysis of a multi-vocal reality.

To fully comprehend cultural change, the situation of the Ainu and the methods they employ must also be related to the transformation of Ainu society over time. This must be understood as a specific historical process where the larger society has penetrated Ainu local society during a considerable period of time. Interaction with the larger society meant, among other things, loss of land and language, the introduction of private land ownership and a new economy. The intervention of the Nihon nation via development programmes and activities has not only triggered various responses by collective and individual actors, but it has also created new networks. Examples are today's alternative land use which has introduced Ainu crops and the new network that exists among Ainu individuals who are engaged in the cultural mobilization.

Naturally, this also relates to restrictions placed upon them by the larger society, where they feel that their land and natural resources are properly assimilated while they themselves are not and where the hierarchical and holistic identity of the Wajin not only makes it difficult for them to enter the larger society – it makes it impossible. Finding themselves part of the process of change, the Ainu react and interpret the events around them, and the actions they take relate as much to the interaction situation as to their knowledge of their own cultural tradition.

In addition, interaction with the larger society also provides alternative or new ways of displaying and strengthening their ethnicity. An example is that tourist production and display have become a central process in the conscious reconstruction of Ainu identity. In several areas they have established Ainu village structures for the express purpose of producing hand-crafted goods and having tourists come and witness Ainu-style practices and activities with roots in their culture. They have also built Ainu-style houses where important village activities, such as the teaching of history and language, Ainu dances, weaving and wood-carving, occur on a weekly basis. In addition they invite the public to take part in field trips to formerly important Ainu areas where the participants, under Ainu guidance, are able to live Ainu-style lives for a couple of days.

While the history of Ainu relations to the larger society is one of increasing economic and political integration, they have not only been able to preserve their own cultural uniqueness, but they are also strengthening it in various ways. The change from a subsistence to a market-oriented economy has thus not worked to alienate them from their own values and ideologies.

When discussing the present situation of the Ainu it is, however, usually claimed that Ainu culture has largely disappeared, and it is argued that they exist as a poorly acculturated and economically and politically marginal minority. Yet this is not how the Ainu perceive themselves. They perceive themselves as central.

The material I have used in this work was obtained from archives, written or taped sources and field material. The main methods employed were fieldwork, including participant observation, censuses, case studies, interviews, both structured and unstructured.

The fieldwork was conducted in Hokkaido and it was divided into three phases, consisting of two shorter periods of three months each, in 1985 and 1986, and a longer period of six months in 1988. Nibutani village in the Hidaka region, in the southeastern part of Hokkaido, functioned as my field base, but I also stayed in other areas, such as Akan and Shirao, in the Kushiro and Iburi regions, as well as the cities of Sapporo, Hakodate and Asahikawa. The criterion for my selection of communities was variation in the degree of personal engagement in Ainu activities and practices and a consequent change in attitude to the policy of assimilation.

My fieldwork approach was to seek an inside view. The main concern was to present their historiography and ethnography in a way that allows incorporation of their own views. Since previous research shows notably little interest in this and since the Ainu do not recognize themselves in their writings, the advantage of this approach is obvious.

Further, since the presentations of the history and ethnography of the Ainu constitute a field within which the Ainu have consistently debated their identity, they also have a central place in my work. To illustrate aspects of inconsistency between the views of the Ainu and the views presented in previous writings about them I used my field material to incorporate Ainu comments and criticism.

The basis from which anthropologists have made their interpretation of the "original" Ainu way of life derives from documents made by feudal lords from Honshu. These documents date back about six hundred years. There is, however, no saying that the cultural and social tradition of the Ainu actually correspond to this picture. It may even be a constructed picture, which is the opinion of the Ainu who have made this a major target of interest.

Studies of their society and culture made by previous researchers, have been carried out as community studies in a functionalist tradition and they have been limited to the local region. The picture emerging from their writings is a static and ahistorical one and their works have encouraged researchers to look for symptoms of cultural decline. Consequently, a presentation of the Ainu as a vanishing people and their culture as a closed chapter was generally accepted, in spite of evidence to the contrary.

A main feature of these works is that they give both scanty and fragmentary information about most aspects of the former Ainu way of life. There has also been a tendency to write the Ainu into pre-conceived notions of "traditional" or primitive hunter-gatherer societies, an evolutionary bias that severely limited the range of phenomena that have been described. For such reasons many aspects of the existing interdependence between economic and social relations, ideas of property and types of economic exchange, political processes, ideas of law and morals, ritual beliefs and practice, have never fully been explained. For the same reason similar problems arise when it comes to accounting for the origins of the Ainu, or when questions of a joint Ainu-Wajin ethnic and territorial past are raised.

The problems of the identity of the Ainu are considerable and since the conclusions arrived at are unsatisfactory the concern has been to clarify certain aspects of the cultural and racial differences and similarities between the Ainu and the Wajin as presented by previous research. From earlier studies about this, one gets the impression that there is stress on the differences rather than the similarities.

The strategy of early research to solve the problem of Ainu identity was from the standpoint of the Ainu relationship to the aboriginal population of the Nihon archipelago. The main aim was to prove that the Ainu were not identical to the aboriginal population of Nihon. The matter was of considerable political importance, since if evidence was found that the Ainu were in fact Nihon's aboriginal population, they must also be regarded as the rightful owners of the land. However, the theoretical and methodological positions taken by early scholars shed no light on the origins of the Ainu, nor do they clarify the confused picture of a joint Ainu-Wajin ethnic and territorial past. A feature of their works is that they have been more concerned with falsifying each other's theories than with answering questions. Although the arguments about the origins of the Ainu do not go beyond hypothesis, as no convincing conclusions can be made on the basis of the craniological, somatological, linguistic and cultural evidence, the view that the Ainu are of Caucasoid origin was, until recently, generally accepted. Today this position has been abandoned and recent research favours Ainu affinity with other Mongoloid peoples. Research into the identity of the Ainu has thus taken a new turn and today focus is on comparison between neighbouring Ainu tribes rather than comparison between the Ainu and neighbouring tribes of other cultures.

The Ainu view of themselves is that they are of the same origin as the Koropok-un-guru a "mythical" people who once inhabited the Nihon archipelago. This theory is in line with the view of early researchers, yet according to them, the Ainu and the Koropok-un-guru are not one and the same people.

Another problem with the identification of the Ainu relates to the Wajin approach to "history". A common feature of Wajin historiography is that only selected parts of the actual historical sequences are presented, giving a picture of the Yamato people, the ancestors of the Wajin, as conquerors and heroes and all other peoples as assimilated or driven away. With their attempts to trace this image as far back in time as possible they have even managed to provide a mythological charter for their position. For the Ainu this has serious consequences since their verbal accounts have been moulded to fit the dominant ideology.

The Ainu of today do not think highly of the existing historiography and ethnography which is why they present their own versions. In these they criticize the way in which their history and ethnography has been used. Their own works are, however, considered to be of little importance. According to official authorities, they are based on personal interpretations of Ainu culture and history, obtained either by personal experience or by interviewing local Ainu people. Their opinion is that the Ainu version of their history and ethnography belongs to the genre of the novel. According to the works of the Ainu, however, their former lifestyle was more elaborate than previous researchers assert. According to the Ainu version, they were neither conquered nor assimilated in the general sense, it was a choice of their own. Either their people chose to abandon their Honshu residence, or else they chose to take up the customs and practices of neighbouring tribes. Yet, in accordance with the incorporation of Hokkaido land and people into the nation-to-be, the official interpretation has proved to be ideal especially when it came to gaining general approval for a policy of assimilation.

When discussing integration it is essential to distinguish between land and people. Generally speaking, the land and its exploitation was a matter of primary concern, while the incorporation of its native people became a matter of secondary importance.

Since the early days of colonization Hokkaido has been developed to receive immigrants, to defend Nihon territory and to provide a base for food supplies, not only for Hokkaido but for the nation as a whole. Today Hokkaido is the major producer of rice and Nihon as a whole has a place among the world's leading capitalist nations. Meanwhile, the Ainu are in the lowest income bracket and their own efforts to alter this condition are legally limited to demands for individual rights.

As a member of the UN, Nihon agrees to abide by the Universal Declaration of Human Rights, and membership in the UN implies that Nihon must ensure basic human rights. In the Ainu case there is a problem since the covenants can only be as effective as the member state permits, and therefore, Ainu measures with respect to the rights of a people are not recognized. Yet, the possibility that the Ainu actually use their knowledge and skills as an instrument or a means to gain recognition as a people cannot be dismissed simply because this does not fit the official ideology in Nihon. My field material suggests that the Ainu have made an official recognition of themselves as a distinct cultural group, the goal of their efforts in achieving equal rights and equal opportunities with the Wajin. Thus, in this sense the cultural mobilization is deeply political.

Most debate about the strategies used by the Ainu in the interaction situation has been concerned with the development of the Ainu from the point of view of the larger society. The people to be developed have been seen as the passive objects of the process rather than active subjects. The Ainu have been seen as agents of the changing conditions of which they are part and the process of change itself has been seen as self-propelling, in the sense that it needs only to be freed from the fetters of tradition or whatever structure may be holding it back. The development programmes for them aim to de-emphasize cultural factors and make them part of one huge national family. This view is in line with the assumption of modernization theories, denying the ideologies and values of "traditional" societies' dynamic intensives. This also includes a tendency to interpret these factors as irrational, that is, as incompatible with strict means-ends calculations. By looking at actually existing change, we find that there is no universal movement from "traditional" to modern but a multitude of regional transformations.

A defining feature of Ainu cultural change is the emphasis placed on ideologies rooted in their cultural mobilization. This includes the introduction of Ainu crops and vegetables, the establishment of national parks in areas of historic importance and the establishment of Ainu knowledge centres, where lectures in their oral language, history and culture as well as in Ainu weaving and wood-carving techniques, are undertaken. This does not necessarily mean that they seek to exit from the nation of which they are part, nor that they strive to exist between two sectors, a "traditional" and a modern. It would be wrong to conclude that their strategies contrast with the life of the present. Such views derive from the assumption that "tradition" and change stand in a dualistic relationship to one another, while in practice there exists a synthesis between the two.

It has been argued, by some, that the essence of Ainu self-identification is "folklore", that is, a mere display of cultural artifacts. Even if there is a special desire among the Ainu to function politically and economically within the larger society, this is a serious misinterpretation of those who fail to see the relationship between culture and identity. While there is a clear desire to remain part of the nation, they wish to do so as a political unit rather than as isolated individuals. In this sense the cultural mobilization implies a degree of political autonomy as well. This might appear simple, but, in a system where multi-ethnicity is seen as a threat to the very existence of society, it is a very serious problem. There is no room for the Ainu to have ethnic status in a society where hierarchical homogeneity is seen as the only acceptable principle of reasoning. Consequently the Ainu are deprived of an identity based on ethnic features, that is, those that derive from or relate to a human group having racial, religious, linguistic and historical traits in common. It has been argued that the position of the Ainu can only be changed in Nihon official ideology via a fuller integration into the larger society and that they must enter contemporary Nihon society on the non-ethnic premises of state organization.

For the Wajin the commercial aspect of Ainu customs, has come to overshadow their cultural contents. Accordingly, substance has been de-emphasized while the display of their culture for tourists and the larger public has become dominant. According to this view, museums, exhibition halls, and the like will remain the only possible forum for the survival of Ainu customs and beliefs. The result is an apparent neat picture of an unproblematic fusion of assimilation and maintenance of "traditional" values and ideologies.

In accounting for the Ainu situation and the changes that have occurred, previous research has adopted the state ideology that ranks rather than analyses the Ainu situation. The premisses that governed Ainu life of the past have been understood as the ultimate cause of their present status as a group of individuals depending on social welfare for their survival. The authorities have made use of the low percentage of Ainu registering as Ainu, together with the high percentage of Ainu engaged in the rural sector, in support of a view that confirms the success of the policy of assimilation. There is, however, reason to believe that this view has been constructed to suit the ultimate purpose of the nation.

In this context the Ainu belongs to a nation that has grounded itself firmly in a territorial and social space inherited from the ancestors of a dominant and sole ethnic group. It is a reality where the Ainu and the Wajin jointly occupy the same national territory and on "equal" terms. Yet, this view does not correspond to the reality in which the Ainu live and operate. But the fact that Ainu and Wajin jointly occupy the same national territory has not resulted in them being equals. Discrimination against Ainu, manifested in Wajin reluctance to marry and employ an Ainu, is a common feature, for if, officially, Ainu are as Wajin as any Nihonjin, they are still outcasts, that is, their social position, their aboriginal status function as effectively as any ethnic stigmatization.

For such reasons the interests of the Ainu and national interests must rather be understood in terms of a contradiction. For the Ainu the stress on cultural factors is an indispensable means of unequivocally defining their own position in the context of the larger society. Here, tourist production and display, manifested in the public arena, where the production of hand-crafted goods, such as Ainu-style clothes and Inau carving, and also the establishment of national parks and the introduction of Ainu crops have become central processes in the conscious reconstruction of their identity.

They establish their own specificity by emphasizing the distinctive content of their culture for tourists and the larger public in a context where such specificity is understood as a variant of the dominant culture rather than as a separate identity. This presentation of their selfhood is notably political, as it is based on the cultural elements that distinguish them from the dominant culture. These cultural elements are used to define their significant otherness.

Although the Ainu, as they are described in the texts produced about them, are seen as indigenous, marginal and peripheral, this does not correspond to their own view of themselves. They do not refer to themselves as marginal or peripheral nor do they talk about themselves as indigenous. Rather they perceive themselves as central. Consequently, the strategies they employ to improve their situation emanate from what they perceive as a central position.

Ainu attitudes to their inheritance differ among themselves. There are those Ainu who register and identify as Ainu as well as those who do not. This difference must be related to specific social and occupational contexts. These different attitudes should be seen as responses to the reality in which they live where their official status as Nihonjin not is accepted by the majority population, who identify them as "Ainu" or "Kyuudojin". This has led to that the Ainu identify in different ways. The strategies they use for identification are of two different kinds. One is used by Ainu who place strong emphasis on their own cultural uniqueness while the other is used by Ainu who stress similarities between themselves and the Wajin.

Although there are Ainu who prefer to be anonymous, this attitude has not resulted in a total rejection of their own cultural inheritance, nor has it worked to alienate them from their own people and therefore it cannot be seen as a carefully planned strategy of acculturation. Besides, both the Ainu who choose to base their identity on ethnic features, and those who do not, are aware that their Nihonjin identity is something which is not accepted by the majority population.

The Ainu who reject their Ainu identity in words may reveal it in practice, that is, at the same time as they choose to identify themselves with respect to their employment situation, such as farmers, peasants, and the like, they take part in Ainu festivities and other Ainu activities. For such reasons it might be argued that their choice of identification is a response to the occupational and situational context in which they live.

This is a possibility that has been overlooked by previous researchers, who have put too much stress on the fact that many Ainu choose anonymity and used this to confirm the view that the Ainu are rejecting their own cultural inheritance. Considering the fact that the Ainu who register and identify as Ainu have shared interests with those who choose anonymity, their different strategies with respect to register and identification can hardly be seen to contrast with shared aims. Instead they contrast with one another on what means serve their purpose best, which makes it questionable to claim that they indicate an indifferent attitude to their Ainu inheritance in general.

As it is now, the two concepts "Wajin" and "Nihonjin" have an identical status, although the Wajin concept is an ethnic concept, while the Nihonjin concept is not. This state of affair is, of course, linked to the holistic and hierarchical identity of Nihon where the national identity, Kokka-shugi, not is separated from the cosmological order. It is constructed out of its myths of history and the deeds of its heroes. According to this model the national identity originates with the ancestors of the Wajin, who according to historians and archaeologists are defined as "the people who founded the empire of Nihon in contradistinction to the primitive inhabitants", who, by the same historians and archaeologists, are described as simple-minded, kindly, stupid and so forth.

In accordance with the annexation of Hokkaido it was decided that all peoples natives to Nihon were to be addressed by the term Nihonjin. On account of the fact that the Ainu had "suffered hard" during the previous periods it was decided that they were entitled to "special treatment", that is, *Hokkaido Kyuudojin Hogoho*. They were singled out by the use of the term "Kyuudojin" which was later inserted before their civil names. Yet, this act can also be seen as a sign of ambiguity on behalf of the authorities – as if they hesitated to recognize the link between themselves and the primitive inhabitants who in the written history is robbed of both pride and dignity. Anyhow, in the colloquial language the term "Ainu" came to replace Kyuudojin and these concepts came to be accepted as references to a people whose culture was considered a variant of the Wajin culture.

Today, this is no longer accepted by the Ainu. Now, "Ainu" has actually become a strictly ethnic concept, based on ethnic features. Yet, this is not accepted by the authorities, who continue to rank the cultures of the nation.

In order to change the official view of themselves as a less-developed people, the Ainu have chosen to reinvestigate their own cultural and historic past. Their concern is to point out potentials within their culture and to make these potentials work to regain lost land and natural resources.

Their position is that they, as well as the Wajin, are not just "Nihonjin". They are also "Kyuudojin", that is, Hokkaido natives, and therefore they are also entitled to have a native status, that is "Ainu". Although, officially, they have actually both a native and a national status, neither of these has rendered them an ethnic status. This is a condition which they do not accept. To make this absolutely clear their strategy is to attach a face to their culture, to put themselves and their culture on show, so to speak. By this act they clearly distinguish themselves and their culture from the majority people and their culture. With this strategy they hope to force the Wajin to accept the reality of the Ainu as it actually is to them. Such a shift of focus is highly relevant, as it will serve to present the actual situation of the Ainu, thereby opening up alternative models for understanding their actions. By questioning the picture of successful assimilation and by stressing that the occupational situation of the Ainu, is a necessity rather than a choice of their own, we find that the strategies employed by the Ainu do in fact serve ethnic purposes. After all, most Ainu do not own the land they work on – it is owned by Honshu companies or else it comes under common property. Further, when asked what kind of occupations they preferred, engagement in occupations and activities tied to their own values were by them seen as the most attractive alternatives.

By focusing on the interests of the Ainu, that is, the way they look upon themselves and the different ways in which they apply their activities, skills and knowledge, we will most likely find that what authorities and others describe as folklore, charismatic leaders and personal interpretations of their Ainu inheritance, presented in the form of novels rather than works of science, are, in fact, carefully planned strategies for achieving ethnic status.

One can of course always ask oneself why the authorities should meet Ainu demand for recognition as ethnic group, especially since by this act they would have to reconsider the view that Nihon is inhabited by one homogeneous people. What would be gained in return for this loss of prestige. The Ainu are a tiny minority. It seems as if they will lose more by acceding the demand than by ignoring it.

In global terms, minorities and indigenous peoples all over the world are today organizing themselves òpposing dominant regimes that have denied them access to land and taken from them their rights. This is not locally and regionally restricted, not even nationally. In their attempts to regain lost land, values, ideologies and lifestyles they join together in organizations working for their rights and interests on a global level. They exchange experiences with one another. They use mass media to win the favour of the public and to put pressure on the regimes that suppress them. The Ainu are no exception to this. Looked upon in this light, it becomes extremely difficult for the authorities to continue to pretend that the culture of the Ainu is a less-developed variant of the majority culture.

Looking back, a hundred years ago when the land of the Ainu was annexed by Nihon, the situation was different. At that time dominant regimes acted as if they were in their full rights to occupy and colonize the land of indigenous peoples, who were in no position to defend themselves against the intruder who were superior in number and had the most effective weapons. It was a time when the claims of those who were numerous and equipped with modern weapons outweighed other claims, like freedom of religion, cultural autonomy and the like. Besides, the cultures and lifestyles of indigenous peoples were at that time seen as primitive and backward. The intruders saw themselves more as saviours than suppressors. To their knowledge they acted as much in the interest of the indigenous peoples as in their own and national interests. Naturally, their acts were in essence political – small and military weak nations had, and still have, problems to survive in a competitive world – in the case of Nihon, policy slogans such as "enrich the nation and strengthen the military" reflected this.

At the time of the annexation of Hokkaido, the development of capitalism was urgent. The feudal regime was abandoned, old Nihon was on the verge of a breakdown. With the Meiji regime Nihon took up competition with other nations of the world. Nihon entered the world market and rapid modernization began.

For the Ainu integration into the larger society meant a general decline of their own lifestyles. While the nation to which they belong flourished they themselves became a marginal minority on the outskirts of the larger society. This was of course not an immediate effect. It is the result of a long and painful integration to which the Ainu have responded in various ways during the years that have passed since 1868. Today, their responses differ in many ways from those of earlier days. The Ainu have only recently come to "realize" that what was good for the nation was not necessarily also good for them. For many years the Ainu accepted this state of affair and their attempt to alter it is fairly recent. This can, to some extent, be explained by Nihon's isolationist policy, which slowed down the awakening process and their attempts to organize themselves. Yet, the fact that the Ainu were positive to integration, with its consequences for their motivations to act in ethnic interests on a large scale, is, perhaps of the greatest importance. This circumstance in combination with the standard position that Nihon consists of one homogeneous population, determine the nature of the cultural mobilization. While other minorities put more stress on political and economic factors in their struggle for better living conditions and are less concerned with how the majority people evaluate the customs and beliefs they themselves have, relying on their own judgments, the Ainu stress these factors and are most concerned with the judgment of the Wajin, due to the hierarchical and holistic identity of Nihon. Their focus on culture serves the following purpose – to gain equal status with the Wajin. Yet, even if their goal is to achieve cultural autonomy their cultural mobilization also implies a certain degree of political autonomy. This is best reflected by their attempts to use part of their land and natural resources in conformity with the values that belong to them.

A recent interpretation
of the Moshir

Noteworthy is also a recent interpretation of the Moshir, given by an Ainu, Naohika Hashine. In 1976, he went to prison after having revolted against Wajin ways of handling Ainu affairs. His thoughts are expressed in a *Letter from Ainu to Native American Friends* (1976). Extracts from the letter:

To the Friends of the Kootenay Nation
I am an Ainu presently imprisoned in one of the prisons in Japan. I should like to express my solidarity and support to our comrades of the Kootenay nation from Ainu Moshir. In the Ainu language this [i. e. Ainu Moshir] means the Ainu nation. However the Ainu Moshir differs from such states as Japan or the United States in that it does not make distinctions between people of different cultures.... We have never possessed nature nor have we turned it into "our territory". We have not established a system in which man controls man. Nature and the earth belong to nobody, because they are living as we are living. Nature and the earth are our mother that has given birth to us and helped us grow up. It is but the Shamo [Japanese] that chopped up into pieces the mother nature and earth, controlled and destroyed them under the name of "possessions". [Shamo is the word Ainu use to call the Japanese. It is a word of denunciation to aggressors.] The Shamo killed and enslaved the Ainu.... The Ainu Moshir will win victory over Japan. (Brother Hashine could not sign this letter because of prison regulations) (Hashine 1976: 1-3).

Interpreted thus the Moshir may stand for a concept which could be likened to "nation" and according to this interpretation, it may well fit the following definition of nation, suggested by Anderson:

An autonomous entity, a socio-cultural concept to depict a common belonging to, a community distinguished by the style in which it is imagined (Anderson 1983: 14-15).

Mr Shigeru Kayano

Name: Shigeru Kayano

Born: June 25, 1915

Place of Birth: Hokkaido Saru-gun Biratori cho Aza Nibutani 26banchi

Address: Hokkaido Saru-gun Biratori cho Aza Nibutani 79banchi 1.

Education: Biratori Elementary School, 1939

Employment:
   April 1939 Sapporo Regional Forest Office
   April 1959 Carving Craftsman (self-supporting)
   April 1971 Writer (novelist) (self-supporting)

Appointments:
   April 1961 Assistant to Mr Kindach Kyosuke, professor of linguistics.
   June 1972 Deputy chief Nibutani Ainu Culture Exhibition Hall
   April 1975 Officer of Biratori cho Town Office
   April 1979 Consulting professor to the National Anthropological Museum
   in Osaka
   April 1981 Consulting professor to the National Nature Children's House;
   Hidaka
   Chief of Nibutani Ainu Culture Exhibition Hall
   April 1983 Chief of the association for Ainu culture Preservation in Biratori
   cho

Cultural Prizes awarded him by the authorities:
   November 1965 The prize for the Preservation of Ainu culture items.
   November 1975 The Kikuchikan Prize (Uwepeker: Folktale)
   November 1976 The Kyoiku Koro Prize (Education)
   November 1978 The Bunka Shorei Prize (Culture)

Visual production:
   In cooperation with NHK (state TV) production:
   1964 "The World of Yukar" (Yukar no Sekai) three films in all (16 mm, each
   30 min.).
   1971 "Ainu Wedding Ceremony" (Ainu no Kekkon-shiki) 16 mm, 34 min

1974 "How to Build a Chise" (Chise Akara) 16 mm, 56 min.

1977 "The Bear Festival" (Iyomante) 16 mm, 163 min.

1978 "The Games of Saru River Ainu Children" (Saru-kawa Ainu Kodomo no Asobi) 16 mm, 50 min.

1978 "How to Build an Ainu Canoe" (Fune Sukari) 16 mm, 50 min.

In cooperation with Turano Production (private):

1987: "Lectures in Ainu Language and Conversation" (Ainu Itak to Kaiwa). Four videotapes, each 30 min.

Glossary of Ainu and Japanese words and concepts

In this glossary the Ainu words are marked with*. Words of uncertain origin, which may be either Ainu or Japanese, are marked with **.

A

Abashiri: a) city in the Abashiri district in Hokkaido; b) district in Hokkaido

*Ainu: "human being"

Ainu Kyokai: Ainu association in Asahikawa

*Ainu Moshir: Ainu native land

*Aiona: the goddess who created and educated the Ainu

**Akan: a) lake in the Kushiro district in Hokkaido ; b) village in the Kushiro district in Hokkaido

**Akita: a) district in Honshu, formerly Ugo district ; b) dog of the Akita race

*Akumi: cloth made of fish skin

Amaterasu: sun-goddess

*Anun Utari: Ainu person from "outside"

Aomori: district in Honshu, formerly Mutsu district consisting of Tsugaru and Shimokita Hanto

*Ape: a) Ape Chise; house father ; b) Ape Huchi; house mother

Asahikawa: city in the Kamikawa district in Hokkaido

*Attus: cloth made of bark

B

Bakufu: Shogunate military administration in Honshu

**Bankinnenshippa: Ainu leader

Basho: Shogunate military administration in Hokkaido

Be: occupational groups of craftsmen and workers

**Biratori: town in the Hidaka district in Hokkaido

Burakumin: Japan's outcast, minority people in Japan also known as Eta
Bushi: Warrior

C

Chigyonushi: tradesmen
Chiho or Schichou: region, district
*Chikabumi: suburb of Asahikawa in the Kamikawa district in Hokkaido
*Chikoikip: beast
*Chise: a) Ainu-style house ; b) nuclear unit
*Chise, Chise-Koro-Kamui: a) the god who protects the house; b) the owl god;
    c) male ancestor god
*Cehorokakep: three-headed gable frame
*Cep: salmon, i. e. main food
*Cip: canoe
*Cipsanke: launching canoes
*Cicira: loach
Cho: administrative unit

D

Daimyou: a) "great name"; b) feudal lord in Honshu
Dewa: today's Yamagata and Akita districts (formerly Ugo and Uzen)
Dojin: natives

E

Ebizu: Ainu
Echizen: Ainu territory in Honshu, included in today's Fukui district
Edo: today's Tokyo
Edo Era: (1603-1867) including the Tokugawa, the Bunka, the Bunsei and the
    Ansei
*Eha: a kind of bean
*Ekashi: a) Ainu leader; b) (Shine) Ekashi Ikir(u); patrilineal kin group
*Ekashi Itak: language of the elders

*Ekashi Itokpa: male ancestor emblem
Emishi: Ainu
Epi-Jomon: archaeological period (Hokkaido only)
*Esoka: bullhead
Etchigo: Ainu territory in Honshu, included in today's Yamagata district
Etchu: Ainu territory in Honshu, included in today's Niigata district
Ezo: Ainu native land
Ezo(jin): Ainu

F

Fukoshu Kyohei: enrich the country, strengthen the military
Fukuyama: included in the Bingo district in Honshu, todays Shimane district
Fune: canoe

G

Gaijin, also Gaikokujin: foreigner
Giri: duty, obligation

H

Hakodate: city in the Oshima district in Hokkaido
Hakubutsukan: museum
Han: the domain of an individual Daimyo
Hanto: peninsula
Hashi: chop sticks
*Hash-uk-Kamuy: the god who provides game
Hayato: people living in the southern part of Japan
Heian: archaeological period (Honshu only)
*Heper: bear cub
**Hidaka: district in Hokkaido
Higashi-Ezochi: east Ezo, areas controlled by the Wajin i. e. the Hiyama,
    Tokachi, Oshima, Iburi, Hidaka, Kushiro and Nemuro districts
Hokkaido: The Northern Sea Circuit

Hokudai: Sapporo State University

Honshu: Japan's main island, also known as Nihon proper and the mainland

Horonai: main trunk railway line exploiting the Horonai coal mine

*Huchi Kamuy: a) fire goddess; b) birth giving goddess ; c) female ancestor goddess ; d) (Shine) Huchi ikir; matrilineal kin group

*Huchi Korpe: female property

I

Iburi: district in Hokkaido

Ienoko: vassal, child

*Ikupasuy: family treasure, offering stick

*Imukusai: necklaces

*Inakibi: Ainu cereal

*Inau: a) offering stick ; b) Kamuy-Nomi Inau; offering stick used in offerings to deities and gods; c) Shiranuppa-Inau; offering stick used in offerings to ancestors

Inu: dog

*Ikir: kin group

*Ikoro: goods of ritual value

*Ir Matina Esap Utar: a group of males descended in the uterine line from a known woman for four generations

*Ir Matainu: a group of females descended in the uterine line from a known woman for four generations

Iroha Jiru Sho: dictionary compiled in the twelfth century

*Isabakiku: club

Ishikari: district in Hokkaido

*Itak: a) Ainu Itak; oral language; b) Ekashi Itak; language of the elders; c) Kamuy Itak; language of the gods

*Itangi: receptacles for sacred things

*Itayaya: green wood

*Itokpa: male ancestor emblem

*Iwory: field of activities for gods and humans

*Iyraykere: Ainu greeting performances

*Iyoibe: useful articles

*Iyomante: offering ceremony to Ainu deities

Izumo: Ainu territory in Honshu, included in today's Shimane district

J

Jinmu: first emperor son of the sun-goddess

Jomon: archaeological period (Hokkaido and Honshu)

K

**Kai: a) boy; b) Ainu territory in Honshu, included in the Ou district; c) Ainu (people) from "Kushi-Kui-Kai" ; d) to carry

Kaikyou: Strait

Kaitakinenka: Hokkaido colonial museum

Kaitakushi: colonization period (1869-1899)

Kaiwa: Ainu conversation

Kaga: Ainu territory in Honshu, included in today's Ishikawa district

Kamakura: archaeological period (Honshu only)

Kameda: area in the Oshima district in Hokkaido

Kamikawa: district in Hokkaido

*Kamuy: Ainu deities:

*Chise-Koro-Kamuy: a) the god who protects the house; b) owl god; c) male ancestor god

*Hash-uk-Kamuy; the god who provides game

*Kamuy Huchi: a) fire goddess; b) bith-giving goddess; c) female ancestor goddess

*Kim-un-Kamuy: bear god

*Metot-us-Kamuy: bear god

*Nupuro-Kes-un-guru: bear god

*Nupuro-Koro-Kamuy: bear god

*Pause Kamuy: supreme gods

*Sekuma-Pause-Kamuy: bear god

*Wakka-uk-Kamuy: the god who provides fish

*Kamuy-Kotan: settlement of the gods, abode of the dead *Kamuy-Kus-Puyuara: holy window to the east

*Kamuy Moshir: land of the gods

Kankokujin: Koreans, minority people in Japan

Kanto: district in Honshu, formerly, Izu, Sagami, Boshu, Shimosa, Hitachi, Shimotsuke, Kotsuke and Musashi, districts (today's Kanagawa, Chiba, Toshigi and Saitama districts)

Kawa: river

Kayano: Ainu leader of today

Kazoku: family

Kekkon-shiki: marriage

*Kema-us-sintoko: receptacles for Ainu treasures

*Ketuni: purification ceremony

Kibori: wood-carving

*Kike: wood shavings

Kimono: Japanese clothing

*Kina: lily root

*Kirepo: a kind of trout

Kodomo-beya: nursery school

Kojiki: records of ancient matters, Japanese chronicle (A. D. 712)

Kokka: the state

Kokka-Shugi; nationalism

Kokumin: a) nation; b) people

*Korokomi: a sort of rhubarb

*Koropok-un-guru: a) a "mythical people" who once populated the Japanese archipelago, ; b) Ainu ancestors; c) dwarf

*Koshamain: Ainu leader

Koshi: a) Ainu territory in Honshu, including the Izumo, Echizen, Kaga, Noto, Etchu and Etchigo, included in today's Yamagata, Niigata, Ishikawa, Toyama, Fukui and Shimane districts ; b) Ainu

*Koshne: state of mind, mental condition

*Kotan: a) Ainu traditional settlements; b) Kamuy Kotan: abode of the dead; c) Sak Kotan: summer village

*Kotan-Koro-guru: Ainu leader

**Kozukai: Ainu leader

Kumaso: people living in the southern parts of Japan

Kumaishi: area in the Hiyama district in Hokkaido

Kunashi Menashi: area in Hokkaido, the battlefield between Ainu and Wajin Kurile, also Chishima: Ainu territory

Kushi: Ainu (people) from Kai, i. e. Kushi-Kui-Kai

Kushiro: district in Hokkaido

Kyokai: association

Kyushu: the southernmost of Japan's five main islands

Kyuudojin: aborigines

Kyuudojin Hogoho: Law for the Protection of Native Hokkaido Aborigines

M

*Maeni Korpe: male property
*Makiri: Ainu knife
*Marimo: lake god
Marimo Matsuri: lake god festival
Mashike: area in the Ishikari district in Hokkaido
*Matikir-Esap-Utar: a group composed of males and females descended in the
    uterine line of a woman for four generations
Matsuri: festival
Matsumae: a powerful Wajin han
Meiji: era (Meiji Ishin, enlightened government)
*Metot-us-Kamuy: bear god
Minshuku: pension
Minzoku: a) nation; b) race; c) people
Mise; tourist shop
*Moshir: a) Ainu native land; b) land of the living and the dead
*Moshir, Ainu Moshir: a) Ainu native land, ; b) land of the living
*Moshir, Kamuy Moshir: land of the gods
**Moshir, Pokna Moshir: the world beneath
Mura: Japanese word for village

N

Nakasone: Japan's former prime minister
Nara: archaeological period (Honshu only)
Nemuro: district in Hokkaido
**Nibutani: village in the Hidaka district in Hokkaido
Nichi Ezochi: west Ezo, Ainu territory controlled by Ainu, i. e. Shiribeshi, Ishi-
    kari, Sorachi, Rumoe, Soya, Kamikawa and Abashiri districts
Nihon: Nipon i. e. Japan, the land of the (rising) sun
Nihon Minzoku: Japanese nation
Nihon Proper: the mainland, i. e. Honshu
Nihongo: Japanese language
Nihonjin: Japanese people, i. e. people who seek their livelihood in Japan (Ni-
    hon)
Nihonshoki: history of Japan, Japanese chronicles (A. D. 720)
*Nikari: chest trinket

*Nima: a vessel, similar to present-day bowl
Niwa: Japanese ornamental garden
Noto: Ainu territory in Honshu, included in today's Ishikawa district
*Nuira: dace
*Nupuro-Kes-un-guru: bear god
*Nupuro-Koro Kamuy: bear god
*Nusa: gathering place for holy things

O

O-cha: Japanese tea
Okhotsk-Satsumon: archaeological period (Hokkaido only)
*Opu: spear
Oshima: district in Hokkaido
Otona: Japanese word for Ainu leader
Ou: Ainu territory in Honshu, formerly, Iwaki, Iwashiro, Rikuzen, Uzen,
    Rikuchu and Mutsu districts (today's Fukushima, Miyagi, Iwate, Akita and
    Aomori disricts)

P

*Pau: sound of gods
*Pause Kaumy: supreme gods
*Pet: river
*Pirika: state of mind, mental condition
**Pokna Moshir: the world beneath
Pon Machi: concubine

R

*Ramat: soul
*Rapuri: cloth made of fish skin
*Reyep also Seta: dog
*Reteruppa: cloth made of helm
*Retunbe: bead necklaces

Ryukyujin: Chinese immigrants also known as Okinawan, minority people in Japan

S

*Sak: non-location
Sakhalin, also Karafutu: Ainu territory
*Sakipe: a kind of trout
Samurai: guardian
San-Ken-Douchou: Three Prefecture (Nemuro, Hakodate and Sapporo) Period
*Sapane-guru: Ainu leader
Sapporo: "capital" of Hokkaido, situated in the Sorachi district
*Saranip: Ainu gathering bag
*Saru: famous Ainu river in the Hidaka district
Sengoku, Sengoku Jidai: epoch of war (1500-1600)
*Set bear cage
*Seta also Reyep: dog
Shakotan: area in the Shiribeshi district in Hokkaido
*Shakushain: Ainu leader
*Shamo: people whom one cannot trust
*Sharante: to imitate
**Shibankinne: Ainu leader
Shichou, or Chiho: region, district
Shi-nou-kou-shou: warrior-farmer- artisan-merchant
*Shinshamo: fellow trades men
Shinto: state religion in Japan till 1946
Shintoko: ornamented fancy sword
**Shiranuka: area in the Kushiro district in Hokkaido
Shiraoi: village in the Iburi district in Hokkaido
*Shirata: external part of wood
Shiro: house or domain of a feudal leader
Shiryoka: exhibition hall
*Shi(n)sham(o): fellow trades-men
*Shitoki also Imukusai: necklaces
Shizunai: a) village in the Hidaka district in Hokkaido, ; b) home of Shakushain
Sho-gakko: elementary school
Shogun: Seii-tai military leader (Generalissimo) in Honshu
Shogunate: ruling body, government

Shokusan Kogyo: industrialization
Shujin: "father" husband, i. e. feudal leader in Honshu
Shujin-Ienoko: lord-vassal
*Soroma: wood anemone
Soya Kaikyou: La Perouse Strait

T

*Tashiro: hatchet
Tatami: mats made of sea grass
Tate: house or domain of a feudal leader
**Teinei Pokna Chiri: hell
Tenno: emperor
Toi: a) Chinese sign for "non-continental people" ; b) barbarians
Tokugawa: a) Tokugawa dynasty (1603-1867) ; b) family name of leader in
    Edo era
Tonden-Hei: colonial military system
Tosho-kan: library
Tsubo: unit of land measure
Tsugaru Hanto: together with the Shimokita Hanto, formerly Mutsu district in
    Honshu, i. e. today's Aomori district
Tsugaru Kaikyou: Tsugaru Strait
Tumulus: archaeological period (Honshu only)
*Tusu: midwife, female medium

U

Uji: a) house; b) tribe; c) clan ; d) domain
*Ukosaino: ritual preparation before hunting
*Un-guru: (Ainu) person
*Upshoro-Kut: a) female ancestor mark; b) hidden girdle
*Urai Teshi: trap
*Uri: cloth made of birtd feather
**Utare: slave
*Utari: fellow
Utari Kyokai: Ainu association in Sapporo

Utasutu: area in the Ishikari district in Hokkaido,
*Uwepeker: Ainu history, consisting of Ainu folk tales and Ainu legend

W

Wajin: the dominant and sole ethnic group in Japan, Nihonjin in the colloquial language
*Wakka-us-Kamuy: the god who provides fish
*Wen: state of mind, mental condition

Y

*Ya: net
Yamato: a) Wajin ancestors ; b) territory of Wajin ancestors, included in today's Nara district
Yasaibatake: kitchen garden
Yayoi: archaeological period (Honshu only)
*Yukar: ode
*Yukar: a) Kamuy Yukar; odes of the gods; b) Yukar Upopo; Ainu legend
Yumasa: a) sword; b) fighting people.

Bibliography

Anderson, B.

1983 *Imagined Communities: Reflections on the Origin and Spread of Nationalism.* Norfolk: Thetford.

Augusta, J.

1960 *Urtidens Människa.* Stockholm: Arena.

Baba, Y.

1980 Study of Minority-Majority Relations: The Ainu and the Japanese in Hokkaido. *The Japanese Interpreter* 1: 60-92.

Barth, F.

1969 *Ethnic Groups and Boundaries: The Social Organization of Cultural Differences.* Boston: Little Brown.

Batchelor, J.

1901 *The Ainu and Their Folklore.* London: The Religious Tract Society.

1902 *Sea Girt Yezo: Glimpses at a Missionary Work in North Japan.* London: Church Missionary Society.

1924 *Ainu Fireside Stories.* Sapporo: Kyobunkan Toyko.

1925 *The Pit-dwellers of Hokkaido and Ainu Place Names Considered.* Sapporo: Kyobunkan Toyko.

1932 *The Ainu Bear Festival.* Sapporo: The Transactions of the Asiatic Society of Japan.

1938 *An Ainu-English-Japanese Dictionary.* Tokyo: Iwanami-Syoten.

1971 *The Ainu Life and Lore.* New York: Johnson Reprint Corporation.

Bell, D.

1975 *The Winding Passage.* Cambridge, Mass.: Cambridge University Press.

Bickmore, A..

1868 The Ainos or Hairy men of Jesso, Sachalin and the Kurile Islands. *American Journal of Science.*

Bird, I.

1881 *Unbeaten Tracks in Japan.* London: John Murray.

Board of Education

1988 *Kaneto: A Man of Burning Spirits.* Sapporo: Sangusha.

Boas, F.

1911 The Mind of Primitive Man. New York: Maxmillan.

1916 The Origin of Totemism. American Anthropologist, 18: 319-26.

1924 Social Organization of the Tribes of the North Pacific Coast. Race Language and Culture. New Yoek Maxmillan.

Brownlie, I.

1971 *Basic Documents on Human Rights.* Oxford: Clarendon Press.

205

Busk, G.
   1867   Description of the Skeleton of an Aino Woman and of Three Skulls of Man of the
          Same Race. *Anthropological Society of London* 3.

Cambell, J.
   1973   *The Masks of God: Primitive Mythology.* London: Souvenir Press.

Chamberlain, B.
   1887   *The Language, Mythology and Geographical Nomenclature of Japan Viewed in the
          Light of Ainu Studies.* Tokyo: Heibonsha.

Chiri, M.
   1956   *Chimei Ainu go shoten* [A Concise Dictionary of Ainu Place Names]. Sapporo: Nire
          Shobo.

   1962   *Bunrui Ainu go Jiten.* [Classified Dictionary of Ainu Language]. Tokyo: Heibonsha.

Chronicles

   A.D. 297   *Accounts of Three Kingdoms.* Sapporo: Hokudai.

   A.D. 712   *Kojiki.* Sapporo: Hokudai.

   A.D. 720   *Nihonshoki.* Sapporo: Hokudai.

Clifford, J. & G. E. Marcus.
   1986   *Writing Culture: The Poetics and Politics of Ethnography.* Berkeley: University of
          Berkeley Press.

Clifford, J.
   1986   Introduction: Partial Truths. In J.Clifford & G. E. Marcus (eds): *Writing Culture.*
          Berkeley: Berkeley University Press.

   1988   *The Predicament of Culture: Twentieth-Century Ethnography, Literature, and Art.*
          London: Harvard University Press.

Cohen, R.
   1978   Ethnicity: Problem and Focus in Anthropology. *Annual Review of Anthropology* 7:
          379-403.

Cornell, J.
   1964   Ainu Assimilation and Cultural Extinction. *Ethnology* 3: 287-304.

Crapanzano, V.
   1977   The Writing of Ethnography. *Dialectical Anthropology* 2: 69-73.

Crawford, G. &. Y. Masakazu.
   1987   Ainu Ancestors and Prehistoric Asian Agriculture. *Journal of Archaeological Science*
          14: 201-213.

Davis, G.
   1987   Japan's Indigenous Indians: The Ainu. *Tokyo Journal* October issue: 7-13, 18-19.

Deriha, K.
   1985   *The Spindles of the Ainu.* Sapporo: Kaitakinenka.

DeVos, G.
   1971   Japan's Outcasts. The Problem of the Burakumin. *Minority Rights Group Report* 3.
          London: Academic Press.

   1975

Ethnic Pluralism: Conflict and Accommodation.In G. DeVos & L. Romanucci-Ross (eds): *Ethnic Identity.* Palo Alto: Mayfield Publishing Company.

Dixon, J. M.

1883   The Tsuishikari Ainos. *Transactions of the Asiatic Society of Japan* XI: 39-50.

Douglas, M.

1966   *Purity and Danger.* London: Routledge & Kegan Paul.

Durkheim, E.

1915   *The Elementary Forms of the Religious Life.* London: Allen & Unwin.

Dönitz, W.

1884   Bemerkungen ueber Aino, Mitteilungen der Deutchen Gesellschaft f. Natur Völkerkunde Ostasiens H. G.

Egenter, N.

1986   Ainu Material Culture: The Last Chance. *Anthropological Newsletter.*

Ekholm Friedman, K.

1991   *Catastrophe and Creation: The Transformation of an African Culture.* London: Harwood Academic Publishers.

Etter, C.

1949   *Ainu Folklore.* Toronto: Wilcox and Follett.

Evans-Pritchard, E. E.

1951   *Social Anthropology.* New York: Free Press.

Fagan, B.

1984· *Clash of Culture.* New York: E. F. Freeman & Co.

Firth, R.

1957   *Man and Culture: An Evaluation of the Work of Bronislaw Malinowski.* London: Routledge & Kegan Paul.

1961   *Elements of Social organization.* Boston: Beacon Press.

1964   *Essays on Social Organization and Values.* London: Athlone Press.

Fisher, F.

1949   *Facts, Fables and Fiction of Hokkaido Japan.* Sapporo: Franciscan Missionaries of Mary Printing Shop.

Friedman, J.

1983   Civilizational Cycles and the History of Primitivism. *Social Analysis* 14: 31-52.

Froome, K.

1983   *Aboriginal Rights in International Law: The Ainu of Japan.* Ottawa Canada: Carleton University Press.

Geertz, C.

1957   Ritual and Social Change: A Javanese Example. *American Anthropologist* 59.

1973   *The Interpretation of Cultures.* New York: Basic Books.

1984   From the Native's Point of View: On the Nature of Anthropological Understanding. *Bulletin of American Academy of Arts and Sciences* 28: 1.

Giddens, A.

1978   *Durkheim.* London: Fontana Press.

Gjerdman, O.
  1926 Word Parallels Between Ainu and Other Languages. *Le Monde Orientale* 20 (1-3): 29-84, Uppsala.
  1959 *Ainu Språket: Ett Inlägg.* Lund: Språkliga Bilder.
Goodrich, L.
  1974 The United Nations in a Changing World. New York: Columbia University Press.
Hall, T.
  1987 Problems of Comparing Native Americans Historically. Paper presented at ASA Meeting, Chicago, 2 August, 1987, Section on Comparative Historical Sociology: Referred Round Table 4: Native Americans.
Hansen, H. H.
  1978 *All Världens Klädedräkter.* Stockholm: Almquist & Wiksell.
Hanihara, K.
  1975 Comparative Studies of Dentition. In S. Watanabe, S. Kono & E. Matsunga (eds): *Anthropological and Genetic Studies on the Japanese.* Sapporo: Hokudai University Press.
Harrison, J.
  1960 Introduction. In S. Takakura: The Ainu of Northern Japan. *Transactions of the American Philosophical Society* 50: 1-9.
Haseba, K.
  1956 Nihonjin no Sosen [The Ancestors of the Japanese]. *Zusetsu Nihon Bunkashi Taikei* 1: 94-105.
Hashine, N.
  1976 *To the Friends of the Kootenay Nation.* (Letter)
Hilger, M. I.
  1967 *Together with the Ainu: A Vanishing People.* Oklahoma: University of Oklahoma Press.
Hirokawa, Z.
  1978 *The People who Settled Previously.* Sapporo: Kaitakinenka.
Hokkaido Government.
  1821 *Official Documents of the Colonization of Hokkaido.*
  1869 *Hokkaido Kaitaku Hiroku Secret Records in the Development of Hokkaido.*
  1899 *Hokkaido Kyuudojin Hogoho* [Law for the Protection of Native Hokkaido Aborigines].
  1927 *Guide to Tourists.*
  1934 *Hokkaido Kyuudojin Hogoho Enkakakushi* [History of the Law for the Protection of Native Hokkaido Aborigines].
  1957 *Noichi Kaitaku Shi* [History of the Land Reform].
  1981 *Hokkaido Encyclopedia.*
  1988a *Passport to Hokkaido.*
  1988b *A Proposal for Legislation Concerning the Ainu.*

I. I. (Anon.)
1969   The Mysterious Race: The Ainu. *The East* 2: 61-69.
Inukai. T.
1933   Higma no Shusei ni Tsuite [On Habits of the Brown Bear]. *Shokubutsu Oyobi Dobutsu* 1(1): 57-64.
Iroha Jiru Sho
       Twelfth Century Dictionary.
Isajiw, W.
1974   Definition of Ethnicity. *Ethnicity* 1: 111-124.
Isamu. Y.
1975   Kikajin: The Naturalized Japanese Citizens who Molded Ancient Japanese Culture. *The East* 1: 41-51.
Kaisawa, K.
1988   *Tongari Boushi* [100th Anniversary of Nibutani Elementary School]. Biratori: Biratori Cho Press.
Kajima, S.
1895   *The Ainu of Japan: An Album of 22 Splendid Photographs of the Ainu with Explanations.* Tokyo: Genrokukan Seisaburo.
Kapferer, B.
1988   *Legends of People, Myths of State: Violence, Intolerance and Political Culture in Sri Lanka and Australia.* London: Smithsonian Institute Press.
Kayano, S.
1974   *Uwepeker Shutaisai* [Compilation of Ainu Stories]. Tokyo: Aldo.
1974   *Kitsune no Charanke* [The Fox's Protest]. Tokyo: Komine Shoten.
1974   *Kaze no Kamui to Okikurumi* [The Window God and Okikurumi God]. Tokyo: Komine Shoten.
1974   *Kibori no Okami* [The Woodcarving God]. Tokyo: Komine Shoten.
1974   *Okikurumi no Bouken* [The Adventures of the Okikurumi God]. Tokyo: Komine Shoten.
1975   *Ore no Nibutani* [My Town Nibutani]. Tokyo: Suzusawa Shoten.
1976   *Chise Akara* [The Building of an Ainu House]. Tokyo: Miraisha.
1976   *Shashinshu Ainu* [Photos of Ainu]. Tokyo: Kokushu Kankoukai.
1977   *Honoo no Uma* [The Flame Horse]. Tokyo: Suzusawas Shoten.
1977   *Ainu no Min wa Shuu* [Ainu Folk-tales]. Sapporo: Hokuto Shoten.
1977   *Ainu no Mingu* [Ainu Artifacts]. Tokyo: Suzusawa Shoten.
1978   *Mono to Kokoro* [Things and Their Souls]. Tokyo: Komine Shoten.
1979   *Hitotubu no Satchiporo* [Salmon Spawn]. Tokyo: Heibonsha.
1980   *Ainu no Ishibumi* [Ainu Monuments]. Tokyo: Asahi Shinbunsha.
1985   *The Romance of the Bear God.* Tokyo: Taishukan.
1987   *Nibutani ni Ikite* [Arrival in Nibutani]. Sapporo: Hokkaido Shinbunsha.
1988a *Kamui Yukar to Mukashibanashi* [Stories of Gods]. Tokyo: Shogakukan.
1988b *Uwepeker* (unpublished).

Keesing R.
  1981   *Cultural Anthropology.* New York: Holt, Rinehart and Winston.
  1987   Anthropology as Interpretative Quest. *Current Anthropology* 28(2): 161-176.
Kindaichi, K.
  1960   *Ainu go Kenkyo* [The Study of Ainu Language]. Tokyo: Sanseido.
Kiyono, K.
  1925   *Nihon Genjin no Kenkyu* [Research on the Aborigines of Japan]. Tokyo: Oka Shoin.
Kodama, S.
  1970   *Ainu Historical and Anthropological Studies.* Sapporo: Hokudai University Press.
Koganei, R.
  1927   Aino Minzoku sono Kigen Narabine Taminzoku tono Kankei [The Origin of the
         Ainu people and their relationship to other peoples] *Jinruigaku Zasshi* 42(5):
         159-62.
Kono, H.
  1955   *Fudoki Nihon* [Old Geographical Guide Book of Japan]. Tokyo: Heiboncha.
Kono, Z.
  1979   *Hokkaido Shi Jiimeijii.* [People connected to Hokkaido History]. Sapporo:
         Hokkaido Shupankikaku.
Kopernicki, I.
  1883   Ainoschädel nach neuem Material. *Krakau Quart* 111: 1.
Kreiner, J. & H. D. Oelschleger.
  1987   *Ainu Jäger, Fisher und Sammler in Japan's Norden.* Köln: Ethnologica.
Kroeber, A.
  1920   Totem and Taboo: An Ethnologic Psychoanalysis. *American Anthropologist* 22:
         48-55.
  1952   *The Nature of Culture.* Chicago: Chicago University Press.
Landor, S.
  1893   *Alone with the Hairy Ainu, or 3, 800 Miles on a Pack Saddle in the Yezo and a Cruise
         to the Kurile Islands.* London: Johnson Reprint Corporation.
Lange, A. & C. Westin.
  1981   *Ethnisk discriminering och social identitet.* Stockholm: Publica.
Lee. R. B. & I. DeVore.
  1975   *Man the Hunter.* Chicago: Aldine Publication Co.
Levin, M. G.
  1958   Ethnic Origin of the People of North-Eastern Asia.In H.N.Michael (ed): *Arctic
         Institute of North America, Anthropology of the North* 3. Toronto: University Press of
         Toronto.
Lévi-Strauss, C.
  1969   *The Elementary Structure of Kinship.* Boston: Beacon Press.
  1983a *The Raw and the Cooked.* Chicago: Chicago University Press.
  1983b *From Honey to Ashes.* Chicago: Chicago University Press.

Lindquist, I.

1960   Indo-European Features in the Ainu Language. *Lund Universitets Årsskrift* 54(1): 3-67.

Malinowski, B.

1922   *Argonauts of the Western Pacific.* New York: Dutton.

Marcus, G. E. & M. J. Fisher.

1986   *Anthropology as Cultural Critique: An Experimental Moment in Human Science.* Chicago: Chicago University Press.

Marwick, M.

1979   The Study of Witchcraft. In A. L. Epstein (ed). *The Crafts of Social Anthropology.* Oxford: .

Masler, D.

1987   Japan's Silent Minorities. *Tokyo Journal* October issue: 14-16.

Matsumoto, Y. S.

1960   The Individual and The Group. *Transactions of the American Philosophical Society* 50: 1-75.

Mauss, M.

1969   *The Gift.* London: Routledge & Kegan Paul.

Mayer, S. I.

1984   *The Rise and Fall of Imperial Japan.* London: Bison Books Ltd.

Miller, A.

1967   *The Japanese Language.* Chicago: Chicago University Press.

Milne, J.

1882   Notes on the Koro-pok-guru or Pit-Dwellers of Yezo and the Kurile Islands. *Transactions of the Asiatic Society of Japan* X.

Morie, E. & K. Nobuhito.

1964   *Hokkaido no Rekishi.* [History of Hokkaido]. Tokyo: Yamakawa Shupansha.

Morin, E.

1973   *Le Paradigme Perdu.* Paris: Editions du Seuil.

Munro, N.

1911   *Prehistoric Japan.* Tokyo: Daiichi Shobo.

1962   *Ainu Creed and Cult.* London: Greenwood Press.

Mutsumi, C. & Y. Takao

1988   *Ainu Conversation Dictionary.* Tokyo: Araki Kioshi.

Myrdal, G.

1944   *An American Dilemma: The Negro Problem and Modern Democracy.* New York: Harper.

Naert, P.

1958   La Situation Linguistique de l'ainou et Indoeuropeen. *Lund Universitets Årsskrift* 53(4): 1-234.

1960   *Aiona: En Bok om Ainu – det Vita Folket I Fjärran Östern.* Stockholm: Natur och Kultur.

Nakane, C.
 1970 *Japanese Society.* California: University of California Press.
Narita, U.
 1988 *Ainu Way of Making Best of Greenwood* (manuscript).
Newell, W.
 1967 Some Problems of Integrating Minorities into Japanese Society. *Journal of Asian and African Studies* 2: 212-229.
Numazawa, F. K.
 1946 *Die Weltanfänger in der Japanischen Mythologie.* Luzern: Josef Stocker.
Nomura, Y.
 1978 *Ainu Way of Thinking.* Sapporo: Utari Kyokai Press.
Ogawa, K.
 1970 *New Intensive Japanese.* Tokyo: Hokusei Press.
Ohnuki-Tierney, E.
 1974 *The Ainu of the Northwest Coast of Southern Sakhalin.* New York: Holt, Rinehart & Winston.
 1976 Regional Variation in Ainu Culture. *American Ethnologist* 3(2): 297-329.
 1981 *Illness and Healing among the Sakhalin Ainu: A Symbolic Interpretation.* Cambridge: Cambridge University Press.
Omoto, K.
 1972 Polymorphism and genetic affinities of the Ainu of Hokkaido. *Human Biology in Oceanica* 1: 278-288.
Parson, T.
 1949 *The Structure of Social Action.* New York: Free Press.
 1957 Malinowski and the Theory of Social Systems. In R. Firth (ed): *Man and Culture. An Evaluation of the Work of Bronislaw Malinowski.* 53-70. London: Routledge and Kegan Paul.
Patterson, O.
 1977 *Ethnic Chauvinism: The Reactionary Impulse.* New York: Stein.
Pelto, Perttii J. & Pelto Gretel, H.
 1978 *Anthropological Research.* Cambridge: Cambridge University Press.
Peng, F. C. C. & P. Geiser.
 1977 *The Ainu: The Past in the Present.* Hiroshima: Bunka Hyoron Publishing Company.
Peterson Royce, A.
 1982 *Ethnic Identity: Strategies of Diversity.* Bloomington: Indiana University Press.
Philippi, D.
 1979 *Songs of Gods, Songs of Humans.* Tokyo: University of Tokyo Press.
Pike, K.
 1954 Language in Relation to a Unified Theory of the Structure of Human Behavior. *Glendale Summer Institute of Linguistics* 1.
Pilsudski, B.
 1912 *Material for the Study of the Ainu Language.* Cracow: Spolka Wydawnicza Polska.

Radcliffe-Brown, A. R.

1948   *A Natural Science of Society.* New York: Free Press.

1952   *Structure and Function in Primitive Society.* London: Oxford University Press.

Refsing, K.

1974   *An Annotated Catalog of Ainu Material in the University of Aarhus.* Lund: Scandinavian Institute of Asian Studies Monographs.

1980   The Ainu People of Japan. *IWGIA Newsletter.* 24: 79-92.

1987   *The Ainu Language: The Morphology and Syntax of the Shizunai Dialect.* Aarhus: Aarhus University Press.

Reischauer, E. O. & Craig, A. M.

1973   *Japan, Tradition and Transformation.* Cambridge: Cambridge University Press.

Sahlins, M.

1976   *Cultural and Practical Reason.* Chicago: Chicago University Press.

1985   *Islands of History.* Chicago: Chicago University Press.

Saito, H.

1912   *Japans Historia.* Stockholm: P. A. Norstedt & Söner.

Sanders, D.

1985   The Ainu as an Indigenous Population. *IWGIA Newsletter* 45: 119-150.

Sanseido

1975   *Sanseido's New Concise English-Japanese Dictionary.* Tokyo: Sanseido.

Scheube, B.

1882   Die Ainos. *Natur und Völkerkunde Ostasiens* 3. 26.

Seligman, B. Z.

1962   Social Organization. Postscript in N. Munro (ed): *Ainu Creed and Cult.* 141-158. Cambridge: Cambridge University Press.

Siebold, H.

1882   Ethnologische Studien über Aino auf der Insel Yesso. *Zeitschrift, Ethnologie* 13.

Sjöberg, K.

1986   The Ainu: A Fourth World Population. *IWGIA Newsletter* 48: 43-99.

Smith, R. J.

1983   *Japanese Society: Traditional Self and the Social Order.* Cambridge: Cambridge University Press.

Spicer, E.

1971   Persistent Identity Systems. *Science* 4011.

Suzumu, H.

1963   *Hokkaido Kinseishi no Kenkyuo* [The Study of Hokkaido History in Premodern Time]. Sapporo: Hokkaido Shupankikaku.

Sternberg, L.

1929   The Ainu Problem. *Anthropos* 24: 755-99.

Sugiura, K. & H. Befu.

1962   Kinship Organization of the Saru Ainu. *Ethnology,* 1(3): 287-301.

Takakura, S.

1942   *The History of Policy Concerning the Ainu Total Entity.* Tokyo: Tokyo University Press.

1960   The Ainu of Northern Japan. *Transactions of the American Philosophical Society* 50: 1-92. Philadelphia.

Tamura, S.

1983   *Ainu Itak.* Tokyo: Tokyo University Press.

Tarentsky, A.

1890   Beiträge zur Craniologie der Aino auf Sachalin. *Memoires de l'Academic Imperiale des Sciences de St. Petersbourg* VII Tome XXXVII. 13.

Thompson, S. I.

1987   The Ainu of Japan. *Cs Quarterly* 11(i): 88.

Tomi, M.

1985   The Ainu: Struggle for Survival and Dignity. *Ampo, Japan Asia Quarterly Review* 1(1): 7.1: 42-46.

Turnbull, S. R.

1982   *The Book of the Samurai, The Warrior Class of Japan.* London: Bison Books Ltd.

Tylor, E B.

1958   *Primitive Culture.* New York: Harper Torchbooks.

Udagawa, H.

1977   *Hokkaido no Kokagaku* [The Archaeologi in Hokkaido]. Sapporo: Hokkaido Shupankikaku.

United Nations.

1978   *International Bill of Human Rights.* New York: United Nation Office of Public Information.

1981   *Human Rights International Instrument.* New York: United Nations Office of Public Information.

Utari Kyokai.

1984   *Counter Plan to a Proposal for Legislation Concerning the Ainu People.*

1987a *Counter Plan to a Proposal for Legislation Concerning the Ainu People.*

1987b *Statement Submitted to the Fifth Session of the Working Group on Indigenous Populations,* Geneva, Switzerland.

1988   *Statement Submitted to the Sixth Session of the Working Group on Indigenous Population,* Geneva, Switzerland.

Van den Berghe, P.

1977   *The Ethnic Phenomenon.* New York: Elsevier.

Van Maanen, J.

1988   *Tales of the Fields: On Writing Ethnography.* Chicago: Chicago University Press.

VeenHoven, A.

1975   Case Studies on Human Rights and Fundamental Freedom. *The Hague* 1.

Voi, K.

1983   *Ainu Itak: Translation of Ainu Oral Tradition.* 1. Asahikawa: Asahikawa Press.

1987 *Ainu Itak* 2. Asahikawa: Asahikawa Press.

Wagatsuma, H.

1975 Problems of Cultural Identity in Modern Japan. In G. DeVos and L. Romanucci-Ross (eds): *Ethnic Identity*. Palo Alto: Mayfield Publishing Company.

Watanabe, H.

1972 *The Ainu EcoSystem*. Tokyo: Tokyo University Press.

1975 Subsistence and Ecology of Northern Food Gatherers, with Special Reference to the Ainu. In R. B. Lee & I. DeVore (eds): *Man the Hunter:* 69-77. Chicago: Aldine Publication Co.

Yamada, G.

1976 *Cultivating the Earth*. Sapporo: Kaitakineka

Yamada, K.

1978 *Looking for a New Land*. Sapporo: Kaitakinenka

Yamanari, K.

1974 *Emishi Tenno Cho no Kenkyu* [The Study of Emishi Japan]. Tokyo: Yoshikawa Kobunkanai.

Index